ANALYSIS OF NUCLEAR LEGISLATION

This study, which is published in two volumes, is part of the series of analytical studies of the major aspects of nuclear energy legislation in force in OECD Member countries. The studies that have been published to date are:

- Nuclear Third Party Liability (first published in 1967 and published in a new edition in 1976);
- Organisation and General Regime governing Nuclear Activities (published in 1969);
- Regulations governing Nuclear Installations and Radiation Protection (published in 1972);
- Regulations governing the Transport of Radioactive Materials (published in 1980).

Also, a Description of Licensing Systems and Inspection of Nuclear Installations in OECD countries was published in 1980.

The present study constitutes both an updating and an expansion of the 1969 study referred to above on the Organisation and General Regime governing Nuclear Activities.

Each study in this series was prepared, to the extent possible, following a standard plan for all countries to facilitate information retrieval and comparison.

The analytical studies are prepared by the Secretariat of the Nuclear Energy Agency in consultation with the appropriate services of the countries concerned.

These studies are based on information available to the Secretariat and neither the Secretariat nor national authorities assume any liability therefor.

INTRODUCTORY NOTE

The present study reviews, as did the study published in 1969, both the national legislation governing nuclear activities in OECD Member countries and the institutional framework within which such legislation is applied in each country.

The Secretariat has decided to update the 1969 study for various reasons. First is the fact that in recent years, nuclear power has developed into a major source of energy for industrial purposes, resulting in a corresponding evolution in the legislative provisions and institutional organisation required to regulate, at national level, the numerous aspects of nuclear activities. Furthermore, the need for a greater involvement on the part of public authorities has been perceived in a number of new areas such as radioactive waste management. Also, the structure and contents of this study have been somewhat reorganised to give a more comprehensive understanding of regulatory policy in each country.

Finally, the second part of this volume contains tables of the major international conventions relevant to nuclear activities.

The NEA Secretariat would like to take this opportunity to thank all those in Member countries whose kind assistance has enabled it to publish this study.

This study has been prepared by Liane Saad and Colin McIntosh of the Nuclear Energy Agency Legal Affairs Section. Dominique Kahn, Katie Schaab and Christian Retemeyer have also helped in its preparation.

VOLUME II

LIST OF COUNTRIES

LIST OF CONVENTIONS

I. THIRD PARTY LIABILITY

 – Paris Convention on Third Party Liability in the Field of Nuclear Energy.
 – Brussels Convention Supplementary to the Paris Convention.
 – Vienna Convention on Civil Liability for Nuclear Damage.
 – Convention relating to Civil Liability in the Field of Maritime Carriage of Nuclear Material.
 – Convention on the Liability of Operators of Nuclear Ships.

II. RADIATION PROTECTION

 – Radiation Protection Convention (No. 115).

III. SAFEGUARDS AND PHYSICAL PROTECTION

 – Treaty on the Non-Proliferation of Nuclear Weapons.
 – Convention on the Establishment of a Security Control in the Field of Nuclear Energy.
 – Treaty establishing the European Atomic Energy Community – Chapter VII (Safety Control).
 – Convention on the Physical Protection of Nuclear Material.

IV. DENUCLEARISATION

 – Antarctic Treaty.
 – Treaty for the Prohibition of Nuclear Weapons in Latin America.
 – Treaty on the Prohibition of the Emplacement of Nuclear Weapons and other Weapons of Mass Destruction on the Seabed and the Ocean Floor and in the Subsoil thereof.

V. MARINE POLLUTION

 – London Convention on the Prevention of Marine Pollution by Dumping of Wastes and other Matter.
 – Oslo Convention for the Prevention of Marine Pollution by Dumping from Ships and Aircraft.
 – Convention on the Protection of the Marine Environment of the Baltic Sea Area.
 – Paris Convention for the Prevention of Marine Pollution from Land-based Sources.
 – Barcelona Convention for the Protection of the Mediterranean Sea against Pollution.

NEW ZEALAND

TABLE OF CONTENTS

I. GENERAL REGULATORY REGIME

Atomic Energy
Act No. 41 of 1945
as amended
by Act No. 13
of 1959

Radiation Protection
Act No. 23, 1965
as amended
by Act No. 90
of 1981

Despite the fact that New Zealand has at present no nuclear power programme, and is unlikely to adopt any such in the near future, various items of legislation exist to regulate dealings with radioactive materials. The two basic Acts are the Atomic Energy Act of 1945, last amended by the Atomic Energy Amendment Act of 1959, and the Radiation Protection Act of 1965, last amended by the Radiation Protection Amendment Act of 1981.

1. MINING REGIME

Act No. 41 of 1945,
Section 5A(1)

Section 2

Under the 1945 Atomic Energy Act, as amended, no-one may prospect for any mineral likely to contain a prescribed substance except pursuant to a miner's right or mineral prospecting warrant issued under the Mining Act of 1926. *Prescribed substance* is defined as uranium, thorium, plutonium, neptunium, or any of their respective compounds, or any such other substance as the Minister of Energy (formerly the Minister of Mines) may prescribe, being a substance which in his opinion is or may be used for the production of atomic energy or research into matters connected therewith.

Section 4(1)

Any person who discovers the existence of any prescribed substance in New Zealand shall, within three months of making the discovery, report it to the Under-Secretary of the Mines Department.

Sections 4A and 4B

Section 5A(5)

Provision is made for the granting, at the discretion of the Minister, of rewards in respect of the discovery of prescribed substances, and of grants to assist persons prospecting for or producing prescribed substances. No-one may mine for any mineral containing any prescribed substance except pursuant to a mineral licence granted under the 1926 Mining Act.

Section 5(1)

In addition, the 1945 Act provides that if the Minister of Energy is satisfied that any person is mining or is about to mine any prescribed substance or is engaged or about to engage in carrying out any physical, chemical, or metallurgical process as a result of which any prescribed substance may reasonably be expected to be isolated or extracted, the Minister may require him, in conducting the mining operations or in carrying out any process as aforesaid, to comply with and observe such terms and conditions as the Minister may think fit to impose.

Section 15

Provision is made for any person authorised by the Minister to have the right of entry on any premises on which mining operations are carried on or with respect to which there are other grounds for suspecting the presence of minerals, concentrates, or other materials containing any prescribed substance, for the purpose of ascertaining whether or not any such materials or substance are in fact present.

2. RADIOACTIVE SUBSTANCES, NUCLEAR FUELS AND EQUIPMENT

a) Prescribed substances

Act No. 41 of 1945, as amended, Section 6

Section 8

The 1945 Act provides that all minerals, concentrates, or other materials containing any prescribed substance which are extracted, isolated, or concentrated by any person shall only be disposed of with the prior written consent of the Minister of Energy and subject to such conditions as he shall impose. As far as uranium is concerned, the Act stipulates in any case that all uranium existing in its natural condition on or below the surface of any land within the territorial limits of New Zealand belongs to the Crown.

Section 7

No prescribed substances may be imported without the prior written consent of the Minister of Energy. However, samples of minerals containing prescribed substances may be imported without such consent if the samples do not exceed five pounds in weight.

b) Fissionable substances, etc.

Section 12

The 1945 Act provides that:
- no person shall, without the prior written consent of the Minister of Science and Technology, import or have in his possession or control any plutonium or other substance from which atomic energy may be produced more readily than from uranium of natural isotope composition;
- no person shall, without the prior written consent of the same Minister import, construct, have in his possession or control, or operate any machine, atomic pile, or apparatus which may be capable of producing atomic energy or which the Minister has, for the purpose of this section, declared to be an essential part of any such machine, pile, or apparatus;
- no person shall, without the prior written consent of the Minister, import, manufacture, or have in his possession or control any material or substance which

9

that Minister has, for the purposes of this Section, declared to be essential to any process for the production of atomic energy.

Section 13

Certain exemptions from the foregoing provisions are, however, laid down. In particular, universities and schools are empowered to carry on experimental work involving small amounts of uranium and thorium or apparatus capable of producing atomic energy at a low rate.

Section 14

Finally, with respect to trade, the Act provides that no person shall, without the prior written consent of the Minister of Science and Technology, export or sell or otherwise dispose of any isotope of uranium, or any plutonium or other substance from which atomic energy may be more readily obtained than from uranium of natural isotope composition, except to the Crown.

c) Radioactive materials

Act No. 23 of 1965,
Section 12
Section 2(1)

In addition to the foregoing provisions of the Atomic Energy Act, the 1965 Radiation Protection Act provides that no-one shall, unless with the prior consent in writing of the Minister of Health, manufacture or otherwise produce, sell, import or export, store or transport any radioactive material. This latter term is defined as *any article containing a radioactive substance giving it a specific radioactivity exceeding 100 kilobecquerels per kilogram and a total radioactivity exceeding 3 kilobecquerels.*

Section 13(1)

Furthermore, no-one may use radioactive material unless he is the holder of a licence under the Act or is acting under the supervision or instructions of a person so licenced.

d) Irradiating apparatus

Section 2(1)
Section 14(1)

The 1965 Act defines irradiating apparatus as: *any apparatus that can be used for the production of X-rays or gamma rays or for the acceleration of atomic particles in such a way that it produces a dose equivalent rate of or exceeding 2.5 microsieverts per hour at a point which could be reached by a living human being* and goes on to provide that no-one may sell any irradiating apparatus to any person, unless at the time of sale the purchaser produces to the vendor a valid licence authorising him to use irradiating apparatus of the kind to which that irradiating apparatus belongs or evidence in writing that he is exempt from obtaining such a licence pursuant to regulations made under this Act.

Section 15

Furthermore, no-one may use any irradiating apparatus for any purpose unless he is the holder of a licence under the Act authorising him to do so, or is a person acting under the supervision or instructions of a person so licensed.

3. PROTECTION OF WORKERS AND THE PUBLIC AGAINST IONIZING RADIATION

Radiation Protection Regulations, 1982

The Radiation Protection Regulations of 1982, made pursuant to the 1965 Radiation Protection Act, provide that the owner of any radioactive material or any irradiating apparatus shall take all reasonable steps to ensure that there is at all times a suitably licensed person responsible for the safe care of the radioactive material or the irradiating apparatus. He should also provide adequate equipment and materials to enable the storage, use, transportation, and disposal of the radioactive material or the irradiating apparatus to be carried out safely.

Section 11

Licensees have a general obligation to take all reasonable steps to ensure that every person who uses any radioactive material or any irradiating apparatus for which the licensee is responsible complies with the provisions of the regulations and with any further condition to which his licence is subject: moreover, they must fully instruct every such person regarding the radiation hazards of his work, and the precautions to be taken in relation thereto.

Section 20(1) and (4)

More specifically, if a licensee, or any person acting under his instruction or supervision, uses a radioactive material, whether unsealed or not, or an irradiating apparatus under conditions in which a dose equivalent or a dose-equivalent commitment exceeding 0.3 of the reference dose-equivalent could be received by any person in any period of one year, then an instrument of a type approved by the Director-General of Health is provided and used to make appropriate measurements of levels of radioactive contamination as often as may be necessary to allow work to be planned and carried out safely.

Section 2(1)

The *reference dose equivalent* means a dose equivalent, received in one year of:

- 50 millisieverts (mSv) in any part of the body except the hands, forearms, feet or lower legs, or
- 500 mSv to the hands, forearms, feet, or lower legs:

provided that the dose equivalent received by any other part of the body does not exceed the difference between 50 mSv and 0.06 of the dose equivalent received by the hands, forearms, feet or lower legs.

In determining the dose equivalent received in any given period, the dose equivalent commitment arising from contamination by any radioactive substance shall be added to the dose equivalent received from external irradiation.

Section 18(1) and (2)

The Regulations provide that no person shall intentionally expose any other person to radiation from any radioactive material or an irradiating apparatus except except for

11

medical reasons or other purposes authorised by the terms of a licence and that every person who is for the time being in control of any radioactive material or an irradiating apparatus shall take all reasonable steps to ensure that:

i) except in the case of exposure to radiation for therapeutic purposes, the dose equivalent received by any person from radiation emanating from the irradiating apparatus or radioactive material is the minimum practicable; and

ii) except in the case of exposure to radiation for therapeutic purposes or for medical diagnostic purposes or as permitted by the terms of a licence, the dose equivalent referred to above does not exceed:

   – the reference dose equivalent, in the case of persons employed to work with such radioactive material or irradiating apparatus (except that in the case of women of child-bearing age the dose equivalent shall not exceed one-quarter of the reference dose equivalent in any period of three months nor during the period of pregnancy following its diagnosis); or
   – 0.1 of the reference dose equivalent, in the case of other persons.

Section 18(3)

If the circumstances are such that sufficient protection cannot reasonably be provided so as to fulfil the requirements referred to in *(ii)* above, the recommendations of the International Commission on Radiological Protection (ICRP Publication 26), shall be followed.

Sections 23 to 25
Section 19

Finally, the Regulations detail restrictions on the use of irradiating apparatus in radiotherapy as well as precautions to be taken with such apparatus when used in radiotherapy or diagnosis. Action is specified that must be taken in the event of possible over-exposure to radiation.

4. NUCLEAR INSTALLATIONS

There are at present no nuclear power plants or other nuclear installations in New Zealand and consequently no laws governing their operation.

5. RADIOACTIVE WASTE MANAGEMENT

Radiation Protection
Regulations, 1982

The 1982 Radiation Protection Regulations provide that every licensee who uses a radioactive material shall dispose of any waste product resulting from such use in accordance with the conditions specified in his licence or, if no such conditions are specified, as the Director-General of Health may require.

Section 14

Every person disposing of the waste product of any radioactive material which, due to the small amounts of activity or concentration involved, is exempted from any licensing requirement must do so:

- by burial at least half a metre deep, in a supervised public refuse tip, or in a place where the earth is unlikely to be disturbed for a period exceeding three times the half-life of the radionuclide that has the longest half-life of those present in the waste product; or
- if the waste product is a gas, by breaking or otherwise opening the container to release the gas in the open air at a distance of at least three metres from any other person or any building; or
- if the waste product has previously been diluted with water to a concentration not exceeding that specified in the regulations, through the public sewerage system in a form soluble in water; or
- if the waste product has previously been diluted by intimate mixture with inert material to a concentration not exceeding that specified in the regulations, by any common method of rubbish disposal.

It is specified that the term *waste product* includes any radioactive material that is no longer intended to be kept or used.

6. NUCLEAR THIRD PARTY LIABILITY

There are no special provisions in New Zealand governing specifically nuclear third party liability: any claim for compensation for damage caused by nuclear activities would be dealt with under the normal rules of law.

7. NUCLEAR SECURITY

Radiation Protection
Regulations, 1982/72
Section 9(2)
Section 11*(g)*
Section 11*(f)*

Under the 1982 Radiation Protection Regulations, licensees are responsible for the safe care of any radioactive material or any irradiating apparatus under their control. A licensee must take all reasonable steps to prevent the loss, or the release beyond his control, of any radioactive material for which he is responsible. In particular, licensees must take all reasonable steps to prevent any unauthorised person from tampering with any radioactive material or any irradiating apparatus for which they are responsible.

8. TRANSPORT[1]

Radiation Protection Act, 1965, Section 12(1)

Section 12(2)

The basic provision governing the transport of radioactive materials in New Zealand is to be found in the Radiation Protection Act of 1965 which provides that no person shall, except with the prior consent in writing of the Minister of Health, manufacture, sell, bring or consent in writing of the Minister of Health, manufacture, sell, bring or cause to be brought or sent into New Zealand, take or send out of New Zealand, store or transport any radioactive material. Any such consent given by the Minister may be made subject to conditions and qualifications.

Radiation Protection Regulations, 1982

More detailed rules concerning transport are contained in the Radiation Protection Regulations of 1982 which replaced and repealed the Transport of Radioactive Materials Regulations of 1973.

Section 3

Section 2(3)

Section 2(4)

The 1982 Regulations provide that no person shall transport any radioactive material into New Zealand or through New Zealand, by any means whatever, unless that radioactive material is packed, labelled, marked, and transported in accordance with the 1973 International Atomic Energy Agency (IAEA) Transport Regulations. It is provided further that if the IAEA Regulations are subsequently amended or replaced, the Minister of Health may adapt the amendment or the substituted regulations for the purposes of the New Zealand regulations, either wholly or in part.

Sections 4 and 5

Exemptions from the provisions of the 1982 Regulations and from the obligation, under the 1965 Act, to obtain prior authorisation for transport, have been made in the case of small (defined) quantities of radioactive material or irradiating apparatus that present little or no risk.

Section 6(1)

A special exemption has been made in the case of any radioactive material that is part of the equipment or stores of a ship or aircraft belonging to a country other than New Zealand, unless any of the radioactive material is removed from that ship or aircraft in New Zealand, or the radioactive material is:

i) part of a nuclear reactor; or

ii) pyrophoric or associated with pyrophoric material; or

---

1. For further details, see Analytical Study in the same series: "Regulations Governing the Transport of Radioactive Materials", OECD/NEA, 1980.

iii) explosive or associated with explosive material; or
iv) a radioactive material that, if transported in accordance with the IAEA Transport Regulations, would require notification to the competent authority; or
v) fissile material that is not exempt from the IAEA Transport Regulations.

Section 6(2)

Also exempt is any radioactive material brought or coming into New Zealand in any ship or aircraft if the destination of that radioactive material is outside New Zealand and the radioactive material:

– is transported, while in New Zealand, in accordance with the requirements of the IAEA Transport Regulations; and

– is not removed from the ship or aircraft except for the purpose of being exported from New Zealand on the next available ship or aircraft; and

– is not a radioactive material coming within any of the sub-paragraphs *(ii)* to *(v)* above.

Section 8(1)

Finally, the 1982 Regulations provide that in any case where the Minister of Health is satisfied that strict compliance with these regulations is not possible, or would involve expenditure or hardship out of proportion to the degree of freedom from radiation hazard to be achieved by such compliance, he may exempt any particular person from compliance with specified provisions of these regulations, or may modify the requirements of any such specified provision if he is satisfied that adequate freedom from radiation hazards can, and will, otherwise be secured.

9. PATENTS

There are no rules in New Zealand dealing specifically with patents in the nuclear field.

II. INSTITUTIONAL FRAMEWORK

1. REGULATORY AND SUPERVISORY AUTHORITIES

a) Minister of Energy

As was seen in Part I of the study, the Minister of Energy has extensive powers under the 1945 Atomic Energy Act with regard to the mining of prescribed substances, including that of imposing terms and conditions for the carrying out of mining operations.

Furthermore, the prior consent of the Minister is required for the disposal of prescribed substances and for their importation into New Zealand.

b) Minister of Science and Technology

This Minister is designated in the Atomic Energy Act (as amended) as being the licensing authority with respect to the possession, use, import, export, etc. of fissionable substances and the possession, control or operation of any machine, or essential part thereof, capable of producing atomic energy.

c) Department of Health

As was seen in Part I, above, this Department is responsible for administering the radiation safety legislation in respect of all sources of ionizing radiation and radioactive materials and is the issuing and supervisory body for licenses in this field as well as the *competent authority* in respect of the transport of radiactive materials. The Division of the Department concerned is in fact the National Radiation Laboratory.

d) National Radiation Laboratory

The Laboratory is the branch of the Department of Health which administers the radiation safety legislation[2] in respect of all radioactive materials and other sources of ionizing radiation. These may be used only by a person holding an appropriate licence or a person working for such a

---

2. Radiation Protection Act, 1965, Radiation Protection Regulations, 1973, Radiation Protection Regulations, 1982.

licensee. Radioactive materials may be manufactured, imported, exported or sold only with permission obtained through the Laboratory, which is also the *competent authority* in respect of the transport of radioactive materials. It provides advisory services on safety to all users of radiation and radioactive materials and additional advice and assistance to medical users, including calibrations and maintenance of the New Zealand primary X-ray measuring standard. It monitors environmental radioactivity, both natural and artificial, and provides radiation monitoring services for those occupationally exposed. The Laboratory publishes codes of safe practice to assist licensees. It provides training courses in radiation safety for groups of professonal and technical workers and has been involved in monitoring and the formulation of emergency plans in connection with visits to New Zealand ports of nuclear powered ships.

2. ADVISORY BODIES

a) Radiation Protection Advisory Council

i) *Legal status*

The Council was set up under the Radiation Protection Act of 1965, and was originally called the Radiological Advisory Council. This name was changed to the present one by the Radiation Protection Amendment, 1977.

ii) *Responsibilities*

Act No. 23 of 1965, Section 10

Radiation Protection Regulations, 1982, Section 8

The functions of the Council are to advise and make recommendations to the Director-General of Health in respect of applications for licences under the 1965 Act which are referred to it by the Director-General.

Moreover, the Council has a duty to advise and make recommendations to the Minister of Health in respect of the exercise of any powers vested in the Minister by the 1965 Act and the 1982 Regulations, of any regulations made or proposed to be made under such legislation, and of any other matter referred to the Council by the Minister.

iii) *Structure*

Radiation Protection Act, 1965

Section 5

The members of the Council are:
- the Director-General of Health;
- a medical practitioner;
- two persons, each of whom shall be either a radiologist or a radiotherapist;

- a person having special knowledge in the use or application of radioactive materials;
- an officer of the Department of Scientific and Industrial Research nominated by the Minister of Science and Technology;
- a qualified physicist.

The members of the Council, other than the Director-General, shall be appointed by the Governor-General on the recommendation of the Minister of Health and shall hold office for a period of five years, save that any such member may from time to time be reappointed.

Section 6(1), as amended

The Council, at its first meeting held after the first day of January in each year, appoints one of its members to act as Chairman.

Section 7(1) to (4)

Meetings of the Council are held at such times and places as the Council or the Chairman may from time to time appoint. At any meeting of the Council four members form a quorum and every question before any meeting of the Council is determined by a majority of the votes of the members present and voting thereon. The Chairman has a deliberative vote and, in the case of an equality of votes, also has a casting vote.

iv) Financing

The Radiation Protection Advisory Council is funded exclusively by monies voted by Parliament.

b) New Zealand Atomic Energy Committee (NZAEC)

i) Legal status

The NZAEC, formed in 1958, was reconstituted by Cabinet in 1966 as an advisory committee responsible to the Minister of Science and Technology. It is not a statutory body.

ii) Responsibilities

The terms of reference of the Committee are as follows:

- to advise the Minister of Science and Technology on any aspects of research, development or application of nuclear science in New Zealand;
- to act as a liaison committee between organisations and departments concerned in planning for the introduction of nuclear power in New Zealand;
- to advise the Minister on international aspects of nuclear science affecting New Zealand, bearing in mind the responsibility of the Minister of Foreign Affairs for the administration of the external and foreign affairs of New Zealand;

- to advise the Minister on any other matters concerning nuclear science which the Minister may refer to it;
- to report annually to the Minister on the activities of the Committee.

iii) Structure

The membership of the Committee is made up as follows:

- two independent persons appointed by the Minister of Science and Technology – one of whom is appointed Chairman;
- two persons from the New Zealand Universities appointed by the Minister;
- the Heads of the Ministry of Energy, Ministry of Works and Development, Foreign Affairs, Department of Scientific and Industrial Research, and Health Department. If an *ex officio* member is unable to attend any meeting of the Committee, he may authorise any other officer of his Department, having the status of a deputy or an assistant Permanent Head, to attend the meeting in his stead.

The Committee is empowered to co-opt specialists as required or to appoint sub-committees. Sub-committees that have been appointed to date are Manpower, Siting and Safety Criteria, Nuclear Law, Nuclear Shipping and Research Reactor. However the Nuclear Powered Shipping Sub-committee is the only one of these which at the present time is continuing to meet.

iv) Financing

The New Zealand Atomic Energy Committee is funded entirely by monies voted by Parliament.

NORWAY

TABLE OF CONTENTS

I. GENERAL REGULATORY REGIME

Although there are as yet no firm plans for nuclear power projects in Norway, it was one of the first countries to embark upon a nuclear research programme and to frame legislation governing nuclear activities.

Act No. 1 of 18.6.1938

As far back as 1938, an Act on the Use of X-rays and Radium etc. was passed to establish rules governing the use of radioactive substances and it is still in force. Other regulations, since repealed and superseded by more recent legislation, provided for the control and supervision of nuclear activities.

Act No. 28 of 12.5.1972, as amended
Regulations of 1.3.1983
Act No. 1 of 18.6.1938
Act of 26.6.1964
Act of 11.6.1976

The nuclear sector is now regulated by an Act of 1972 concerning Nuclear Energy Activities which provides for a licensing system for nuclear installations, fuels and radioactive substances. In addition, the Regulations of 1st March 1983 govern the use of such activities; these Regulations were made pursuant to the Act of 1938, the Act of 1964 on Medical Goods and the Act of 1976 relating to Product Control. Radiation protection aspects are regulated by the provisions of the above-mentioned Act of 1938 on the Use of X-rays and Radium, etc. and regulations made under that Act.

1. MINING REGIME

Act No. 16 of 14.12.1917
Chapter II

Under the General Concessions Act on the acquisition of waterfalls, mines and other immovable property, general prospecting activities may be carried out by the State, local authorities and Norwegian nationals and companies. A mine may not be exploited without authorisation from the Ministry of Industry; the State and local authorities are exempted from this requirement. While existing legislation contains no express provisions giving the State direct control over the ownership and distribution of products obtained from mining, the Ministry of Industry, when granting mining concessions, enjoys wide powers to impose such conditions as appear to be necessary in the public interest. In effect, uranium prospecting in Norway is almost entirely undertaken by the State.

2. RADIOACTIVE SUBSTANCES, NUCLEAR FUELS AND EQUIPMENT

Act No. 28 of 12.5.1972
Regulations of 1.3.1983
Act No. 28 of 12.5.1972,
Section 1(*a*), (*b*) and (*c*)

The Act of 1972 concerning Nuclear Energy Activities lays down the general regime for radioactive substances and nuclear fuels, while the production, import and sale of radioiosotopes are subject to the Regulations of 1st March 1983. Under the Act of 1972, nuclear fuels mean fissionable materials in the form of uranium or plutonium metal, alloy or chemical compound; radioactive products mean other radioactive materials (including waste) which are made or have become radioactive by radiation incidental to the production or utilisation of nuclear fuels; nuclear substances mean nuclear fuels, other than natural or depleted uranium, as well as radioactive products, except radioisotopes used for industrial, commercial, agricultural, medical or scientific purposes.

Section 10
Regulations of 1.3.1983
RD[1] of 25.9.1953

The Nuclear Energy Safety Authority (*Statens Atomtilsyn*), set up in accordance with the Act of 1972 and under the Ministry of Petroleum and Energy, is the supervisory authority in connection with the licensing of nuclear materials. The State Institute of Radiation Hygiene (*Statens Institutt for Strålehygiene* – SIS), under the Ministry of Health and Social Affairs, is also competent with respect to radioactive substances.

Act No. 28 of 12.5.1972,
Section 5(1) and (2)

The 1972 Act provides that it is unlawful to manufacture, own, store, handle, transport, sell or otherwise hold or dispose of nuclear substances without a permit from the Ministry of Petroleum and Energy unless such activities are already covered by a concession to construct, own or operate a nuclear installation.

Section 5(2)
Section 8(1)
Section 8(2) and (3)

Permits may be granted for a given or undetermined period and may cover one or more of the above activities involving nuclear substances. No permit includes the right to export such material unless expressly provided, and any such permit is granted subject to such conditions as are considered necessary in connection with safety and the public interest. The conditions for granting a permit may be modified if circumstances so require.

Section 5(1)
Section (9)

The Ministry may make exceptions to the obligation to obtain a permit, provided that certain conditions are complied with. In addition, a permit may be revoked if its requirements are being substantially or repeatedly disregarded.

Section 5(3)
Section 6

It is provided that the King may decide that any activities involving nuclear fuels or radioactive products other than

---

1. RD = Royal Decree.

nuclear substances should be subject to notification or licensing. He may issue rules regarding the manufacture, handling, packaging, storage, etc. of nuclear substances, nuclear fuels or radioactive materials.

Regulations of 3.1.1983, Section 1

As mentioned above, the Regulations of 1st March 1983, issued by the Ministry of Health and Social Affairs govern the production, import and sale of radioisotopes. They apply to radioisotopes used for industrial, commercial, agricultural, medical or scientific purposes.

Section 2
Section 3

The production of radioisotopes is subject to permission by the State Institute of Radiation Hygiene (SIS), which issues the detailed conditions for all dealings involving such materials. In addition, all imports of radioisotopes must be approved by the Institute; a valid permit from the Institute is required for each import.

Regulations of 1.3.1983, Section 5

The Institute for Energy Technology (*Institutt for Energiteknikk* – IFE formerly the *Institutt for Atomenergi*) has a general permit to import radioactive substances.

Acts No. 29 and 30 of 13.12.1946

It should also be noted that imports and exports of any kind are subject to a permit under temporary prohibition Acts of 1946 concerning import and export.

Regulations of 1.6.1979, Section 3.1.c

Regulations made in 1979, pursuant to the Act on Drugs and Poisons of 1964[2], exempt from approval radioisotopes for medical uses which are produced or imported by the Institute for Energy Technology.

3. PROTECTION OF WORKERS AND THE PUBLIC AGAINST IONIZING RADIATION[3]

Act No. 1 of 18.6.1938

Legislation on radiation protection in Norway stems from a series of laws and regulations, the most important being the Act of 1938 on the Use of X-rays and Radium etc., which provides the basis for protection in this field.

Act No. 1 of 18.6.1938
RD of 23.1.1976
RD of 25.9.1953

The Ministry of Health and Social Affairs is the competent authority in matters of radiation protection; the State Institute of Radiation Hygiene (SIS) which is attached to the Ministry, is responsible, *inter alia,* for ensuring that work involving ionizing radiation is properly carried out and co-ordinates its activities with the Labour Inspectorate.

---

2. Under the Act of 1964 all pharmaceutical products must be approved by the Ministry of Health and Social Affairs before they are distributed or sold.

3. For further details see Analytical Study in the same series: "Regulations Governing Nuclear Installations and Radiation Protection", OECD/NEA, 1972.

Regulations of 4.6.1974
Regulations of 22.10.1974
Regulations of 1.7.1975
Regulations of 24.6.1977
Act No. 47 of 14.6.1974

Several Regulations made under the Act of 1938 provide for radiation protection in a number of activities covering, in particular, industrial radiography, industrial gauges and X-ray crystallography. Other Regulations issued in 1975 and 1977 concern the use of ionizing radiation in schools and approval of radiographs respectively. The latter were made in pursuance of an Act of 1974 on approval etc. of health personnel.

RD of 23.1.1976
Regulations of 31.3.1978
Regulations of 1.7.1981

A Royal Decree of 1976, pursuant to the Act of 1938, prescribes regulations on the supervision and use of installations, apparatus, material and substances which release ionizing or other radiation representing a danger to health (this Decree repealed another Royal Decree of 22nd October 1948 on the supervision of X-ray installations and radium). Regulations were issued in 1978 by the Labour Inspectorate in implementation of Act No. 4 of 4th February 1977 on the protection of workers and their environment. These Regulations prescribe protective measures during work involving ionizing radiations, and supersede other regulations on the subject dated 21st November 1947. Another series of Regulations issued in 1981 pursuant to the Act of 1938 lay down measures for protection when handling different types of radiation sources.

Regulations of 15.5.1973

In addition, detailed Regulations were issued in 1973 by the State Institute of Radiation Hygiene concerning the use of radioactive sources on drilling platforms used for drilling of petroleum in Norwegian internal waters, territorial waters etc.

The public is protected in many ways through the radiation protection regulations, as mentioned above. In addition, the SIS, which is charged with supervising radiation protection measures, deals with protection of the public by carrying out regular controls and tests of radiation-emitting equipment as well as by testing consumer goods.

Act No. 28 of 12.5.1972
Section 49

It should be pointed out that, in connection with public safety measures, the Act of 1972 provides that the King may decide that municipal and county authorities in the area where a nuclear installation is to be sited, should collaborate with the operator for protection of the neighbouring population, and that an emergency plan be prepared for relief measures in the event of an incident.

Section 15

Under the Act of 1972, the operator of a nuclear installation must take all necessary measures to ensure that no damage is caused as a result of radioactivity or the hazardous properties of nuclear fuel or radioactive products on the installation site; he must also ensure that the installation does not endanger the public safety after operations have ceased.

25

RD of 23.1.1976
Section 1
Section 3
Section 5

The Decree of 1976, made under the Act of 1938 on the Use of X-rays and Radium, etc., lays down detailed provisions on the supervision and use of installations, apparatus, material and substances which release ionizing and other radiation representing a danger to health. The text specifies the authority competent in matters of supervision in accordance with the Act of 1938, namely, the SIS, as well as the types of devices concerned and the duties of the persons using them.

The following are subject to supervision by the SIS:

- all installations, apparatus, material and substances which produce ionizing radiation and are used for medical, veterinary, scientific, industrial or other purposes;
- waste and discharges of substances which produce ionizing radiation; and
- use of lasers, radar, microwaves and other electromagnetic radiation representing a danger to health.

Section 4

Such installations, apparatus and materials cannot be sold or used without prior notification to the SIS, which may prohibit transactions or use before an authorisation has been granted to this effect. Furthermore, the SIS must be notified of new installations, or extensions or major alterations to existing facilities, and permission must be obtained from the SIS before they are used.

Section 3

Installations, facilities and other devices exempted by the Minister of Defence are not subject to this control.

Regulations of 31.3.1978

The 1978 Regulations issued by the Labour Inspectorate concerning protective measures provide for regular medical examinations of persons working with ionizing radiation, radiation dose measurements, the keeping of lists of staff exposed to radiation and submission of reports in their respect to the Labour Inspectorate.

RD of 2.11.1979

A Royal Decree, made in 1979 in implementation of the Act of 1938, prescribes the qualifications required for using X-ray devices for medical purposes.

Act No. 1 of 18.6.1938,
Section 1
and RD of 23.1.1976,
Section 1

Regulations of 1.7.1981

Finally, in 1981, the SIS issued three sets of Regulations also in pursuance of the Act of 1938 and the Regulations of 1976. These concern respectively:

- protection against radiation arising from the use and handling of unsealed radioactive sources;
- inspection of gammaradiography equipment; and
- protective measures against radiation in case of accidents connected with gammaradiography.

4. NUCLEAR INSTALLATIONS[4]

Act No. 28 of 12.5.1972
Section 4

The legal system governing nuclear installations is laid down by the Act of 1972 concerning Nuclear Energy Activities. It is provided that no person may construct, own or operate a nuclear installation without a licence.

Section 10

The competent authority in matters of licensing is the Ministry of Petroleum and Energy; the Nuclear Energy Safety Authority advises the Ministry in connection with the safety aspects of nuclear installations and makes recommendations on licensing applications. It is furthermore empowered to put into effect all measures it considers necessary for reasons of safety.

Section 11
Section 4

A licence for a nuclear installations covers both construction and operation. However, before construction and operation of an installation, the operator concerned must carry out certain procedures to obtain the authorisation or approval of the Nuclear Energy Safety Authority; the latter exercises continuous supervision over all the operations and ensures that all the conditions prescribed by the licence are being complied with. Licences are granted for a specific site and are, as a rule, limited to a given period.

Section 14

In connection with the inspection of nuclear installations, the Nuclear Energy Safety Authority may at any time demand access to any such installation and its surrounding area.

5. RADIOACTIVE WASTE MANAGEMENT

Act No. 28 of 12.5.1972,
Section 11
Section 13(1)
Regulations of 1.3.1983,
Section 2

In accordance with the Act of 1972 concerning Nuclear Energy Activities, the Nuclear Energy Safety Authority continuously supervises the operation of nuclear installations. In this framework, the Authority must ensure that radioactive waste disposal operations are carried out in compliance with the safety requirements in force. The State Institute of Radiation Hygiene is also charged with continuous supervision of radioactive waste disposal operations and sites and prescribes conditions governing waste disposal in connection with radioactive materials.

Act No. 6 of 31.3.1981,
Section 49

The Pollution Control Authority, set up under the Pollution Control Act of 1981 is competent in connection with

---

4. For further details see "Description of Licensing Systems and Inspection of Nuclear Installations", OECD/NEA, 1980.

waste and other polluting materials. The Act prescribes measures to counteract environmental pollution and to improve waste treatment, including radioactive waste.

Section 29
Section 30
Section 6

Under the Act, no person may abandon, store or transport waste in a way which results in damage to the environment, and no person may operate a storage site or facility for waste treatment which can lead to pollution without permission from the Pollution Control Authority. It is provided that radiation will be regarded as pollution to the extent determined by that Authority.

6. NUCLEAR THIRD PARTY LIABILITY[5]

Act No. 28 of 12.5.1972,
as amended

The regulations on nuclear third party liability are embodied in the Act of 1972 concerning Nuclear Energy Activities. The Act enabled Norway to ratify the Paris Convention on Third Party Liability in the Field of Nuclear Energy and its Brussels Supplementary Convention. In addition, the Act was amended to enable Norway to ratify the Brussels Convention relating to Civil Liability in the Field of Maritime Carriage of Nuclear Material.

7. NUCLEAR SECURITY

Section 51
Section 53

Although there are at present no specific regulations covering nuclear security, the Act of 1972 concerning Nuclear Energy Activities provides that the King may issue the provisions required to ensure and to ascertain by supervision that nuclear installations, nuclear fuel and radioactive products are solely used for peaceful purposes. It is also provided that persons engaged in activities in accordance with the Act have the duty to preserve secrecy concerning confidential technical information they acquire during the course of their work.

---

5. For further details see Analytical Study in the same series: "Nuclear Third Party Liability", OECD/NEA, 1976.

8. TRANSPORT[6]

Act No. 28 of 12.5.1972
Act No. 1 of 18.6.1938

The basic framework for the rules governing activities involving the transport of nuclear fuels and certain other radioactive materials is determined in the Act of 1972 concerning Nuclear Energy Activities; the transport of radioactive materials not covered by the Act of 1972 falls within the scope of the Act of 1938 on the Use of X-rays and Radium etc.

Act No. 4 of 18.6.1965
RD of 5.4.1963

The Norwegian State Railways (NSB) is the competent authority for the carriage of radioactive materials by rail, while the Minister of Communications is competent for the transport of such materials by road. The Maritime Directorate of the Ministry of Commerce and Shipping is the authority responsible for issuing regulations on the maritime carriage of dangerous goods. Regulation of the transport by air of radioactive materials is the responsibility of the Civil Aviation Administration.

The different modes of transport are regulated by rules specific to each mode as summarised in the following paragraphs.

Norwegian State
Railway's Print No. 425

The carriage by rail of radioactive materials within Norway is carried out in accordance with the provisions of the International Atomic Energy Agency (IAEA) Regulations for the Safe Transport of Radioactive Materials. The international carriage of such materials is regulated by the International Regulations concerning the Carriage of Dangerous Goods by Rail (RID).

RD of 12.2.1976
Regulations of 20.12.1979

On 15th December 1975, Norway ratified the European Agreement concerning the International Carriage of Dangerous Goods by Road (ADR) and its provisions now regulate both international and domestic transport by road of radioactive materials.

Regulations of 30.11.1979

As far as maritime transport is concerned, the relevant provisions of the International Maritime Dangerous Goods Code issued by the International Maritime Organisation – IMO have been applied to the sea transport of radioactive materials in Norway by virtue of regulations made in 1979 by the Maritime Directorate.

Regulations of 15.5.1979

Under regulations issued by the Civil Aviation Administration the carriage by air of radioactive materials is governed by the Restricted Articles Regulations of the International Air Transport Association (IATA).

---

6. For further details see Analytical Study in the same series: "Regulations Governing the Transport of Radioactive Materials", OECD/NEA, 1980.

9. PATENTS

Act No. 9 of 15.12.1967   Although the Act on Patents of 1967 contains no special provisions concerning the nuclear field, it is provided that the Government may order, when in the public interest, that the right to a particular invention be surrendered to the State.

II. INSTITUTIONAL FRAMEWORK

In Norway, responsibility for nuclear matters is vested mainly in the Ministry of Petroleum and Energy, the Ministry of Industry and the Ministry of Health and Social Affairs. It should be noted tht the former Ministry of Industry was divided into a Ministry of Industry and a Ministry of Petroleum and Energy on 11th January 1970. The Ministries are assisted in their work by bodies which have advisory and supervisory duties.

Several other Ministries also have certain responsibilities in the nuclear field when activities connected with such questions are within their competence.

1. REGULATORY AND SUPERVISORY AUTHORITIES

A. MINISTERIAL LEVEL

a) Ministry of Petroleum and Energy

The Ministry of Petroleum and Energy is the competent authority in matters of nuclear energy policy. It is responsible for providing guidelines for research and development in the nuclear field and for issuing licences in respect of nuclear installations.

The Ministry also has general co-ordinating functions and deals with budgetary matters concerning research and development in the field of nuclear energy.

b) Ministry of Industry

The Ministry of Industry deals with matters concerning prospection for deposits of uranium, thorium and other ores or minerals which may be of use for the exploitation of nuclear energy.

c) Ministry of Health and Social Affairs

The Ministry of Health and Social Affairs is responsible for the protection of public health and is therefore competent to deal with questions of radiation protection. In this capacity it is responsible not only for drafting legislation in this field, but also for ensuring that work involving ionizing radiation is properly carried out.

The Ministry performs its licensing and control functions and, to some extent, drafts regulations through the State Institute of Radiation Hygiene.

d) Ministry of Culture and Science

The above Ministry has certain responsibilities in nuclear research in the field of nuclear chemistry and nuclear physics.

e) Ministry of Commerce and Shipping

RD of 5.4.1963

The Ministry of Commerce and Shipping is the competent authority for issuing regulations on the maritime carriage of dangerous goods and for issuing import and export licences.

f) Ministry of Foreign Affairs

The above Ministry is responsible for international relations and agreements in the nuclear field. It also co-ordinates Norwegian participation in this field in international organisations.

g) Other Ministries

The Ministry of Justice, the Ministry of Agriculture, the Ministry of Communications and the Ministry of Local Government and Labour may also be called on to deal with legislative or certain administrative questions connected with nuclear energy.

B. SUBSIDIARY LEVEL

a) Nuclear Energy Safety Authority

Act No. 28 of 12.5.1972,
Section 10

Regulations of 9.2.1973,
Section 1

The Nuclear Energy Safety Authority (*Statens Atomtilsyn*) was set up by the Act of 1972 concerning Nuclear Energy Activities; it is placed under the Ministry of Petroleum and Energy for administrative purposes. It advises the Ministry as the highest specialised agency on questions of nuclear safety and is the supervisory authority in that field. It also prepares recommendations for the Ministry concerning all applications for concessions and permits involving nuclear activities.

The Authority may, on its own initiative, put into effect all measures it considers necessary for reasons of safety and is responsible for ensuring that all rules and conditions connected with safety precautions are complied with.

Act No. 28 of 12.5.1972,
Sections 11 and 13

In this connection, the Authority is responsible, from the safety viewpoint, for the licensing aspects of nuclear installations. It must exercise continuous supervision over the construction and operation of nuclear facilities, and is responsible for authorising their entry into service.

Section 15
Section 14

The Authority is also empowered to issue the necessary instructions to ensure compliance with licensing conditions; and any safety measures taken by the operator of a nuclear installation are subject to the Authority's approval. It may also demand access at any time to a nuclear installation for purposes of inspection.

Section 10

Regulations of 9.2.1973,
Section 2

The Nuclear Energy Safety Authority is managed by an Executive Board whose members are appointed by the King for a period of four years. The Board consists of a Chairman, a Vice-Chairman and six other members and is convened by its Chairman as and when necessary.

Section 4

The Authority has a Secretariat charged with the conduct of day-to-day business under the responsibility of an Administrator.

Section 5

The Board prepares proposals for annual budgets and annual reports as well as statements of accounts for submission to the Ministry.

b) State Institute of Radiation Hygiene

RD of 25.9.1953

Act No. 1 of 18.6.1938
RD of 23.1.1976

The State Institute of Radiation Hygiene (*Statens Institutt for Strålehygiene* – SIS) was set up in 1939 under the Ministry of Health and Social Affairs. Certain of the Institute's responsibilities are defined in a Royal Decree of 1953. In accordance with the 1938 Act on the Use of X-rays and Radium etc., and the Royal Decree of 1976 it is the competent authority for radiation protection in Norway.

Act No. 1 of 18.6.1938
RD of 23.1.1976

Regulations of 1.3.1983,
Sections 2, 3 and 4

The SIS is empowered to licence and control all facilities and apparatus emitting ionizing radiation with regard to radiation protection and public health and may issue the necessary regulations for this purpose.

Under the Regulations of 1983, the SIS is the authority responsible for granting permits for the production, import and sale of radioisotopes. Furthermore, the Institute issues detailed conditions governing their production, storage, labelling and quality control, as well as conditions regarding disposal, radiation protection and facilities and equipment connected with such materials.

In addition to the above duties, the SIS is charged with research and educational work in the fields of dosimetry, radiation hygiene and other related topics.

The SIS is managed by a Director who is responsible for its day to day work. He is appointed by the Government. Heads of departments are appointed by the Ministry of Health and Social Affairs; other employees are appointed by the Institute.

The research activities conducted by SIS are carried out in the three following sectors: medical radiation physics, industrial radiation physics and medicine.

2. ADVISORY BODIES

Royal Norwegian Council for Scientific and Industrial Research

Parliamentary
Resolution of 10.6.1946

The Council (*Norges teknisk-naturviten-skapelige forsk-ningråd* – NTNF), which was set up in July 1946, is charged with encouraging scientific and industrial research and advising the Government and Ministerial departments in this field.

The Ministry of Petroleum and Energy charges the Council with reviewing the annual programme and budget proposals as well as the long term plans of the Institute of Energy Technology (IFE); it submits recommendations to the Government in this respect.

The Council which is attached to the Ministry of Industry receives the necessary funds for its activities from four different Ministries: Industry, Petroleum and Energy, Environment, as well as Local Government and Labour. It consists of forty members appointed for four years; twelve such members represent various Ministries, twelve represent universities and research institutes and thirteen represent industry and ship-building; finally three members represent the employees. The Council appoints an Executive Board of eight members, one of whom is elected Chairman, and is assisted in its work by nineteen specialised Standing Committees; one of these is concerned among other things with fundamental nuclear research.

3. PUBLIC AND SEMI-PUBLIC AGENCIES

Institute for Energy Technology (IFE)

i) *Legal status*

RD of 30.5.1947

The IFE (*Institutt for Energiteknikk*) was set up in 1948 as the *Institutt for Atomenergi* (IFA) and became an independent foundation in 1953 under the Ministry of Industry (as from 1978 under the Ministry of Petroleum and Energy); in 1980, its name was changed to its present one, in line with the developments in its work in recent years and adapted to national goals, as specified by the authorities.

ii) *Responsibilities*

The Institute's mandate, as defined in 1980 is to "conduct research and development, analyses, etc., within the field of energy, including nuclear research and other fields particularly suited to the Institute's competence".

The IFE is the national centre for nuclear research and development and as such, it carries out work in nuclear safety, environmental protection, waste management and materials technology.

The IFE owns and operates the JEEP II reactor, a 2MW, heavy water cooled and moderated research reactor, as well as the 20 MW Halden Boiling Water Reactor which is used in an International Project, set up in 1958 under the auspices of the OECD Nuclear Energy Agency for the purpose of carrying out a joint programme of research and experiments between national centres and nuclear power manufacturing industries from OECD Member countries in connection with the operation of a boiling water reactor.

IFE also produces and distributes radioisotopes; it has a gamma radiation plant in operation and arranges courses in data processing and isotope applications.

The activities of IFE are geographically divided between two sites, Halden, where the OECD International Reactor Project is located, and Kjeller which is the main research centre.

The research and development activities are performed in the following sectors:

- energy and systems technology;
- petroleum technology;
- International Halden Reactor Project;
- materials technology;
- isotopes and chemistry;
- industrial chemistry;
- physics.

The Institute also operates a waste treatment plant which processes radioactive waste from its own activities and from outside sources.

iii) *Structure*

The Institute is managed by a Board consisting of six members, one appointed by the Government, one by the firm Norsk Hydro A/S and two by the Royal Council for Scientific and Industrial Research (NTNF). The remaining two members are chosen by and from among the staff and are appointed by the Government.

A Managing Director, appointed by the Board, is entrusted with the day to day running of the Institute which has a staff of 520 people.

iv) *Financing*

The Institute's yearly expenditure is covered by grants from the Ministry of Petroleum and Energy and by income from research and development work undertaken on a contractual basis with other national and foreign firms and institutions; at present the ratio is 40% and 60% respectively.

In connection with the Halden International Reactor Project, the majority of the programmes are financed by contributions from Signatory countries to the Halden Agreement and Associated Parties.

PORTUGAL

TABLE OF CONTENTS

I. GENERAL REGULATORY REGIME

Decree No. 113-C/81
of 4.9.1981

There is no framework Act governing the nuclear sector in Portugal. Instead, there are a series of laws, regulations and orders covering nuclear activities, which provide for detailed provisions in their respect. At present, overall responsibility for the nuclear sector is vested in the Minister of Industry, Energy and Exportation.

D.L.[1] No. 548/77
of 31.12.1977

Although the institutional framework for such activities will be described in the following Chapter, it should be mentioned here that in 1977, the Ministry of Industry was reorganised. It was decided to create new departments and to suppress others, including the Junta de Energia Nuclear (JEN). The tasks of the JEN, which was formally abolished by Decree, were distributed to other existing departments in the Ministry and to new bodies set up for that purpose.

1. MINING REGIME

D.L. No. 37.986
of 27.9.1950

D.L. No. 40.135
of 20.4.1955

In Portugal a number of Decree-Laws have been issued since 1950 to regulate prospection for and exploitation of radioactive ores. Already in 1955, the Minister of Finance was authorised by Decree-Law to fix export taxes for radioactive materials and their concentrates.

D.L. No. 41.995
of 5.12.1958,
Section 2(e)

Section 3(a)

Section 3(j)
D.L. No. 48.568
of 4.9.1968,
Section 1(1)(a)

The JEN was given wide powers to organise, orient and promote exploration for radioactive ores and other source materials required for its activities. It was also competent to propose to the Government the necessary legislation for exploiting and developing research on source materials to further the national purpose, and in general, to secure mining concessions. JEN was also empowered to supervise all activities involving the mining of radioactive ores.

Decisions No. 2 and 3
of 19.3.1971

D.L. No. 49.398
of 24.11.1969,
Section 1(1)(b)

Two Decisions respectively define the rules to be complied with for concluding contracts related to the prospecting for and exploitation of radioactive ore deposits and the licensing of bodies engaged in such activities. In particular, private firms are required to take out licences.

Decree No. 67/77
of 6.5.1977,
Section 5

Order No. 126/78
of 22.5.1978,
Section 1(1)(c)

Decree No. 67/77
Section 2

The responsibilities of JEN concerning mining have now been divided between the National Uranium Enterprise (*Empresa Nacional de Urânio* – ENU), the General Directorate for Energy (*Direcção Geral de Energia*) and the General Directorate for Geology and Mines (*Direcção Geral de Geologia e Minas*), both within the Ministry of Industry, Energy and Exportation.

---

1. D.L. = Decree-Law.

2. RADIOACTIVE SUBSTANCES, NUCLEAR FUELS AND EQUIPMENT

D.L. No. 49.398
of 24.11.1969

Activities involving production of and trade in radioactive substances and nuclear fuels are governed by a Decree-Law made in 1969.

Order No. 126/78
of 22.5.1978, Section 1

The General Directorate for Energy (DGE) within the Ministry of Industry, Energy and Exportation is the body responsible for controlling the production of and trade in nuclear fuels for industrial uses.

D.L. No. 44.060
of 25.11.1961

The production of and trade in radioactive substances and radiation-emitting appliances are subject to prior authorisation by the Committee for Protection against Ionizing Radiation.

D.L. No. 41.995
of 5.12.1958,
Section 39

There are exemptions from certain customs formalities for imports of radioisotopes, radioactive substances and radiation-emitting appliances.

D.L. No. 49.398
of 24.11.1969,
Section 1(1)

Sections 1(2) and 2(2)

Section 4(1)

The import and export of concentrates of radioactive substances, the fabrication, import and export of nuclear fuels, the treatment of and trade in irradiated fuels and other activities of an industrial nature are subject to licensing. These licences are issued for a limited period on a case-by-case basis, upon proof that the establishments concerned have the necessary technical knowledge and financial resources. Their premises are subject to inspection by the competent authorities. In addition, contracts, the purpose of which is the establishment, modification or transfer of associations concerned with the above-mentioned activities, are subject to ministerial approval.

3. PROTECTION OF WORKERS AND THE PUBLIC AGAINST IONIZING RADIATION[2]

D.L. No. 44.060
of 25.11.1961, as
amended
by D.L. No. 45.132 of
13.7.1963
and an Order of 3.3.1965

Order No. 53/71
of 3.2.1971,
Section 28

Regulations for the radiation protection of workers and the public are embodied in a Decree-Law of 1961. Its provisions stipulate in detail the measures to be taken and fixes the standards to be observed. In addition, an Order approving general health and safety regulations for workers in industrial facilities provides that premises where radioactive substances or radiation-emitting devices are used, handled or produced must be kept in compliance with the special safety regulations in force.

---

2. For further details see Analytical Study in the same series: "Regulations Governing Nuclear Installations and Radiation Protection", OECD/NEA, 1972.

D.L. No. 548/77
of 13.12.1977,
Section 64

D.L. No. 361/79
of 1.9.1979
Section 26

Until the energy sector was reorganised, the Committee for Protection against Ionizing Radiation was the competent authority in matters of radiation protection. Its abolition will be defined later by another Decree-Law. It is foreseen that this Decree-Law will determine the transfer of responsibilities to the General Directorate for Health (*Direcção Geral de Saúde*) as well as the competence of the Ministry of Industry, Energy and Exportation in such matters. Also, another Decree-Law lays down that the Department for Radiological Protection and Safety (*Departamento de Protecção e Segurança Radiológica*) within the National Laboratory of Industrial Engineering and Technology (*Laboratorio Nacional de Engenharia e Tecnologia Industrial* – LNETI) has some responsibilities in the radiation protection field.

D.L. No. 44.060
of 25.11.1961, Annex I
as amended by Order
of 3.3.1965

The 1961 Decree-Law provides for different radiation protection standards for members of the public and for workers. A distinction is also made within each category according to the proximity of the group or individual to the radiation source and to the type of work involved.

Annex I

For persons living in the vicinity of establishments containing radiation sources and individual members of the population, the maximum permitted radiation dose is 0.5 rem per year, while for the population as a whole, the maximum accumulated dose is 5 rem per person over a period of thirty years.

Annex I
Section 5

The radiation dose for persons working in controlled areas must not exceed 12 rem per year, while persons who occasionally enter a controlled area or who, in view of their activity are exposed elsewhere to a radiation source must not receive a radiation dose in excess of 1.5 rem per year. Physical control of radiation doses received by workers and their medical supervision must be organised by the person responsible for the installation concerned. Persons under eighteen years of age must not engage in work exposing them to radiation.

Section 4

Finally, radioactive substances and radiation-emitting appliances must be the subject of protection measures and be used in such a way as to reduce as far as possible the doses received by workers.

4. NUCLEAR INSTALLATIONS[3]

D.L. No. 49.398
of 24.11.1969

The licensing and operation of nuclear installations in Portugal are governed by the Decree-Law of 1969 which lays

---

3. For further details see: "Description of Licensing Systems and Inspection of Nuclear Installations", OECD/NEA, 1980.

Decree No. 487
of 5.12.1972

D.L. No. 48.568
of 4.9.1968

down the licensing system for all nuclear industrial activities, and a Decree of 1972 made in implementation of the Decree-Law which stipulates the licensing procedure for nuclear power plants. Another Decree-Law of 1968 lays down the system for inspecting nuclear installations.

D.L. No. 548/77
of 31.12.1977
Section 7

The General Directorate for Energy (DGE) and the Protection and Nuclear Safety Bureau (*Gabinete de Protecção e Segurança Nuclear* – GPSN) are involved, both within the Ministry of Industry, Energy and Exportation, in the licensing, operation and inspection of nuclear installations.

Decree No. 487/72
of 5.12.1972,
Section 2

Order No. 126/78
of 31.5.1978,
Section 1(1)*(a)* and *(c)*

According to the Decree of 1972 these tasks were within the competence of the General Directorate for Electricity Services (DGSE) and JEN; they have been transferred to DGE and GPSN, respectively, as provided by an Order of 1978.

Section 1

Nuclear power facilities must be established in compliance with the Decree-Law of 1969. The licensing procedure takes place in three stages, each one resulting in delivery of a prior licence for site approval, construction and operation respectively.

Section 2

Section 3

Sections 6 et 7

The application for a preliminary licence for site approval must contain all the information required to assess the technological, economic and safety aspects of the installation concerned and the local population is informed of the application by notification in the Official Gazette. When the Government grants a preliminary licence, the applicant must apply to the DGE for a construction licence and attach a preliminary safety report. Requests for a construction licence are examined from the viewpoint of the design of the facility, construction techniques, safety, etc. The Government takes its decision on the granting of the construction licence following submission of a report by the DGE. The operating licence is then issued on the basis of a final safety report.

D.L. No. 48.568
of 4.9.1968

Section 1

Nuclear facilities are inspected regularly, in accordance with the provisions of the Decree-Law of 1968. The inspections are scientific and technical and are intended to check the effectiveness of radiation protection measures and nuclear safety.

5. RADIOACTIVE WASTE MANAGEMENT

At a present there are no particular regulations concerning waste management in Portugal.

6. NUCLEAR THIRD PARTY LIABILITY

Decree No. 33
of 11.3.1977

Portugal ratified the Paris Convention on Third Party Liability in the Field of Nuclear Energy but has not yet enacted national nuclear third party liability legislation[4].

7. NUCLEAR SECURITY

Although there are no specific provisions on the subject in domestic legislation, at international level, Portugal acceded to the Non-Proliferation Treaty on 15th December 1977 and has concluded the subsequent safeguards agreement and subsidiary arrangements with the IAEA which came into force in mid-1979.

8. TRANSPORT[5]

Order No. 20.558
of 6.5.1964

There are as yet no specific regulations concerning the transport of radioactive materials in Portugal. However, an Order of 1964 provides for the application of the IAEA Regulations for the Safe Transport of Radioactive Materials, regardless of the mode of transport used. The latest (1973) Edition of the Regulations is applied, as laid down in the above Order.

9. PATENTS

There are no specific provisions concerning patents in the nuclear field.

---

4.   A Bill on Nuclear Third Party Liability, also taking into account the provisions of the Brussels Supplementary Convention is presently under preparation.
5.   For further details see Analytical Study in the same series: "Regulations Governing the Transport of Radioactive Materials", OECD/NEA, 1980.

II. INSTITUTIONAL FRAMEWORK

D.L. No. 358/76
of 14.5.1976
D.L. No. 548/77
of 31.12.1977

In Portugal, responsibility for the control and management of nuclear activities is vested in the Minister of Industry, Energy and Exportation, as mentioned in Chapter I. A Decree-Law of 1976 provides for the general organisation of the Ministry of Industry, Energy and Exportation, in accordance with the needs of the national industry and energy sector and its structure; the Decree-Law also provides for greater involvement of the State in such matters. In 1977, a new structure was established on the basis of the above Decree-Law, setting up new departments within the Ministry and providing for the abolition of others, in particular the Junta de Energia Nuclear.

Section 7

The 1977 Decree-Law provides for a number of centralised departments and regional delegations. It set up the National Laboratory of Industrial Engineering and Technology (LNETI) which is responsible for technological research and development in support of the different industries, as well as the General Directorate for Energy (DGE) and the Protection and Nuclear Safety Bureau (GSPN). The DGE is generally in charge of the production, transport, distribution and use of the different forms of energy, including nuclear energy. The GSPN for its part, is responsible for control and inspection of nuclear power plants and related materials and equipment.

Order No. 126
of 22.5.1978

The Minister of Industry and Technology (now the Minister of Industry, Energy and Exportation) reorganised the energy sector, in particular, to combine nuclear energy with the overall energy sector and to merge nuclear activities with other industrial and research activities.

Sections 1 and 7

In connection with the responsibilities previously discharged by the Junta de Energia Nuclear, the Order provides that they shall be divided between the LNETI, the DGE, the Protection and Nuclear Safety Bureau (GSPN) and the General Directorate for Geology and Mines (DGGM).

1. REGULATORY AND SUPERVISORY AUTHORITIES

a) Minister of Industry, Energy and Exportation

The Minister of Industry, Energy and Exportation is the authority responsible, under the Government, for all nuclear activities in Portugal.

D.L. No. 548/77
of 31.12.1977
Section 1

In addition to providing for the overall structure of the Ministry of Industry, Energy and Exportation, the Decree-Law of 1977 lays down in detail the responsibilities and tasks of the Minister. He is empowered to prepare and propose the energy and industry plan within the general national development programme; he supervises and directs the management of public and nationalised companies in the industry and energy sector, without prejudice to the competence of other Ministers concerned, and he promotes R and D in that sector as well as technological agreements on scientific and technical co-operation; and finally, he controls activities in the industrial and energy sectors.

Section 3
Section 15
Ordinance No. 204/79
of 16.7.1979

More generally, he proposes the industrial and technological policy and is responsible for having it carried out in the framework of the general policy determined by the Government. The Minister may also set up under his control specialised institutes for the purpose of encouraging industrial and energy development. In addition he has established by Ordinance a number of research and development services in the nuclear field, within the Ministry, covering, *inter alia,* nuclear physics and instrumentation, reactors, nuclear fuels, radioisotopes, radiochemistry and radiobiology.

b) Minister of Finance

D.L. No. 40.135
of 20.4.1955

The Minister of Finance is generally competent, jointly with the Minister of Industry, Energy and Exportation for the financing of public industrial activities. He is also authorised to fix customs duties in connection with radioactive ores and their products.

Decree No. 490/76
of 23.6.1976
Decree No. 67/77
of 6.5.1977, Statute
Section 26
Section 34

As regards the National Uranium Enterprise (ENU), the Minister of Finance, jointly with the Minister of Industry, Energy and Exportation fixed by Decree the authorised capital of the Company, and is empowered to increase this capital by another joint decree. Together with the Minister of Industry, Energy and Exportation he appoints the Supervisory Commission of ENU and may authorise the latter to take out loans in national and foreign currency and to issue shares.

D.L. No. 361/79,
Section 13

In connection with the National Laboratory of Industrial Engineering and Technology (LNETI), the Minister of Finance and the Minister of Industry, Energy and Exportation are empowered to fix by Order the conditions of operation of the LNETI Administrative Board.

c) Minister of Labour

Decree No. 67/77
Section 36

The Minister of Labour is the authority responsible for matters involving working conditions in industrial facilities.

He is, *inter alia,* empowered to approve the statute of the ENU personnel, jointly with the Minister of Industry, Energy and Exportation.

d) Minister of Social Affairs

Notwithstanding the plans concerning abolition of the Committee for Protection Against Ionizing Radiation (see Part 3 concerning radiation protection in preceding Chapter), the Minister of Social Affairs will continue to have a relevant role in the field of protection against ionizing radiation.

2. ADVISORY BODIES

Co-Ordinating Group on the Licensing of Nuclear Installations

Ordinance of 30.3.1976

The Co-ordinating Group on the Licensing of Nuclear Installations (*Grupo de Coordenação para as Actividades de Licenciamento de Centrais Nucleares*) was set up pending the revision, currently in progress, of Decree No. 487 of 5th December 1972, on the licensing procedure for nuclear power plants.

Order No. 50/79 of 19.2.1979, Section 6(b)

The Co-ordinating Group, which was set up during this transitional phase, is responsible for the preparation of reports on the status of present licensing activities, for recommending measures for improving the licensing procedure and for proposing measures for the transfer of this procedure to the new bodies to be responsible for this task.

3. PUBLIC AND SEMI-PUBLIC AGENCIES

D.L. No. 548/77
Order No. 126/78

As mentioned above, the Ministry of Industry, Energy and Exportation, was reorganised into different new departments, some of which are untrusted with the tasks of the JEN. While these departments are within the Ministry, they enjoy a measure of autonomy under the supervisory authority of the Minister of Industry, Energy and Exportation and, in view of their scientific and technical responsibilities, it is appropriate to discuss them in this part of the Study.

a) General Directorate for Energy

D.L. No. 548/77

The area of responsibility of the DGE, as already specified, covers the operational aspects of the overall energy sector, namely, the production, transport, distribution and use of the various forms of energy, including nuclear energy.

Section 20

The tasks of the DGE are the following:

− to provide technical support to the members of the Government responsible for formulating the policy for the sector assigned to the DGE;
− to propose and to implement, within that policy, actions intended to develop and promote industrial enterprise in its sector;
− to study and to propose legislation regulating the activities within its field of competence;
− to study and to propose measures for the improvement of laboratory and production processes in its sector, and also to provide technological assistance to industrial undertakings while ensuring that the regulatory provisions involved are observed;
− to promote and to elaborate draft national standards, regulations and technical specifications connected with products and facilities within its field of competence.

Order No. 126/78
Section 1

The Order of 1978 specifies the tasks previously discharged by the JEN which are now the responsibility of the DGE:

Ordinance No. 172/79
of 25.6.1979

− relations with foreign nuclear governmental organisations, as well as national representations in international organisations, without prejudice to the specific responsibilities of LNETI;

Order No. 126/78
Section 1

− licensing and inspection of nuclear installations in accordance with Decree-Laws No. 48.568 and 49.398 of 1968 and 1969 respectively, without prejudice to the specific responsibilities of the GPSN;
− preparation of technical and economic studies on nuclear plants and fuels as well as activities connected with safeguards for nuclear materials;
− generally assess for the Minister of Industry, Energy an Exportation matters in relation to the management of uranium ores and concentrates.

b) General Directorate for Geology and Mines

The DGGM is generally responsible for the stock-taking and management of mineral resources.

D.L. No. 548/77

The DGGM has been given the same duties as those entrusted to the DGE (see above) in connection with its own scope of activities.

Order No. 126/78
Section 2

The Order of 1978 specifies the tasks prevously discharged by the JEN which now are the responsibility of the DGGM, namely mining and prospecting activities in the nuclear field, with the exception of the tasks entrusted to the National Uranium Enterprise under Decree No. 67 of 6th May 1977.

c) Protection and Nuclear Safety Bureau

Order No. 126/78
Section 7
D.L. No. 548/77,
Section 23

The activities of the JEN connected with the safety of nuclear power plants, as laid down by Decree-Law No. 487/72 of 5th December 1972, have been assigned to the GPSN. The GPSN is responsible for control and surveillance in the field of the peaceful uses of nuclear energy, and in particular it must:

- control the safety of nuclear reactors and power plants, assess the effectiveness of the different safety techniques as well as verify from the viewpoint of quality control the materials, systems and components used;
- undertake the inspections required to ensure the protection of workers and the general public against the hazards of ionizing radiation arising from the construction, operation and decommissioning of nuclear reactors and power plants;
- promote and prepare draft national standards, regulations and technical specifications relating to nuclear installations.

d) National Laboratory of Industrial Engineering and Technology

D.L. No. 548/77

The LNETI was set up within the framework of the reorganisation of the Ministry of Industry, Energy and Exportation. It incorporates the General Directorate of Nuclear Engineering and Physics and the Central Services, formerly with the JEN.

i) *Legal status*

Section 24
D.L. No. 361/79
of 1.9.1979,
Sections 1 and 2

The LNETI is an agency for technological research and development which provides technical support to the different industrial sectors in the ambit of the Ministry of Industry, Energy and Exportation. It is endowed with legal personality, owns property and enjoys administrative and financial autonomy.

47

ii) Responsibilities

The responsibilities of the LNETI are the following:

D.L. No. 548/77
Section 24

- to undertake applied research in accordance with the objectives of the national programme;
- to provide technological assistance to industrial undertakings, with a view to improving manufacturing processes and supplying innovative techniques;
- to provide the analytical assistance required for quality control of products and related inspection and technical surveillance;
- to collect, co-ordinate and disseminate technical information of interest to the Ministerial services and undertakings concerned;
- to train specialists in techniques of interest to the different sectors of industry.

D.L. No. 361/79,
Section 5
Section 6
and Ordinance
No. 172/79

In particular, the LNETI co-ordinates and carries out R and D technical programmes and projects, directly related to industrial development, through contracts with national undertakings or in association with national and international bodies. LNETI is also responsible for promoting, participating in and ensuring co-operation with similar foreign and international agencies in the field technology, energy and industry, and participates in and implements scientific and technical international co-operation agreements.

iii) Structure

D.L. No. 361/79,
Section 8

The High Council for Engineering and Industrial Technology (*Conselho Superior de Engenharia e Tecnologia Industrial*) is the LNETI's supervisory body. The governing bodies of LNETI are the President, the General Board of Management (*Conselho geral*) and the Administrative Board (*Conselho administrativo*).

Section 8
Section 15

The High Council for Engineering and Industrial Technology was set up by the Decree-Law establishing the structure of LNETI. Its composition, tasks and operating procedure will be fixed by ordinance of the Minister of Industry, Energy and Exportation. The meetings of the High Council are chaired by the Minister; the members include representatives of the Ministry's central departments, universities and public institutions whose work is directly connected with the LNETI's as well as representatives of trade unions and financial and other organisations interested in technological and industrial development.

Section 16

The High Council's responsibilities are to contribute to the determination of the scientific and technological policy in industry and energy; to establish the priorities in the development of LNETI's activities and to give its opinion on LNETI's planned programme and projects.

Section 11 *The General Board of Management* includes the directors of the institutes and departments incorporated in LNETI, the directors of external relations, administrative and financial services and staff representatives from among senior technical executives. The President of LNETI is Chairman of the General Board of Management. He is assisted by a Vice-Chairman.

Section 12 The General Board meets regularly every two months and is responsible, *inter alia,* for planning the working programme of LNETI.

Section 13 *The Administrative Board* is chaired by the President of LNETI, who is assisted by the Vice-Chairman, and includes the Director of the Financial Services, a representative of the General Directorate for Public Accounts and the head accountant of LNETI.

The Administrative Board meets regularly twice a month and is competent, *inter alia,* to authorise expenditures for the running of LNETI and investments.

Section 21 The LNETI departments responsible for nuclear activities are the Energy Institute and the Protection and Radiological Safety Department.

Section 23 In the Energy Institute, the *Nuclear Energy and Engineering Department* deals with the promotion of and carries out R and D in the engineering field and the *Nuclear Science and Technology Department* is responsible for the promotion of and carries out R and D in the applications of nuclear science and technology for peaceful purposes. The *Protection and Radiological Safety Department* deals with the radiological safety of nuclear installations and radioactive equipment, radiation protection and co-ordinates studies on environmental radioactivity monitoring.

iv) *Financing*

Section 51 In addition to funds allotted from the general State budget, the revenue of LNETI is derived from remuneration for services supplied to public and private undertakings as well as income from property and profits from patented inventions.

e) National Uranium Enterprise

i) *Legal status*

Decree No. 67/77 of 6.5.1977, Statute Section 1

Decree No. 67/77 Section 2

ENU is a public corporation, endowed with legal personality and enjoys administrative and financial autonomy, under the overriding authority of the Minister of Industry, Energy and Exportation. It is governed by the law applicable to public undertakings, by its Statute and subsidiarily by private law.

49

Section 3

ii) Responsibilities

The purpose of ENU is to:

– prospect for, explore and exploit uranium deposits;
– to set up and to operate facilities for recovery and treatment of uranium ores and to market the products obtained.

Section 4

ENU may also carry out activities related to its main purpose, in particular by providing services in connection with the use of uranium in the peaceful applications of nuclear energy.

iii) Structure

The governing bodies of ENU are the Board of Management and the Supervisory Commission.

Section 13
Section 14

The Board of Managements is made up of three to five Administrators, one of whom is appointed by the Council of Ministers on the proposal of the Minister of Industry, Energy and Exportation. The members of the Board are appointed for a three-year term which is renewable.

Section 21
Section 19

The Board of Management meets regularly once a week and is responsible, *inter alia,* for defining the policy and objectives of ENU.

Section 26

The Supervisory Commission is made up of three members, one of whom is elected Chairman, and two deputies. The members are appointed by joint ordinance of the Ministers of Finance and Industry, Energy and Exportation for a three-year term which is renewable.

The Commission meets regularly once a month and is responsible, *inter alia,* for ensuring that the operating rules of ENU are observed and for supervising its management. It also examines the accounts of ENU.

iv) Financing

Section 6
Section 7

The funds of ENU are made up of authorised capital, the amount of which was fixed by joint Decree-Law No. 490/76 of 6th June 1976 of the Ministers of Finance and Industry, Energy and Exportation. This capital may be increased or reduced by joint Ministerial Decision. Revenue is also derived from property administered by it and from services supplied.

50

SPAIN

TABLE OF CONTENTS

I. GENERAL REGULATORY REGIME

Decree-Law of
22.10.1951
(BO¹ of 24.10.1951),
Section 7

Act No. 25/1964
of 29.4.1964
(BO of 4.5.1964)

After the end of World War II, Spain was aware that nuclear energy production would be playing an important role in the next decade, and therefore set up a public body, the Junta de Energia Nuclear (Nuclear Energy Commission), with full powers over nuclear matters. At the same time, Spain expanded its legislation in the field of atomic energy and in particular, on 29th April 1964, adopted the Act on Third Party Liability in the Field of Nuclear Energy, referred to as the Nuclear Energy Act. This is an outline Act leading to the introduction and development of a general programme of action in the nuclear field.

Act No. 15/1980
of 22.4.1980
(BO of 25.4.1980);
Decree No. 2967/1979
of 7.12.1979
(BO of 14.1.1982)

Since the early 1970s or so, the Spanish authorities have been amending the previous legal and institutional regime. The nuclear sector has been reorganised by separating research from industrial and commercial activities. The Junta de Energia Nuclear has been made responsible for research and development whereas the Nuclear Safety Council has been entrusted with tasks relating to nuclear safety control and radiation protection, and the National Uranium Enterprise (ENUSA) with industrial activities in the nuclear fuel cycle, except for radioactive waste management, to be dealt with by the Junta.

1. MINING REGIME

Decree of 23.12.1948
as amended by Act of
17.7.1958;
Act No. 25/1964
of 29.4.1964,
Section 19

With the Act of 17th July 1958, referred to as the Freedom of Mining Act, radioactive ore prospecting and mining activities became open to any private individual.

Decree-Law of
22.10.1951,
Sections 3 and 4

Until then, Spain had had a system whereby the Junta de Energia Nuclear held exclusive mining rights whilst prospecting activities remained free.

Act No. 25/1964
of 29.4.1964,
Section 19

Individuals and firms wishing to search for and mine radioactive ores must apply for an exploration licence and a mining concession to the Ministry of Industry and Energy. The applications are accompanied by a report drawn up by ENUSA (see below) and are governed by the general law on mining. ENUSA is responsible for supervising these activities

---

1. **BO** = *Boletin Oficial del Estado:* Official State Gazette.

and may submit proposals for any suitable measures to the Ministry of Industry and Energy. The Ministry keeps a record of the quantities of radioactive ores mined.

These rules do not apply to ENUSA, the company that has taken over the mining activities formerly carried out by the Junta de Energia Nuclear. ENUSA may purchase from private individuals an annual quota of radioactive ore, which is fixed by the Minister of Industry and Energy. The ores are classified under two categories, depending on whether or not the uranium is associated with another mineral.

2. RADIOACTIVE SUBSTANCES, NUCLEAR FUELS AND EQUIPMENT

Act No. 25/1964 of 29.4.1964, Section 22s

Under the Nuclear Energy Act of 29th April 1964, private enterprises are allowed to produce and market nuclear substances and equipment.

Section 5

Decree No. 3322/1971 of 23.12.1971 (BO of 15.1.1972)

Since in theory the Junta de Energia Nuclear was not empowered under its own rules to carry out nuclear industrial and marketing activities, a company was set up in 1971 for this purpose: the National Uranium Enterprise (ENUSA). This is a company established under private law which, among other things, is responsible for producing and emergency-stockpiling nuclear substances.

Act No. 15/1980 of 22.4.1980 (BO of 25.4.1980), Section 3

Act No. 25/1964 of 29.4.1964, Sections 22 and 31

Decree No. 2967/1979 of 7.12.1979, Section 11

The Minister of Industry and Energy authorises the manufacture of nuclear or radioactive components after examining a report drawn up by the Nuclear Safety Council. He is also responsible for granting import and export licences with foreign firms regarding nuclear substances.

In the case of ENUSA, the Minister of Industry and Energy approves the standard form contracts for agreements between the company and third parties, and he is consulted regarding the selling prices of nuclear substances to be applied by ENUSA.

3. PROTECTION OF WORKERS AND THE PUBLIC AGAINST IONIZING RADIATION

Order of 22.12.1959 (BO of 28.12.1959)

Order of 10.7.1962 (BO of 25.7.1962)

Radiation protection was mentioned for the first time in Spanish regulations in 1959. The Order of 22nd December 1959 contains standards for protection against ionizing radiation. Legislation on radiation protection has since

Order of 9.3.1971
(BO of 16.3.1971)

Act No. 25/1964
of 29.4.1964

expanded and the Order, as amended by an implementing Order in 1962, was supplemented by a further one in 1971, laying down general rules on safety and hygiene in the workplace. General provisions concerning protection against ionizing radiation have likewise been included in the Nuclear Energy Act of 29th April 1964.

RD[2] No. 2519/1982
of 12.8.1982
(BO of 8.10.1982)

In 1982, a Royal Decree approved new radiation protection regulations. The Regulations were made pursuant to the radiation protection principles laid down by the Nuclear Energy Act of 29th April 1964, as amended.

Section 2

These Regulations replace the different standards which existed on the subject, in particular, those specified in the above-mentioned Orders of 22nd December 1959 and 10th July 1962 respectively which provided for lower or threshold limits similar to the threshold limits prescribed by the 1982 Regulations. The latter contain detailed administrative and technical provisions applicable to nuclear and to radioactive installations as well as to the use of radiation-emitting equipment. The new standards conform to international regulations on radiation protection and nuclear safety, in particular the recommendations of the International Atomic Energy Agency (IAEA). The Regulations also take into account the recent Euratom Directives.

Sections 8 to 12
Sections 13 to 15
Sections 40 to 46
Sections 59 to 62

The Regulations fix the basic radiation protection measures for occupationally-exposed workers as well as for the population as a whole and on an individual basis; they contain provisions on radioactive waste, medical supervision, inspection of installations as well as on activities which may lead to exposure to radiation. Non-compliance with the Regulations is subject to various penalties. The three annexes contain definitions as well as tables giving radiation exposure dose limits.

The Minister of Industry and Energy, the Minister of Health and the Nuclear Safety Council are the authorities responsible for ensuring implementation of the Regulations, without prejudice to the special duties of other Ministries or national agencies.

Act No 15/1980 of
22.4.1980,
Section 2

Decree No 53/1963
of 10.1.1963
(BO of 19.1.1963)

Radiation protection is a matter for the Nuclear Safety Council. In particular, the latter is responsible for radiation protection checks both within and around atomic facilities. In addition, the Directorate-General of Civil Protection organises radioactivity warning networks which take the action required when any abnormal increase in radioactivity is observed.

---

2. RD = *Real Decreto:* Royal Decree.

4. NUCLEAR INSTALLATIONS[3]

Decree No 157/1963
of 26.1.1963

Act No 25/1964
of 29.4.1964

Decree No 2072/1968
of 27.7.1968

Decree No 2869/1972
of 21.7.1972
(BO of 24.10.1972)

In Spain there is no State monopoly for the production of nuclear power, and private industrial concerns may also become nuclear operators. The first enactment governing the operation of nuclear facilities appeared in 1963 as a Decree regulating industry in general. However, it was not until 29th April 1964, when the Nuclear Energy Act was adopted, that special regulations concerning nuclear installations were issued. The Decree of 27th July 1968 establishing a system for licensing industries producing and using nuclear power was superseded by the Decree of 21st July 1972 concerning the approval of the Regulations on nuclear and radioactive installations.

Act No 15/1980
of 22.4.1980

These enactments were followed by the Act of 22nd April 1980 setting up a Nuclear Safety Council, and this is now the basic law in force and supersedes the Decrees and the Act mentioned above.

Section 3
Section 2(b)

The various types of licence required for nuclear and radioactive installations falling within the first category are issued by the Minister of Industry and Energy, subject to any special rules laid down by the Autonomous Communities. Prior to issuing the preliminary licence for site approval, the Minister consults the local authorities concerned, the Autonomous Communities, Pre-autonomy Bodies or, failing this, the Provinces concerned, whose opinions are forwarded to the Nuclear Safety Council. The latter draws up a report for the Minister of Industry and Energy. Construction and operating licences, both provisional and final are granted by the Minister according to a technical report by the Council.

Section 3

All the licences required for minor nuclear facilities (so called "radioactive" installations) are granted by the Director-General for Energy, unless otherwise required by the Autonomous Communities.

The Nuclear Safety Council has taken over responsibility for the safety of nuclear installations from the Junta de Energia Nuclear. With the competent authorities, it contributes to the development of nuclear legislation on the subject and in particular, proposes criteria concerning emergency and physical protection plans for nuclear facilities. The inspectors of the Nuclear Safety Council monitor the safety and radiation protection of nuclear installations.

---

3. For further details see: "Description of Licensing Systems and Inspection of Nuclear Installations", OECD/NEA, 1980.

5. RADIOACTIVE WASTE MANAGEMENT

RD No. 2519/1982

The 1982 Decree on radiation protection contains several provisions concerning radioactive waste.

Section 53
Section 55

It provides in particular that installations whose activities are likely to produce significant quantities of radioactive waste must be equipped with adequate facilities for storage, treatment and disposal of such waste. In addition, radioactive waste disposal requires an administrative permit and any operation of this type must be undertaken in compliance with the terms of the permit.

Decree No. 2967/1979
of 7.12.1979

In accordance with a Decree of 1979, the Junta de Energia Nuclear is the authority responsible for radioactive waste management.

6. NUCLEAR THIRD PARTY LIABILITY[4]

Act No. 25/1964
of 29.4.1964
Ch. VII to X

Decree No. 2177/1967
of 22.7.1967
(BO of 18.9.1967) as
amended by
Decree No. 742/1968
of 28.3.1968 and
Decree No. 2864/1968
of 7.11.1968
(BO of 25.11.1968)

The Spanish outline Act of 29th April 1962 on Nuclear Energy laid the foundations for the rules governing nuclear third party liability. It was supplemented by an implementing Decree of 22nd July 1967 approving the regulations on cover for nuclear damage risks, which was itself amended by a Decree of 28th March 1968 and then by a Decree of 7th November 1968.

At international level, Spain has ratified the Paris Convention of 29th July 1960 on Third Party Liability in the Field of Nuclear Energy and the Brussels Supplementary Convention of 31st January 1963. It has signed the Vienna Convention of 21st May 1963 on Civil Liability for Nuclear Damage and acceded to the Brussels Convention of 17th December 1971 Relating to Civil Liability in the Field of Maritime Carriage of Nuclear Material.

7. NUCLEAR SECURITY

Act No. 25/1964
of 29.4.1964
Decree No. 2869/1972
of 21.7.1972

General provisions regarding nuclear safety are set out in a rather brief form in the outline Act of 29th April 1964 on Nuclear Energy and in the Decree of 21st July 1972.

---

4. For further details see Analytical Study in the same series: "Nuclear Third Party Liability", OECD/NEA, 1976.

Special provisions concerning each particular nuclear installation are set out in the decisions concerning licences issued by the Ministry of Industry and Energy.

Act No. 25/1964
Section 23

The Ministry of Industry and Energy is informed of all operations carried out on nuclear sustances and has a special record of them kept.

Section 40
Sections 87 and 91

Any loss, abandonment or theft of radioactive substances must be notified to the competent authorities as soon as possible. Criminal and administrative penalties may be imposed, depending on the seriousness of the offence, either by the Directorate-General or the appropriate body of the Ministry of Industry, or by the Minister of Industry and Energy, or even by the Council of Ministers if the person has disclosed secret information in the field of nuclear energy.

At international level, Spain applies the safeguards system established by the IAEA and has concluded with the latter various safeguard transfer agreements for nuclear installations on Spanish territory.

8. TRANSPORT[5]

Act No. 25/1964 of
29.4.1964 as amended by
Act No. 25/1968
of 20.6.1968
(BO of 21.6.1968)

The 1964 Nuclear Energy Act contains specific provisions concerning the transport of radioactive substances in general. Subsequent Decrees have supplemented the basic provisions of the 1964 Act as regards certain transport modes, e.g. road or rail, in order to bring Spanish legislation into line with the international agreements ratified by Spain. The other transport modes, inland waterways, sea and air, are still governed by the original provisions of the 1964 Act.

Decree No 2676/1973
of 19.10.1973
(BO of 31.10.1973)
Decree No. 1754/1976
of 6.2.1976
Decree No. 2101/1976
of 10.8.1976
(BO of 9.9.1976)
Decree No. 1999/1979
of 26.6.1979

For road transport of radioactive substances, a 1973 Decree specified the competent authorities for implementing the European Agreement concerning the International Carriage of Dangerous Goods by Road (ADR) to which Spain became a party on 22nd November 1972. In order to meet the specific requirements of Spanish road transport, two Decrees were issued on 6th February and 10th August 1976 to apply the National Regulations for the Transport of Dangerous Goods by Road, which are based on the ADR. A Decree dated 29th June 1979 amended that of 6th February 1976 to take account of the amendments made to the ADR in November 1977, following the 1973 revised edition of the IAEA Regulations on the Safe Transport of Radioactive Materials.

---

5. For further details, see Analytical Study in the same series: 'Regulations Governing the Transport of Radioactive Materials', OECD/NEA, 1980.

For rail transport, Spain, on 19th November 1974, ratified the International Convention concerning the Carriage of Goods by Rail (CIM) and therefore applies the International Regulations concerning the Carriage of Dangerous Goods by Rail (RID) within its territory.

Decree No. 1558/1977 of 4.7.1977
Act No. 15/1980 of 22.4.1980, Section 3

Responsibility for the transport of radioactive materials is shared by the Ministry of Industry and the Ministry of Transport and Communications. The former is responsible for issuing licences, in the light of a report submitted by the Nuclear Safety Council.

Act No. 25/1964 of 29.4.1964, Section 22
Section 23

The Ministry of Industry is also responsible for issuing approval certificates, and for licensing shipments of radioactive materials with foreign under-takings. Further conditions may also be imposed by other government departments, including the Ministry of Trade. Any parties transporting radioactive substances or concentrates must report their activities to the Ministry of Industry, which keeps a running record of all the information received.

RD No. 2519/1982

The 1982 Regulations on radiation protection provide in a Supplementary Section that any transport of radioactive material which is not governed by specific regulations, is subject to the provisions of the 1982 Regulations supplemented by the technical standards in the latest edition of the IAEA Transport Regulations.

Decree No. 1558/1977 of 4.7.1977, Section 11

The Minister of Transport and Communications has general responsibility for all transport.

Act No. 15/1980 of 22.4.1980, Section 2

The Nuclear Safety Council is responsible for monitoring and enforcing safety and radiation protection requirements in the field of transport. To this effect, it helps the competent authorities to draw up criteria relating to emergency and physical protection plans for the transport of nuclear substances.

9. PATENTS

Act No. 25/1964 of 29.4.1964, as amended by Act No. 25/1968 of 20.6.1968

Regulations concerning patents, trademarks and inventions in the field of nuclear energy have been incorporated in the amended 1964 outline Act on Nuclear Energy.

Section 81

Patent applications are filed in accordance with the normal procedure as laid down by Spanish legislation on industrial property.

Section 82

Patents are issued by the Industrial Property Registration Office, after it has examined a report by the Junta de Energia Nuclear.

Section 83

On the basis of a report by the Junta de Energia Nuclear, the Ministry of Industry may grant exemption from the need to provide evidence of commissioning and operation, as required by the industrial property legislation, to any patent owner who has submitted a request to this effect to the Industrial Property Registration Office.

II. INSTITUTIONAL FRAMEWORK

Nuclear activities are carried out in Spain under the control of various Ministers, each being responsible for the area assigned to him under Spanish law. It should be noted, however, that the Minister of Industry and Energy clearly plays a major role since he is generally responsible for enforcing current nuclear legislation.

Decree-Law
of 22.10.1951,
Section 7
Act No. 15/1980
of 22.4.1980;
Decree No 2967/1979
of 7.12.1979

When the Junta de Energia Nuclear was set up in 1951, it was the first specialised body with full powers over nuclear matters. Since then, the Junta has relinquished its duties concerning industrial aspects of the nuclear fuel cycle to ENUSA and those concerning nuclear safety control and radiation protection to the Nuclear Safety Council.

1. REGULATORY AND SUPERVISORY AUTHORITIES

a) Minister of Industry and Energy

Act No 25/1964
of 29.4.1964,
Section 3

The Minister of Industry and Energy applies nuclear legislation, except for responsibilities expressly assigned to other ministries, by delegating his powers to the Directorates-General for Energy and Mining and Fuels and to the competent bodies in nuclear matters.

Section 6*(a)*
Decree No. 2175/1964
of 16.7.1964 as amended
by
Decree No. 3237/1974
of 24.10.1974
(BO of 29.10.1974),
Sections 2 and 3

Since 1962, the Minister of Industry and Energy has acted as the supervisory authority for the Junta de Energia Nuclear. The latter must submit its opinions via the Minister to the Government regarding nuclear matters falling within its province. The Minister of Industry appoints the members of the Board of the Junta de Energia Nuclear either directly or on a proposal from the ministries concerned.

Act No. 15/1980
of 22.4.1980,
Section 5

In the case of the Nuclear Safety Council, the Minister of Industry and Energy submits proposals to the Government regarding the appointment of the governing bodies and the Council's Secretary-General. The appointments must be approved by the Parliament.

Act No. 25/1964
Section 17
Section 18

Together with the Minister of National Education or other government department or body concerned, the Minister of Industry and Energy sets safety standards for the operation of nuclear research and training centres. To this end, the Minister of Industry and Energy has the power to carry out any inspection he deems necessary. In any case, he may limit the quantities of nuclear substances held by the said centres.

Section 21
Section 24
Decree No. 3322/1971
of 23.12.1971,
Section 11
Decree No. 2967/1979
of 7.12.1979

As already stated, the Minister of Industry and Energy is responsible for classifying radioactive ore deposits on the basis of reports drawn up by ENUSA. On a proposal from the Minister of Industry and Energy, the Sub-Committee on Economic Affairs determines the characteristics of concentrates. The Minister of Industry and Energy is consulted when the terms under which ENUSA wishes to sell nuclear substances to third parties are to be fixed and approves the draft agreements drawn up for such transactions. The Minister of Industry and Energy is also responsible for determining the size of and management arrangements for the uranium reserve supplies maintained by ENUSA. Generally speaking, the Minister supervises the implementation of the national plan for uranium exploration and prospecting.

Act No. 15/1980,
Section 3

It is also recalled that the Minister of Industry has the power to grant licences for constructing and operating first-category nuclear installations and the Directorate-General for Energy of the Ministry of Industry is the competent body for all other licences, such as those for the transport of radioactive substances and for manufacturing nuclear components, after consulting the competent authorities including the Nuclear Safety Council.

– *Directorate-General for Energy*

Act No. 15/1980
of 22.4.1980,
Section 3

The Directorate-General for Energy is responsible for planning, co-ordinating and implementing Spanish electronuclear development, with the help of the competent bodies.

2nd Supplementary
Provision;
Act of 29.4.1964, Section
93

It is also responsible for official procedures relating to administrative licences and, after receiving an opinion from the Nuclear Safety Council, it issues the necessary licences other than those for first-category nuclear and radioactive installations, subject to any special provisions in the rules of the Autonomous Communities. Finally, it may impose administrative penalties if the relevant nuclear requirements are not met.

b) Minister of the Interior

The Minister of the Interior is the supervisory authority for the Directorate-General for Civil Protection.

Decree No. 53/1963
of 10.1.1963
(BO of 19.1.1963)

The Directorate-General for Civil Protection is responsible for setting up an emergency warning network in the event of an increase in radioactivity on Spanish territory, especially in areas where nuclear facilities are located.

c) Minister of Finance

Act No. 24/1964
of 29.4.1964,
Section 68

Section 56

The Minister of Finance takes decisions regarding the financing of expenditure to be met by the State under national nuclear legislation and international nuclear conventions. He approves the financial security to cover nuclear risks. The Minister of Finance is responsible for authorising Spanish nuclear insurance pools.

– *Directorate-General of Insurance*

Decree No. 2177/1967
of 22.7.1967

This Directorate-General is responsible for the *Insurance Compensation Consortium,* whose task is to share in covering nuclear risks should insurance companies be unable to meet the entire cost. It undertakes reinsurance in accordance with directives of the Minister of Finance. The Consortium is a member of the Executive Committee of the nuclear insurance pools.

A special Nuclear Risks Department has been set up under the Consortium for the purpose of compensation. It is financially independent and is managed by a govenment committee chaired by the Director-General of Insurance. The committee meets either in plenary Session or a standing committee.

An appeal against the decisions of the Department lies to the Insurance Compensation Consortium, with the possibility of a further appeal to the Insurance Arbitration Court.

The plenary committee is responsible for applying the measures adopted for covering nuclear risks. It authorises reinsurance and pays damage in excess of one million pesetas. The sale of assets of the Department and its expenditure must be approved by the Committee.

The standing committee is responsible for claims of less than one million pesetas.

2. PUBLIC AND SEMI-PUBLIC AGENCIES

a) Nuclear Safety Council

Act No. 15/1980
of 22.4.1980

In accordance with the guidelines of the National Energy Plan and the Resolution on Nuclear Energy adopted on 28th July 1979 by the Spanish Parliament, the Nuclear Safety Council was set up under the Act of 22nd April 1980.

It is generally responsible for the regulation and supervision of nuclear installations. In this context, it therefore takes over the tasks previously carried out by the Junta de Energia Nuclear under the Nuclear Energy Act of 29th April 1964.

i) *Legal status*

Section 1
RD No 1157/1982
of 30.4.1982
(BO of 7.6.1982)
Section 1

The Nuclear Safety Council is independent of public administration. A Royal Decree of 1982, made under the Act of 1980, defines the statute of the Council.

The Decree provides that the Council is a body governed by public law and that it enjoys legal personality and administration and financial autonomy.

ii) *Responsibilities*

Act No. 15/1980
3rd Supplementary
Provision
RD No. 1157/1982,
Section 1

The Nuclear Safety Council is intended to be an independent body with sole powers in the field of safety and radiation protection. Nevertheless, it may delegate powers to the Autonomous Communities in accordance with procedures laid down by the Council itself.

Chapter II
Act No. 15/1980
Section 2*(i)*
Section 2*(k)*

The Council maintains contacts with similar bodies abroad and advises the Spanish Government on the commitments it has entered into with other States or international organisations in the field of nuclear safety and protection against ionizing radiation.

The Council has extensive powers:

Section 2*(l)*

In the field of research, it draws up plans concerning nuclear safety and radiation protection and monitors their implementation.

Section 2*(a)*
Section 2*(e)*

In regulatory matters, the Council co-operates with the Government to draw up or review rules concerning nuclear protection. Jointly with the competent authorities, it draws up and approves the criteria relating to emergency plans and those for the physical protection of nuclear and radioactive installations as well as those concerning the transport of nuclear substances and radioactive materials.

Section 2*(b)*
Section 3-3

By virtue of its administrative powers, the Council submits reports on the issuing of the licences required for nuclear and radioactive installations, the transport of nuclear substances or radioactive materials and the manufacturing of nuclear or radioactive components to the Ministry of Industry and Energy before the latter takes any decisions. In the case of preliminary licenses (siting) the Nuclear Safety Council examines beforehand the reports prepared either by the Autonomous Communities or the Pre-Autonomous Bodies, or failing this, by the Provinces concerned. The opinions given by the Nuclear Safety Council must be followed when they are against the applications being granted. Any conditions contained in favourable opinions must also be complied with.

Section 2*(c)* and *(d)*
Section 2*(h)*

In the field of radiation protection, the Nuclear Safety Council has the power to supervise nuclear or radioactive installations, component manufacturing plants and transport, to ensure that the safety requirements are complied with. Where it notes that there is a safety risk, it has the right either to suspend the activities of the enterprises concerned or to propose to the Ministry of Industry and Energy that it should revoke the previously granted licences. These measures may be accompanied by recommendations for the imposition of penalties. Courts and government departments may consult the Council on matters concerning nuclear safety and radiation protection.

Section 2*(g)*
Section 2*(m)*

The Council also checks on irradiation levels in the area surrounding nuclear and radioactive installations and in the areas through which nuclear or radioactive materials are transported. It monitors the cumulative doses received by persons exposed to radiation in the course of their work, and grants or renews the necessary licences. The Council is kept informed of incidents due to radiation and gives its opinion on the steps to be taken.

Section 2*(j)*
Section 11

The Nuclear Safety Council is also responsible for informing the public of its administrative activities and of matters relating to radiation protection. Finally it reports each quarter to the Senate and the Chamber of Deputies on its activities.

iii) *Structure*

The Nuclear Safety Council consists of a Chairman and a Board composed of four members assisted by a General Secretariat.

Section 5

The Chairman and the Board members are appointed for a period of six years, renewable by the Government, after consultation of the Minister of Industry and Energy and on a favourable opinion of at least three-fifths of the members of the competent committee of the Chamber of Deputies.

Section 4

The Chairman and members are selected in the light of their expertise in nuclear safety and radiation protection. One of the four members is appointed Vice-Chairman by the Board on a proposal from the Chairman and replaces the latter in his absence.

Section 5

The Secretary-General of the Nuclear Safety Council is appointed by the Government on a proposal from the Ministry of Industry and Energy and after a favourable opinion by the competent committee on the Chamber of Deputies. He takes part in the Council's meetings in a consultative capacity.

RD No. 1157/1982, Section 45

The Council meets at least once a fortnight in regular session. Extraordinary sessions may be convened by the Chairman or at the request of a member of the Board.

Section 8
3rd Transitional Provision

The Nuclear Safety Council engages the necessary qualified staff and lays down the procedures for absorbing staff of the Junta de Energia Nuclear. For the purpose of carrying out specific tasks or for a set period of not more than one year, it may also call on persons outside the Council, both Spanish and foreign.

iv) Financing

Section 2

The Council's funds come from appropriations under the general State budget and from the Council's own resources. Other resources may also be allocated in some cases.

Section 10-2
Section 10-3

The Nuclear Safety Council obtains funds through a special charge for services rendered, which has been established especially for this purpose. This charge is made on studies carried out by the Council in respect of the issue of licences, and on inspections of nuclear and radioactive installations, and in relation to the transport of nuclear or radioactive substances, the manufacturing of nuclear or radioactive components and type-approval of radioactive equipment.

Section 10-8

It is also levied on the issue or renewal of licences for operating staff at nuclear and radioactive facilities. The charge, usually paid to the competent collecting centre, is payable by persons who have applied for the said licences. The entire proceeds are used to cover the cost of the services rendered by the Council on behalf of third parties.

b) Junta de Energia Nuclear

Decree-Law of 22.10.1951, Section 1

The Junta de Energia Nuclear (JEN) was set up in 1951, in the expectation of growing nuclear power applications in Spain.

This body, which was to be given major technical, financial and staff resources, had been envisaged as an instrument for promoting nuclear industrial development and to this end, had been given broad powers.

Recently, because of the growth in nuclear activities connected with the need to meet energy requirements, and the corresponding increase in regulations warranted on safety grounds, the Government decided to split up the complex structures of the JEN into separate bodies in the nuclear field. As a result, the Junta remains responsible for the tasks connected with promotion and research in the peaceful uses of nuclear energy, whilst those connected with the industrial aspects of the nuclear fuel cycle have been entrusted to the National Uranium Enterprise (ENUSA). Likewise, regulatory and supervisory duties for nuclear installations have been passed on to the Nuclear Safety Council.

At the moment, additional regulations concerning the functional reorganisation of the Junta are being discussed.

i) Legal status

Decree-Law of
22.20.1951,
Section 7
Decree-Law of 25.3.1957,
Section 13
Act No. 25/1964 of
29.4.1964,
Section 5
Decree No. 87/1968 of
18.1.1968
(BO of 22.1.1968)

The Junta de Energia Nuclear is a public body which at first used to report to the Prime Minister, then from 1957 onwards to the Directorate-General of Nuclear Energy, and since 1962 is under the direct supervision of the Minister of Industry and Energy.

Act of 17.9.1958,
Section 1
Act No 25/1964,
Section 5

Since 1958 the Junta de Energia Nuclear has had legal personality and enjoys administrative and financial autonomy.

ii) Responsibilities

The Junta de Energia Nuclear remains a research centre, a consultative body and a representational body at domestic and international levels in industry. Nevertheless, its responsibilities are now restricted to the following:

– *Nuclear research and development*

Section 6(e)

Section 6(j);
Decree No. 2967/1979
of 7.12.1979,
Section 1

The Junta de Energia Nuclear owns basic research laboratories and pilot plants at which, with the agreement of the ministerial departments concerned, it conducts fundamental and applied research activities. Equipped with all the services required for executing its nuclear duties, it grants technical assistance to ENUSA with scientific research into the successive stages in the nuclear fuel cycle. It advises and also offers technical assistance to private industry within the scope of its responsibilities. The Junta helps to promote and develop nuclear energy by subsidising other Spanish research centres.

Section 16
Section 17

With a view to co-ordinating research work and the training of highly specialised staff for the problems raised by atomic energy, it has set up an *Institute of Nuclear Studies* for the purpose of providing advanced training in nuclear sciences. The Junta awards study grants to enable scientific and technical experts to further their studies at universities and higher technical colleges both in Spain and abroad.

Section 82
Section 83

No invention relating to the nuclear field may be patented without having been the subject of a report by the Junta de Energia Nuclear. On the basis of this report, the Ministry of Industry decides whether the applicant for the patent should be exempted from the need to provide the evidence of commissioning and operation required under industrial property law.

Section 4

In general, the Junta de Energia Nuclear is responsible for planning, coordinating and drawing up the Spanish action programme in the field of nuclear energy in liaison with the Directorate-General of Energy.

– *Advisory role*

Section 6(a)

The Junta de Energia Nuclear advises the Government, through the Minister of Industry, on all civil nuclear problems falling within its scope.

Section 66

In the event of a nuclear incident, the Junta de Energia Nuclear must prepare a technical report on the surrounding circumstances. The report is to be attached to claims filed by or on behalf of the victims.

Section 6(m)
Section 7

As a highly specialised body in the nuclear field, the Junta participates in the framing of nuclear legislation and submits to the Minister of Industry proposals for legislation relating to the development of nuclear energy. Generaly speaking, whenever matters falling within its competence are being studied or dealt with, the Junta will always be represented at meetings of joint consultative committees not answerable to the Ministry of Industry and Energy.

– *Representational role*

Section 6(n)
Section 6(1)
Section 7

For matters within its competence not covered by the Minister of Industry or other authority, the Junta de Energia Nuclear represents the Government in the implementation of nuclear provisions. The Junta maintains exclusive official relations in its particular field with the equivalent nuclear bodies abroad with which it co-operates in implementing technical and scientific nuclear programmes. Generally, in international relations, it acts in liaison with the Ministry of Foreign Affairs.

– *Residual responsibilities for industry*

As a result of the reorganisation of the nuclear sector the duties previously assigned to the Junta de Energia in relation to the nuclear fuel cycle and concerning nuclear installations and radiation protection have been transferred to ENUSA and the Nuclear Safety Council respectively.

Decree No. 2967/1979
of 7.12.1979,
Section 3-2

However, the Junta is not entirely excluded from these activities since it remains responsible for the disposal of radioactive waste.

iii) Structure

Act No. 25/1964
of 29.4.1964,
Section 8

The Junta de Energia Nuclear is run by a Chairman and a Board assisted by an Executive Committee, a Director-General and Heads of Departments, and also a Secretariat.

JEN Board Decision
of 7.1.1955

Section 15

The Junta de Energia Nuclear also has power to establish all departments, divisions, sections or units required for carrying out its duties, such as the Auxiliary Committee on Plant Biology and Industrial Applications, which is responsible for centralising work on radioisotopic applications in agriculture. It appoints permanent staff and may recruit temporary, scientific, technical or administrative staff where necessary.

Decree No. 1613/1979
of 26.6.1979 as amended
by Decree No 2000/1980
of 3.10.1980
(BO of 7.10.1980),
Section 2
Act No 25/1964,
Section 11

Since the Decree of 3rd October 1980 regarding the Ministry of Industry and Energy, the Secretary-General for Energy and Mining Resources acts as the *Chairman of the Junta.* He also chairs the Board and the Executive Committee of the Junta and represents it in all official and legal acts.

Act No. 25/1964
as amended by Act No.
25/1968,
New Section 9;
Decree No. 2175/1964
of 16.7.1964
as amended by
Decree No. 3237/1974
of 24.10.1974
(BO of 29.11.1974),
Sections 2 and 3
Section 4

The Board of the Junta consists of a maximum of seventeen members. The Minister of Industry and Energy personally appoints the two Board members representing his Ministry and those representing scientific, technical or industrial circles, and on a proposal from the ministerial departments and bodies concerned, the other Board members. The normal term of office of Board members is four years. A Vice-Chairman is selected by the Minister of Industry and Energy from among the Board members on a proposal from the Chairman of the Junta, after receiving the Board's opinion.

Act No. 25/1964
of 29.4.1964,
Section 10

The Board sets up an Executive Committee and specifies its tasks. It is consulted when the Director-General is appointed by the Minister of Industry and Energy on a proposal from the Chairman of the Junta. On a proposal from the Director-General, it approves the appointment of Heads of Department and the technical Secretary-General of the Junta, who acts as secretary to the Board and attends Board meetings in a consultative capacity.

The Board is the top executive body of the Junta. It is responsible for drawing up its general programme of action and the corresponding budgets. It gives its opinions on matters submitted to it.

iv) Financing

Section 13

The Junta's budget is funded from both external and internal sources.

External funds consist of ordinary and extraordinary appropriations entered in the general State budget and funds from autonomous bodies transmitted through the Government. Both Spanish and foreign legal persons and private individuals may contribute through donations or subsidies. Further finance may be provided by contractual agreement or as a result of a court order.

The Junta's own resources consist of the proceeds of sales, fees for services rendered to third parties, and income from its shareholdings in national and international companies.

Section 12

Decree No. 2697/1979
of 7.12.1979
(BO of 14.1.1980),
Section 1

In the performance of its duties, the Junta may carry out all necessary financial transactions. It has a shareholding in the National Uranium Enterprise.

c) Institute of Nuclear Studies

Act No. 25/1964
of 29.4.1964
as amended by Act No.
25/1968
of 20.6.1968,
New Section 16

Following the Nuclear Energy Act of 29th April 1964, an Institute of Nuclear Studies was set up under the Junta de Energia Nuclear with a view to co-ordinating research and training in the nuclear field.

The Junta makes technical facilities and staff available to the Institute for the specialised training of future nuclear experts. The training is intended merely to supplement the basic training received at universities and higher technical education establishments.

d) National Uranium Enterprise

Decree No. 259/1969
of 20.2.1969
Decree No. 3322/1971
of 23.12.1971

The National Uranium Enterprise (ENUSA) was set up by a Decree of 23rd December 1971 for the general purpose of assuming responsibility for the various stages of the nuclear fuel cycle, with the technical co-operation of the Junta de Energia Nuclear.

Decree No. 2967/1979
of 7.12.1979

Section 5-1

The Decree of 7th December 1979 implementing the guidelines of the national energy plan widened ENUSA's scope in the nuclear fuel cycle by redefining its tasks to make them more independent of those of the Junta. The growth in the nuclear industry had made it necessary to transfer responsibilities from the Junta to a unit which would efficiently secure uranium supplies for nuclear facilities.

i) Legal status

ENUSA is a state enterprise in the form of a limited liability company.

ii) Responsibilities

Decree No 2967/1979 of 7.12.1979, Section 5-1

Section 2

In general, ENUSA implements the national uranium exploration and prospecting plan. It has direct responsibility for the following tasks:

- prospecting and mining radioactive deposits with a view to processing ore into uranium and thorium concentrates;
- converting uranium concentrates into uranium hexafluoride;
- uranium enrichment;
- manufacturing nuclear fuel and reprocessing irradiated fuel.

Section 3-2

Section 1

In the case of radioactive waste disposal, however, the Decree of 7th December 1979 confirmed the previous duties of the Junta. The research and development activities on the various stages in the nuclear fuel cycle are to be undertaken with the Junta's technical assistance.

Section 8

In order to meet Spain's energy requirements and remedy any interruption in uranium supplies, ENUSA must establish reserve stocks of natural and enriched uranium. The size of these stocks and relevant conditions will be fixed by the Ministry of Industry and Energy in accordance with the national energy plan.

Sections 6 and 7

Uranium supplies to nuclear power plants and uranium enrichment and the conversion of uranium concentrates into uranium hexafluoride are guaranteed by ENUSA for a period of ten years. To this effect, the enterprise will have to establish permanent emergency stocks corresponding to the domestic consumption for twelve and six months respectively.

iii) Financing

Section 1

The National Industry Institute has a majority shareholding in ENUSA. The Junta, holds the remainder of the shares.

Section 14

Agreements concerning the supply of goods and services are concluded with third parties on the basis of a standard form contract approved by the Ministry of Industry and

Energy. Financial conditions are fixed at regular intervals by ENUSA and forwarded, with the opinion of the Ministry of Industry and Energy, to the Government Committee on Economic Affairs. ENUSA's assessment of selling prices includes detailed grounds for all price components and ancillary costs, such as the financing of emergency stocks, investment costs for uranium ore exploration, transport costs and charges, and the profit margin. A reserve payment system should enable ENUSA to meet its commitments.

SWEDEN

TABLE OF CONTENTS

I. GENERAL REGULATORY REGIME

Act 1958 No. 110
Act 1984 No. 3

The basic framework within which nuclear activities are governed in Sweden is to be found in two pieces of legislation, the first dating from the 1950s, namely the Radiation Protection Act of 14th March 1958 and the second, promulgated on 12th January 1984, the Act on Nuclear Acitivities which replaces the Atomic Energy Act of 1st June 1956. Various Ordinances have also been passed and they too will be discussed where appropriate in the following paragraphs.

The first Chapter reviews the legislation governing nuclear activities in Sweden, while the following Chapter will consider the institutional framework within which such activities are carried out.

1. MINING REGIME

Act 1974 No. 890
Section 1

Under the Act of 13th December 1974 concerning Certain Mineral Deposits, a special licence (concession) is required for the exploration for or exploitation of deposits of minerals containing uranium or thorium.

Section 2

Applications for concessions are submitted to the National Industrial Board and considered by the Government or authority appointed by the Government.

Section 6

A concession may be granted only to someone who is considered suitable from the standpoint of the public interest to carry on the exploration or exploitation to which the concession refers. Within an area covered by a concession, no other person may be granted a concession for the same group of subtances.

Section 10

A concession may be combined with stipulations necessary for protecting public interests or individual rights or which are otherwise required in order to promote prospecting for and the preservation of natural resources in a manner serving the interests of the public. A concession may be made conditional upon exploration or exploitation operations taking place on a certain scale and it may be stipulated in the concession that the State shall be entitled to participate in the undertaking or that the concession-holder shall pay a fee or a share of the production to the State or observe other similar conditions.

Section 11

A concession may not be transferred without the consent of the authority granting the concession.

Section 12
Section 40

A concession may be revoked by the authority granting the concession if directions or conditions laid down in the concession are disregarded or if there are other special reasons. The Inspectors of Mining exercise supervision over compliance with the provisions in, or made by virtue of, the Act relating to exploration and exploitation.

Section 40

Concession-holders or others carrying on activities under the Act shall on demand furnish the Inspectors of Mining with such information and documents as are needed for supervision. The Inspectors of Mining may issue regulations to secure compliance with the provisions in, or made under the Act relating to exploration and exploitation.

The supervisory authority shall be entitled to access to a mine or plant where activities covered by the Act are carried on and may inquire into circumstances of significance concerning the implementation of orders or conditions in respect of such activities.

2. RADIOACTIVE SUBSTANCES, NUCLEAR FUELS AND EQUIPMENT

Act 1984 No. 3

The Act of 1984 on Nuclear Activities governs among others the possession of and trade in radioactive substances and nuclear fuels, wastes and equipment.

Sections 1 and 5

The definition of *nuclear activity* under the Act also covers the export of nuclear substances, products made from nuclear substances or goods containing such substances. The same applies to export of equipment or material that has been specially designed or prepared for processing, use or production of nuclear substances to the extent prescribed by the Government. Consequently, such export is subject to a licence. The Government is empowered to require an export licence for products which are not directly intended for but otherwise are of essential importance for the production of nuclear devices (so-called dual use products). A licence is also required, to the extent prescribed by the Government, for the transfer of technology, i.e. assignment or transfer of a right to manufacture outside Sweden certain equipment or material.

Section 5

Nuclear activities included in the definition are subject to a licence in certain cases prescribed by the Government.

Act 1958 No. 110
as last amended by
Act 1984 No. 4
Section 2
Ordinance 1958 No. 652

Furthermore, under the Radiation Protection Act, as amended, no radiological work may be carried out without a licence, nor may anyone possess X-ray equipment or any other technical device designed to emit ionizing radiation, carry out trade with radioactive substances or acquire, possess or assign them without a licence. Exemptions may,

73

however, be granted for radioactive substances with a specific activity not exceeding certain values, and for uranium and thorium or their compounds intended for use in laboratories for chemical analyses, or for teaching or research.

Act No. 110, as amended, Section 1

Radiological work is defined as work with radioactive substances, work involving the use of X-ray equipment or other technical device designed to emit ionizing radiation, and work at a plant for the production of nuclear energy.

Section 1

It is further provided that, if necessary from the point of view of radiation protection, the Government may prescribe that the provisions of the Act shall, either wholly or partly, be applicable also to certain types of technical devices intended to emit non-ionizing radiation or to work involving the use of such devices.

Section 2
Act 1984 No.4

It should be noted that a licence under the Radiation Protection Act is not normally required in respect of any activity already covered by a licence under the 1984 Act. However, when a licence is granted under this latter Act, the radiation protection authority prescribes any conditions necessary for radiation protection.

Ordinance 1958 No. 652

Control of importation of radioactive materials is the responsibility of Customs officials, acting in accordance with regulations made by the general Customs Administration in agreement with the State Institute for Radiation Protection (*statens strålskyddinsitut*).

3. PROTECTION OF WORKERS AND THE PUBLIC AGAINST IONIZING RADIATION

Act 1958 No. 110

The authority responsible for all aspects of radiation protection is the National Institute for Radiation Protection which enjoys extensive powers under the Radiation Protection Act.

Section 5

The Institute attaches, in compliance with the Radiation Protection Act, such conditions to licences issued under the 1984 Act as it thinks fit for securing the safety of the population as a whole as well as that of individuals or groups of individuals particularly likely to be exposed to radiation hazards in connection with licensed activities. Conditions thus imposed differ widely as they are dependent on the particular circumstances under which radioactive substances are being used and on the purpose they serve in each individual case. The standards laid down are based on international guidelines such as the Recommendations of the International Commission on Radiological Protection (ICRP) and on the Institute's own research and practical experience.

Act 1984 No.3
Sections 19 to 21

The 1984 Act on Nuclear Activities provides that each nuclear power plant shall have a local safety committee which shall be given insight into the work of safety and radiation protection at the plant. This insight shall enable the committee to gather information on the work on safety and radiation protection that has been done or is planned at a plant and to compile material to inform the public of this work. The licence-holder shall, at the request of the Committee, furnish the Committee with information on facts and give it access to available documents, to the extent necessary for the Committee to fulfil its duties. The Committee shall, with some restrictions, also have access to plants and sites.

a) Protection of workers

Instruction 1972 No. 164
(reprinted 1978: 436)
as amended

The central administrative authority responsible for the protection of workers in general is the Workers Protection Board. Its function is to promote the measures necessary for the protection of workers in the field of safety technology, occupational hygiene or industrial medicine. At the same time, the Board supervises the application of rules and regulations pertaining to labour legislation.

Instruction 1973 No. 847
as amended

The Labour Inspectorate is responsible for the local supervision of working conditions; its officials report to the Workers Protection Board but are not subordinate to it in every respect.

These two bodies are competent for the protection of workers in general, and the National Institute for Radiation Protection is responsible for minimizing the risks involved in radiological work. The Radiation Protection Act provides the guidelines for regulations issued and for measures adopted by the Institute, for the purpose of protecting the health and safety of the workers. The basic aim is to ensure that doses received by occupationally exposed persons are kept to the lowest practicable level.

Act 1958 No. 110
Section 10

The licensee himself or the managers of a nuclear installation are responsible for the strict observance of all radiation protection measures with regard to workers within a nuclear installation or in any other place where nuclear substances are handled. They must ensure that all operations with nuclear materials are carried out properly and that all protective devices are provided for, or attached to, certain kinds of equipment.

Section 18
Section 11

The radiation protection authority may order that apparatus and equipment, whose use is regulated by the Radiation Protection Act, may not be put into operation until special measures prescribed by the National Institute for Radiation Protection have been taken. This is in addition to a provision which requires manufacturers and sellers of X-ray apparatus and of other equipment emiting ionizing radiation to ensure that the equipment is provided with appropriate protective devices against radiation hazards when delivered for use.

Section 12

Finally, it is forbidden for certain categories of persons who are particularly susceptible to radiation damage to engage in radiological work. At the same time, a system is established for the persons actually carrying out radiological work which provides for a permanent control of their state of health and of dose levels received.

b) Protection of the public

In addition to any safety regulations that may be laid down by the National Institute for Radiation Protection for the protection of the public with regard to any given radiological work, special legislation exists concerning protective measures to be taken in the event of accidents occurring in nuclear installations.

**Act 1960 No. 331
as amended
Section 2(1)
Section 2(2)**

The Act on Protective Measures against Harmful Effects caused by Nuclear Incidents provides for special measures to be implemented by the County Government Board for dealing with this kind of emergency situation. Thus, in the first place, the Boards have to ensure that all necessary measures will be taken to protect the public from ionizing radiation. An officer with the power to take decisions on behalf of the Council must be appointed for cases where immediate action must be taken and where delay in taking such decisions would have detrimental effects.

Section 3

The owner of the installation himself, or his representative, has the obligation to notify immediately local police authorities and the County Government Board or the officer designated under the Act of any occurrence that might require special measures.

Section 4

In order to carry out radiation measurements for ascertaining the scale of dispersal of radioactive substances, the Boards are empowered to adopt measures which may encroach upon individual rights which are otherwise protected by law.

**Section 5
Sections 6, 7 and 8**

Finally, with a view to limiting radiation damage to the greatest possible extent in the case of an accident, the Boards are authorised to exercise a certain number of special powers such as to order evacuation, curfews, restrictions on the right to consume water and foodstuffs, etc.

4. NUCLEAR INSTALLATIONS

1984 Act No. 3
Ordinance 1984 No. 14

The licensing procedure for nuclear installations in Sweden is laid down primarily in the 1984 Act on Nuclear Activities and the Ordinance concerning Nuclear Activities. Such installations may not be erected, possessed or operated without a licence issued by the Government or the authority designated by the Government. This authority is the Swedish Nuclear Power Inspectorate (*statens kärnkraftinspection –* SKI) which comes under the Ministry of Industry.

Act 1984 No. 3

The 1984 Act replaces inter alia the 1956 Nuclear Energy Act, the 1977 Act on special permits to load nuclear reactors with nuclear fuel, and the 1980 Act on Public Insight into the Safety Work at Nuclear Power Plants. On the other hand, the 1958 Act on Radiation Protection remains basically unchanged.

Section 3

Like the 1956 Act, the 1984 Act is legislation on safety which is based on a system of licensing, conditions and supervision of nuclear activities. According to the fundamental provisions of the 1984 Act, these activities should be conducted in such a manner as to meet safety requirements and to fulfil the obligations that follow from Sweden's international agreements for the purpose of preventing the proliferation of nuclear weapons.

The main provisions of the Act deal with safety, waste handling and final storage, export of substances and equipment etc. in the nuclear energy field, public insight into the safety work at nuclear plants, and the decommissioning of nuclear power plants.

Sections 1 and 5

The Act contains a definition as to what is meant by *nuclear activity* and thus subject to licensing. Nuclear activity means construction, possession or operation of a nuclear plant, i.e. reactors and plants for the recovery, production, handling, processing, storage or final storage of nuclear substances and waste.

Section 4

As already stated, the aim of the Act is to provide for safety in nuclear activities. Thus it is prescribed that safety shall be maintained by the adoption of whatever measures are required in order to prevent defects in or malfunction of equipment, incorrect action or whatever else that might lead to a radiological accident or to prevent illicit dealings with nuclear substances or waste.

Section 15

A licence to conduct a nuclear activity can be revoked if stipulated conditions or directives have not been observed in some essential respect. It can also be revoked if the provisions concerning research and development are not observed and particular reasons exist from the viewpoint of safety, or there exist other particular reasons from the viewpoint of safety.

Finally, it should be noted that, apart from the nuclear licensing procedure proper, nuclear installations are subject to the provisions of other legislation such as the 1947 Building Act (a new Act is currently under preparation), and the 1969 Environmental Protection Act, the 1983 Water Regulations Act, and the 1977 Work Environment Act.

Act 1947 No. 385
as amended
Section 136a

In particular, the location of a nuclear power installation at a new site would be subject to the provisions of the 1947 Building Act which provides that permission is required for the new establishment of certain industrial operations, including nuclear power installations, (as well as, if the Government so decided, uranium mining for instance or plants for waste management) which are of essential importance to energy conservation or for the country's land and water resources. Applications for such permission are dealt with by the Ministry of Housing and the Licensing Board for Environmental Protection issues the conditions and directives which are to apply. In all cases, however, the municipality concerned must approve of the industrial establishment before permission will be given.

5. RADIOACTIVE WASTE MANAGEMENT

The Act of 1984 on Nuclear Activities contains provisions concerning radioactive waste handling and final storage or disposal.

Act 1984 No. 3
Section 6

In particular, no permit for loading a reactor with nuclear fuel shall be granted unless the reactor owner demonstrates that a method for handling and final storage of the spent nuclear fuel and radioactive waste deriving from the fuel exists which can be approved, from the viewpoint of safety and radiation protection. He must also have an R and D programme of work prepared for the safe handling and final disposal of the spent nuclear fuel from the reactor and the resulting radioactive waste.

Section 10
Section 14

The 1984 Act also provides that a licensee must take the necessary measures to maintain safety in view of the nature of the activity and the conditions under which it is conducted. As regards nuclear waste, he shall take the necessary measures to handle and safely dispose of nuclear waste or nuclear substances arising from the waste which are not recycled. He must also take the necessary measures to decommission and dismantle in a safe manner plants which are no longer in operation. Unless they are waived, these obligations must be complied with even when a licence is revoked or its period of validity has expired.

Sections 11 and 12

An important feature of the 1984 Act is that each holder of a licence to own or operate a reactor shall ensure that such comprehensive research and development work is conducted as required in order to handle and finally safely dispose of nuclear waste arising from the activity and to decommission and dismantle the plant in a safe manner. Therefore the licence holder must prepare or have prepared a research programme defining the measures intended to be taken within a period of at least six years. It shall, as from 1986, be submitted to the Government, or the authority designated by it every third year for scrutiny and evaluation.

Act 1981 No. 669
as amended
Act 1984 No. 5
Section 1

It is further specified in the 1981 Act concerning the financing of future costs of spent fuel etc. that the holder of a licence to own or operate a nuclear reactor under the Act on Nuclear Activities, is responsible, inter alia, for the costs so as to ensure that *(i)* nuclear fuel irradiated in the reactor and radioactive waste deriving therefrom is handled and disposed of in a safe manner; *(ii)* the reactor will be shut down and dismantled in a safe manner; and *(iii)* such research and development activities are conducted as are required to ensure compliance with these obligations.

Section 3
Ordinance 1981 No. 671

The 1981 Act provides that the owner of a nuclear reactor shall, in consultation with other reactor owners, establish a calculation of the costs required to carry out the activities described in the above paragraph. The calculation shall be submitted evey year to the National Board for Spent Nuclear Fuel. (*nämnden för hantering av använt kärnbränsle*).

Section 2

In addition to the costs resulting from his obligations, above, the operator is also responsible in respect of any costs incurred by the State with regard to waste management research and development, planning or surveillance and inspection.

Sections 5 and 6

In order to ensure the availability of adequate funds, the operator must pay an annual fee to the State for such time as the reactor is in operation. The amount of this fee is established on the basis of various criteria, including the amount of energy produced by the reactor, and is calculated so that the aggregate amount of fees paid during the operating life of the reactor will cover the total cost of all aspects of the management of the spent-fuel produced by the reactor.

Section 7
Section 8
Section 9

Fees are to be paid to the authority designated by the Government and deposited in an interest-bearing account with the National Bank of Sweden. Loans may, subject to appropriate conditions, be granted to operators out of this fund and fees paid by an operator may of course be used to reimburse the costs incurred by him or on his behalf in respect of measures referred to above.

Section 10

Matters relating to supplementary research and development activities, surveillance and inspection of final disposal operations, loans to operators and handling of collected fees are to be supervised by the Government or the authority designated by it.

6. NUCLEAR THIRD PARTY LIABILITY

Act 1968 No. 45
and implementing
Ordinance
1981 No. 327 (replacing
Ordinance 1968 No. 46)

The basic legislation on nuclear third party liability in Sweden is contained in the Nuclear Third Party Liability Act of 1968 which implements the provisions of the 1960 Paris Convention on Third Party Liability in the Field of Nuclear Energy and the Brussels Convention Supplementary to the Paris Convention.

Act 1974 No. 249

In order to enable Sweden to ratify also the 1971 Brussels Convention relating to Civil Liability in the Field of Maritime Carriage of Nuclear Material, Sections 3, 4 and 15 of the 1968 Act were amended and a new Section 14a was introduced in 1974, which amendments entered into force on 15th July 1975.

Act 1982 No. 1275

Further amendments to the 1968 Act were adopted in 1982. Sections 1, 12 and 31 were amended in order to enable Sweden to ratify the 1982 Protocols to the Paris Convention and the Brussels Supplementary Convention respectively. These amendments will enter into force when the Protocols are operational.

Also in 1982, Sections 9, 17, 30, 32 to 35 and 37 were amended and a new Section 31a was added. These amendments which were not dependent on the 1982 Protocols entered into force on 1st April 1983. They include an increase of the liability of operators, earlier limited to 50 million Swedish kronor per incident, to 500 million kronor. As regards installations that only produce, treat or store unirradiated uranium, or incidents occurring in the course of transport of such uranium, the maximum liability is 100 million Swedish kronor per incident.

In addition, a State liability was introduced over and above the compensation available under the Paris Convention and the Brussels Supplementary Convention. If, in the case of a nuclear incident for which the operator of a nuclear installation located in Sweden is liable, the amounts available under the two Conventions are insufficient to allow compensation in full, the State will indemnify the victims up to a ceiling of 3,000 million Swedish kronor per incident. This extra State indemnification will apply to nuclear damage sustained in Sweden, Denmark, Finland or Norway and also to damage within the territory of any other Contracting Party

80

of the Brussels Supplementary Convention to the extent that such State provides additional compensation out of public funds for damage caused in Sweden.

Ordinance 1981 No. 327
Section 1

Two Decisions adopted on 27th December 1977 by the Steering Committee of the OECD Nuclear Energy Agency and relating to the Paris Convention were implemented in Sweden in 1981 by an Ordinance on nuclear third party liability. The first Decision concerns the exclusion of certain kinds of nuclear substances from the application of the Paris Convention, and the second, the similar exclusion of small quantities of nuclear substances while in transport.

7. NUCLEAR SECURITY

Act 1984 No. 3

As mentioned under "Nuclear installations" above, the 1984 Act on Nuclear Activities provides that such activities should be conducted in fulfilment of the Swedish commitments under international agreements for the purpose of preventing the proliferation of nuclear weapons. Sweden is a Party to the Treaty on the Non-Proliferation of Nuclear Weapons and on 1st August 1980, ratified the Convention on the Physical Protection of Nuclear Material.

8. TRANSPORT[1]

Act 1984 No. 3
Act 1958 No. 110
as amended
Section 22
Ordinance 1958 No. 652
amended *inter alia* by
Ordinance 1976 No. 246

In Sweden, the Act on Nuclear Activities of 1984 and the Radiation Protection Act of 1958 are the basic Acts regulating the transport of radioactive materials, in particular by imposing licensing requirements. It is also provided in the 1958 Act that regulations concerning transport, customs examination and transit conveyance shall be laid down by the Government or by an authority appointed by the Government. This authority is the National Institute for Radiation Protection.

Act 1982 No. 821
Ordinance 1982 No. 923

Provisions concerning carriage of dangerous goods were made in 1982 and entered into force on 1st January 1983. As to radioactive goods, the provisions are valid only to the extent that they are compatible with the 1984 Act on Nuclear Activities and the 1958 Radiation Protection Act respectively and with provisions or conditions prescribed by virtue of these Acts.

---

1. For further details see Analytical Study in the same series: "Regulations Governing the Transport of Radioactive Materials", OECD/NEA, 1980.

9. PATENTS

On 1st January 1968, new co-ordinated Acts on patents came into force in Denmark, Finland, Norway and Sweden.

Act 1967 No. 837   The Swedish Act No. 837, which was published on 1st December 1967, contains no special provisions as regards patents in the nuclear field.

II. INSTITUTIONAL FRAMEWORK

Under the Swedish Constitution, Ministers are responsible for making proposals regarding matters within their competence and of course for giving advice on these matters, but a Minister acting alone has virtually no actual powers. All decisions are taken by the Government as a whole.

Various national bodies exist with responsibilities in the nuclear field, ranging from regulatory or supervisory duties to an advisory function. As a general rule, these bodies enjoy considerable independence within the broad framework laid down by the Government.

1. REGULATORY AND SUPERVISORY AUTHORITIES

a) Minister of Industry

The Minister of Industry is responsible for supervising the development of nuclear energy in Sweden. (At present a Minister has been designated to handle energy issues within the Ministry of Industry.)

The Minister of Industry is also responsible for industrial research and development and holds, on behalf of the State, the capital of Studsvik Energiteknik AB, a state-owned company which is the main body dealing with applied nuclear research and development in Sweden. The Minister of Industry has general responsibility for overseeing the licensing procedure for nuclear fuel and nuclear installations. However, the national body responsible for administering the licensing procedure under the Act on Nuclear Activities is the Swedish Nuclear Power Inspectorate.

b) State Nuclear Power Inspectorate

i) *Legal status*

Instruction 1974 No. 427 as amended

On 1st July 1974, the Swedish Atomic Energy Board (*delegationen för atomenergifrågor*) was renamed the State Nuclear Power Inspectorate (*statens kärnkraftinspektion*). At the same time its composition and functions were changed slightly. It remains, however, a governmental body governed by public law and comes under the authority of the Ministry of Industry.

ii) *Responsibilities*

Ordinance 1984 No. 14

The Inspectorate has extensive licensing and inspection responsibilities and is charged with following developments in the nuclear field, in particular with regard to questions of safety, and with examining the need for research and development in the field of the safety of the transport of fissile material and the safety of nuclear installations whether in general or in connection with specific installations for which a licence has been requested or granted. The Inspectorate is further responsible for exercising such functions with respect to the supervising of nuclear fuel and special fissionable material as result from Sweden's international commitments.

iii) *Structure*

Instruction 1974 No. 427, Section 3

Section 5

The Inspectorate is governed by a Board of Directors consisting of the Head of the Inspectorate and six other members appointed by the Government which nominates the Chairman and Vice-Chairman. In addition to the civil servants permanently employed there, the Inspectorate may, in case of need, employ temporary staff or make use of experts and consultants.

Section 4

Section 6

The Inspectorate, in addition to its Department of Administration and an Information Secretariat is divided into two main offices – the Office of Inspection and the Office of Regulation and Research. The latter has four divisions – licensing and safety assessment, spent fuel and waste management, systems and reliability analysis, and research. The Inspectorate also has specialised advisory committees such as a committee on reactor safety, a committee on safeguards and one on reactor safety research.

Section 8

The Board of Directors, which is responsible for deciding on all safety questions of major importance, is competent to take decisions when at least half the members, including the Chairman, are present. Decisions are taken by simple majority, the Chairman having the casting vote.

Section 8

If a question is of such urgency that the Board is unable to meet quickly enough, a dicision can be taken if at least half of the members, including the Chairman, have been consulted. If even this is not possible, decisions can be taken by the Director General of the Inspectorate in the presence of the subordinate directly responsible. Any such decisions must, however, be put on the Agenda of the next meeting of the Board.

Sections 9 and 10

Any business not put forward for decision by the Board of Directors is decided by the Director General of the Inspectorate or his delegated representative.

iv) Financing

Ordinance 1975
No. 421 as amended

Funding for its regulatory activities as well as for the safety research initiated and administered by the State Nuclear Power Inspectorate is covered by the statutory fees payable by applicants for licences and licensees.

c) State Institute for Radiation Protection

i) Legal status

Instruction 1976 No. 481
as last completed by
Ordinance 1981 No. 711

The State Institute for Radiation Protection is a governmental body coming under the Ministry for Agriculture. Originally set up in 1965, the rules relating to its composition and competence were modified somewhat by an Ordinance of 1976. It is the competent authority referred to in the Swedish Radiation Protection Act of 1958.

ii) Responsibilities

Section 2

The Institute is the central authority responsible for matters concerning protection against ionizing and non-ionizing radiation. In addition to its licensing and inspection responsibilities under the 1958 Radiation Protection Act (see Part I above), the Institute is charged with:

Section 3

- acquiring detailed and accurate knowledge about the risks linked with radiation, for which purpose it must attentively follow developments in the fields of biological radiation effects and radiation physics;
- acting as the central co-ordinating body with respect to applied radiation protection research;

- conducting applied research and development work in the field of radiation protection;
- taking account of international norms in the field of radiation protection;
- acting as a co-ordinating body for the different radiation interests in the country and in so doing co-operating with authorities and groups interested in radiation protection questions;
- disseminating information regarding the dangers and difficulties which can be caused by radiation.

Ordinance 1976 No. 246
amending
Ordinance 1958 No. 652

An Ordinance of 1976 provides that the government empowers the State Institute for Radiation Protection to issue regulations pursuant to the 1958 Radiation Protection Act including those concerning transport, customs examination and transit conveyance of radioactive materials.

iii) Structure

Section 4
Section 24

The Institute is governed by a Board, the Chairman of which is the Director General of the Institute, there being a maximum of ten other members appointed by the Government. The Director General of the Institute is also appointed by the Government, for a maximum of six years.

Sections 5 and 24
Section 6

There are three departments set up within the Institute, namely an administrative department inspection department, and a research and development department. Each of these has its own Head – appointed by the Government on the proposal of the Director General of the Institute – one of whom acts also as the Deputy to the Director General. In addition to the civil servants permanently employed there, the Institute may, in case of need, employ temporary staff or make use of experts and consultants.

Sections 12 and 13

The Board, which is responsible for deciding all radiation questions of major importance or which concern basic principles, has the power of decision when at least half the members, including the Chairman, are present. Decisions are taken by simple majority, the Chairman having the casting vote.

Section 13

If a question is one of such urgency that the Board is unable to meet quickly enough, a decision can be taken if at least half of the members, including the Chairman, have been consulted. If even this is not possible, decisions can be taken by the Head of the Institute in the presence of the subordinate directly responsible. Any such decisions must, however, be put on the Agenda of the next meeting of the Board.

Sections 15 to 18

Any business not put forward for decision by the Board is decided by the Director General, his Deputy or other delegated representative.

iv) *Financing*

Ordinance 1976 No. 247
last amended by
Ordinance 1982 No. 561

Funding for the Institute's activities is provided in part by fees paid by applicants and licensees in a similar way to the State Nuclear Power Inspectorate. For the rest, funds are allocated by the Government.

d) National Board for Spent Nuclear Fuel

Instruction 1981 No. 672
last amended by
Instruction 1984 No. 18

The National Board for Spent Nuclear Fuel (*nämnden för hantering av anvant kärnbränsle*) is a governmental created on July 1st 1981 further to the passing of the 19ծ. Act concerning the financing of future costs of spent fuel etc. (see above, Part I, section 5). The supervisory and financial duties laid down in the Act have been delegated by the Government to the Board which is entrusted *inter alia* with:

Section 2

- following developments within the nuclear power field especially with respect to spent fuel and its waste products and to decommissioning;
- scrutinising and evaluating the research programme according to the Act on Nuclear Activities;
- initiating research and development work so as to widen the base for decisions on waste management actions;
- disseminating information regarding the work concerning spent fuel and radioactive waste from the fuel and decommissioning;
- proposing to the Government a fee in *öre*/kWh on electric power delivered from nuclear plants. This fee is determined yearly and paid by the utilities to the Board. The fees are accumulated in a fund administered by the Board;
- administering the funds paid in.

e) Swedish Plant Inspectorate

The Swedish Plant Inspectorate was set up in 1975 as a non-profit-making Government-owned company to assist *inter alia* the Nuclear Power Inspectorate in its supervision of the safety aspects of nuclear installations. In particular, it performs independent inspection and testing of pressure components and lifting devices.

2. ADVISORY BODIES

a) Advisory Research Committee

An Advisory Research Committee was set up within the State Institute for Radiation Protection. The members of this Committee are the Director General of the Institute, who is the Chairman, plus a maximum of twelve other members appointed by the Government and whose mandate is for a maximum of three years. The Committee is charged with selecting its own Vice-Chairman. Its tasks are to prepare research programmes in connection with applied research into radiation protection and to plan co-ordination and follow up research for which the Institute is responsible. The Committee may call on experts to help with particular questions.

b) Advisory Nuclear Accident Emergency Committee

This Committee is also attached to the National Institute for Radiation Protection. Its principal task is to advise the Institute on protection measures against nuclear accidents and on emergency planning in the event of such accidents.

The members of the Advisory Nuclear Accident Emergency Committee are the Director General of the Institute, who is the Chairman, together with other members, the number of which is decided by the Government, and whose mandate is limited to a maximum of three years; they are also appointed by the Government. The Committee is empowered to collect from the authorities and departments concerned the information necessary to carry out its tasks.

c) Association of Municipalities with Nuclear Reactors

The Municipalities in Sweden enjoy extensive powers in political life and community planning, including the right to veto the siting of an industrial plant (nuclear reactor, waste repository etc.) within its area. In the 1970s, there was a rapid expansion of nuclear power in four Swedish Municipalities[2] and in 1977 representatives of these Municipalities approved the setting up of a special co-operation agency, the Association of Municipalities with Nuclear Reactors (*kärnkrafts-kommunernas samarbetsorgan-KSO*).

---

2. Oskarshamm, Kävlinge, Varberg, Osthammar.

The main duties of KSO are:
- to take the initiative in calling, according to need, one to three meetings a year for the permanent KSO members;
- to inform the four nuclear power Municipalities of relevant experience and knowledge gained both in Sweden and abroad;
- to complete and facilitate the work of the local safety committees[3].

KSO is run by a Board of eight persons, two from each nuclear power Municipality. So far, the persons appointed have been the Chairman and Vice-Chairman of the local government in question, although other politicians have been called in to participate in the work of KSO.

3. PUBLIC AND SEMI-PUBLIC AGENCIES

a) Studsvik Energiteknik AB

i) *Legal status*

In 1947, the decision was taken to associate private enterprise and Government interests in a company for applied nuclear research and development, *Aktiebolaget (AB) Atomenergi.*

Until 1969, four sevenths of the capital of AB Atomenergi were owned by the State (Ministry of Industry), and the remainder owned by about seventy other shareholders. The private shareholders, however, reached an agreement with the Government to transfer their shares to the State and the company, renamed *Studsvik Energiteknik AB* in 1978, is now 100% state-owned. It has a share capital of 30 million kronor and employs about 900 persons.

ii) *Responsibilities*

The company performs research and development in the energy field in Sweden and a major activity is research and development work to support the Swedish nuclear programme, which is based on light water reactors. It also pursues related industrial and commercial activities.

3. These are committees attached to each nuclear power station or according to the 1984 Act on Nuclear Activities, installations for the management, storage or final disposal of nuclear waste. The members of the committees, representing local institutions, are appointed by the Government. Their primary duty is that of controlling the safety of work carried out at the power station and they are closely associated with the Municipality concerned.

To a considerable extent the company works for customers in Sweden and abroad on the basis of research contracts carried out for industry, utilities and authorities. The company represents Sweden in international collaboration in the nuclear field.

The company, which carries out applied nuclear research mainly at its centre at Studsvik, near Stockholm, has two research reactors, one of which is R2, a materials testing reactor of 50MW.

The company also owns shares in technical companies at home and abroad.

iii) Structure

The company is governed by a Board of Directors consisting of eight members and four alternates appointed by the Ministry of Industry.

The General Manager of the Company is appointed by the Board of Directors.

The company's activities are conducted through two commercial divisions – the Nuclear Division and the Energy Technology Division.

The Nuclear Division, responsible for Studsvik's nuclear research and service activities, is divided into four operational units covering marketing, fuel technology, reactor technology and waste technology respectively.

The Energy Technology Division, whose work extends over almost the entire spectrum of energy, also includes marketing and fuel technology units as well as a unit dealing with industrial technology.

iv) Financing

The Company's activities are mainly financed by its own sales and the former governmental grants are being reduced gradually.

b) State Power Board

Electricity production in Sweden is in the hands of the State, local authorities and a number of private undertakings.

The State Power Board (*statens vattenfallsverk*) which was set up in 1909 by the government, controls about 45% of total power production. It operates the Ringhals and Forsmark nuclear plants.

c) Swedish Nuclear Fuel Supply Company

The Swedish Nuclear Fuel Supply Company, (*svensk kärnsbränsleförsörjning AB*) in which both private and public interests are represented, deals with questions of common concern to its owners within the nuclear fuel cycle. Its activities, which cover nuclear waste disposal and the supply of materials and services, range from research and development through commercial arrangements to full scale common technical facilities.

It is managed by a Board of Directors, the Chairman of whom is appointed by the Government.

SWITZERLAND

TABLE OF CONTENTS

I. GENERAL REGULATORY REGIME

Federal Order of
18.12.1946

It was in 1946 that the peaceful use of nuclear energy was first regulated by the Swiss Confederation in the form of a Federal Order, dated 18th December 1946, encouraging research in the field of nuclear energy.

Federal Constitution
Article 24 *quinquies*

Federal Tribunal,
13.8.1973
(ATF[1] 99I*a*, 247)
and 23.3.1977
(ATF 103I*a*, 325)

Given the complexity of the issues raised by the use of nuclear technology and the fact that large sums of money are required to put it into effect, the Federal Parliament in June 1957 authorised the Constitution to be amended so that nuclear legislation should fall within the sole jurisdiction of the Confederation, and this was approved in a referendum and by all the cantons in November 1957. Cantons therefore, are not responsible for nuclear safety questions and have a residual jurisdiction only with regard to the licensing of nuclear installations (construction policy, etc.). This division of jurisdiction beween federal and cantonal authorities was sanctioned by the Lausanne Federal Tribunal in decisions in 1973 and 1977.

In Switzerland, the development and use of nuclear energy is not a State monopoly, and a large place is left to private industry. However, many local communities have a direct or indirect interest in the operation of nuclear installations.

Federal (Order of
6.10.1978 (RS[2] 732.0)

Section 3

Legislation was initially limited and concerned mainly the field of radiation protection. More recently, given public reaction to the use of atomic energy, the legislature has had to intervene in the economic sphere. Thus, the Federal Order of 6th October 1978, adopted temporarily pending a comprehensive revision of the Atomic Energy Act of 23rd December 1959, introduced a so-called need requirement: the general licence to construct a nuclear power plant may be refused if it seems that the setting up of the installation is not essential to meet the energy needs of the country. On 18th March 1983, Parliament prolonged the validity of the Federal Order of 6th October 1978 until 31st December 1990.

Act of 23.12.1959

Federal Order of
6.10.1978

Nuclear legislation in Switzerland is based essentially on a Federal framework Act, the 1959 Act on the peaceful use of atomic energy and protection against radiation (discussions as to the reorganisation of the Act have been going on for several years), as completed in 1978 by the above-mentioned Federal Order. A series of Ordinances has been adopted to regulate problems of implementation in the nuclear energy field.

---

1. ATF = Official Gazette of the Federal Tribunal's Decisions.
2. RS = *Recueil Systématique du droit fédéral.*

1. MINING REGIME

Ordinance of 18.1.1984
(RS 732.11)

There are in Switzerland no special mining regulations relating to nuclear ores. Nuclear ores are not considered as nuclear fuels within the meaning of the new Ordinance on definitions and licences in the atomic energy field.

Act of 23.12.1959,
Section 3

Source materials may be acquired by the Confederation to ensure that nuclear installations are supplied, and for scientific research.

2. RADIOACTIVE SUBSTANCES, NUCLEAR FUELS AND EQUIPMENT

Given the special properties and possible uses of nuclear fuels, Swiss nuclear legislation contains more detailed rules with regard to them than to other radioactive substances.

a) Nuclear fuels

Act of 23.12.1959
Fed. Council Ordin. of
18.1.1984
(RS 732.11)
Ordin. of 30.6.1976
(RS 814.50)

The Federal Atomic Energy Act of 1959 contains the basic provisions as to the possession and use of nuclear fuels (and residues), while their import and export is governed by the Federal Council Ordinance of 18th January 1984 on definitions and licences in the atomic energy field. However, these provisions do not apply to amounts of fuel weighing less than 1 gramme or to the shipment of uranium-bearing ores, which are governed by the Federal Council's Radiation Protection Ordinance of 30th June 1976.

Act of 23.12.1959.
Section 4
Ordin. 5/18.1.1984,
Sections 11 and 12

The possession, transport, import and export of nuclear fuels are subject to authorisation by the Confederation, the Federal Energy Office being the body competent to deal with applications. It grants licences on the advice of the principal Nuclear Safety Division (DSN). It is also the DSN which certifies that the regulations on the transport of dangerous goods have been complied with. A licence from the import and export branch of the Federal Office of Foreign Economic Affairs is also necessary in the case of exports of fissile materials and nuclear equipment. In accordance with the new 1984 Ordinance on definitions and licences, any proposed export of sensitive nuclear equipment or products is considered in the light of the London Club guidelines on nuclear transfers, subject to the provisions relating to the transfer of nuclear technology, and is submitted to the Federal Energy Office, the Foreign Affairs Department and the Federal Office of External Economic Affairs for joint authorisation.

Act of 23.12.1959,
Section 9

Section 39

The revocation of a licence to possess nuclear fuels results in a transfer of the nuclear materials either to another licence-holder or to the Confederation. If necessary, the Confederation may arrange for such materials to be seized at the operator's expense.

Section 8

Ordin. of 14.3.1983
(RS 732.22)

Act of 23.12.1959,

Sections 37 and 38

The possession of nuclear fuels is subject to supervision by the Confederation, to which end the Confederation or any bodies designated by it may take all necessary steps to protect persons, property and important rights. In practice, supervision is mainly carried out by the principal Nuclear Safety Division of the Federal Energy Office. The Federal Council has the general task, in the context of the possession and use of nuclear fuels, of laying down implementation standards and setting up any necessary bodies.

b) Radioactive substances and equipment

Fed. Council Ordin.
of 30.6.1976
(RS 814.50),

Section 1

Ordin. of 18.1.1984

The Federal Council's Radiation Protection Ordinance of 30th June 1976, regulates the possession and use of radioactive substances and equipment containing such substances, as well as quantities of nuclear fuel with an activity of less than 1 curie and shipments of uranium-bearing ores. Two different regimes are provided for in the Federal Council Ordinance, according to the potential risk of contamination linked to the different uses of nuclear materials and equipment.

Fed. Council Ordin.
of 30.6.1976
(RS 814.50),
Section 4

Section 87

Section 90

Section 17

Section 13 and 23

i) A *licence* from the Federal Office of Public Health is required for the possession of nuclear materials and equipment whose specific activity exceeds given thresholds, and for all medical uses of ionizing radiation as well as all uses of radioactive substances for pharmaceutical, alimentary or agricultural purposes, and, generally, in everyday objects. In the case of radio-pharmaceutical products, the Federal Office of Public Health grants licences for medical uses – after first approving them and subject to their being registered with the Inter-Cantonal Office for the Control of Medicines – after consulting a joint panel of experts composed of representatives of the Inter-Cantonal Office for the Control of Medicines on the one hand, and representatives of the Confederation nominated by the Federal Department of the Interior on the other. Licences for irradiated foodstuffs will only be granted by the Federal Office of Public Health, or the Federal Veterinary Office in the case of meat products, after biological tests have shown such products to be harmless. Radioactive substances and equipment for restricted use only, must be licensed by the Federal Office of Public Health unless the Office waives the need for such a licence and, if applicable, the mandatory declaration. If licences are revoked, the cantonal authority concerned may, at the request of the competent supervisory bodies, take all necessary steps for radiation protection.

Section 14
Section 17

ii) The regime consisting of a *mandatory declaration* to the Federal Office of Public Health is applicable to the possession of radioactive materials and equipment exempted from the licensing procedure, and to radioactive substances and equipment for general use which have not been exempted by the Federal Service of Public Hygiene from the declaration requirements.

Section 15
Section 17

Activities connected with the use of radioactive substances and of equipment containing such substances must be notified to the Federal Office of Public Health. If trading activities involve substances and equipment approved for general or restricted use, such substances and equipment must also be declared unless expressly exempted by the Federal Office of Public Health.

Section 21 as amended
by Fed. Ordin. of
28.11.1983

In the case of undertakings governed by the Federal Insurance Act, control of the possession of radioactive substances and equipment is entrusted to the Swiss National Accident Insurance Office and in other cases, to the Federal Service of Public Health.

Section 22

The Federal Office of Public Health licenses and controls the import and export of radioactive substances and equipment containing such substances. Imports and exports must be carried out through the customs offices designated by the Directorate-General of Customs.

Section 111

The Federal Department of the Interior is responsible for laying down implementing provisions relating to the possession and marketing of radioactive substances and equipment.

3. PROTECTION OF WORKERS AND THE PUBLIC AGAINST IONIZING RADIATION

Act of 23.12.1959
Fed. Council Ordin.
of 30.6.1976
(RS 814.50),
amended by Fed. Ordin.
of
28.11.1983

Radiation protection is regulated by two basic enactments, the Federal Atomic Energy Act of 1959 which lays down the fundamental principles in this field, and the Federal Council's Radiation Protection Ordinance of 1976 which repealed the previous Ordinance dealing with this subject-matter dated 19th April, 1963. The 1976 Ordinance covers all the health protection measures which should be observed with respect to the various types of use of ionizing radiation accoi ding to the different categories of individuals exposed to such radiation.

Act of 23.12.1959
Sections 11 and 37
Section 38
Section 8

Several government authorities and federal bodies are concerned with questions relating to protection against radiation. The Federal Council has been given regulatory and administrative powers. In particular, it lays down the rules

95

Fed. Council Ordin.
of 30.6.1976,
Sections 7 and 8

relating to protection against ionizing radiation, and sets up the administrative, supervisory and research bodies required for the protection of health. The Federal Council oversees the application of its regulations, and may take any additional measures required to ensure the protection of persons and property. Members of the medical profession wishing to use ionizing radiation for medical purposes must prove that they are properly qualified. The Federal Council appoints experts to check on the professional ability of dental practitioners with a foreign qualification which is not equivalent to a Federal degree, and of chiropractors wishing to use radioactive sources and equipment generating ionizing radiation.

Section 20
Sections 40 and 43
Section 55
Section 46
Section 31
Fed. Council Ordin.
of 30.8.1978,
Section 2
Fed. Council Ordin.
of 30.6.1976,
Section III

The Federal Department of the Interior, and the Federal Department of Transport, Communications and Energy are responsible for implementing regulations in the field of radiation protection. After consulting the competent supervisory bodies whose activities they co-ordinate, these Departments lay down guidelines as to how the supervision required in the field of radiation protection should be carried out. The Federal Department of the Interior concentrates particularly on the protection of persons, and thus is concerned with health risks which may affect certain groups of persons – workers or patients – or the population as a whole, when exposed to ionizing radiation. Those who, in their work, handle radioactive substances or use radiation-producing equipment, are required by the Federal Department of the Interior to have received adequate radiation protection training. The Department determines the content of the courses given in this field as well as the exams. Finally, in consultation with the Federal Commission for Protection against Radiation, the Federal Department of the Interior ensures that there is no conflict between the definitions and values adopted in the field of radiation protection, and the standards used generally. These standards are in line with the recommendations of the International Commission on Radiological Protection (ICRP).

Commission Regulation
(unpublished) of
19.12.1966
Fed. Council Ordin.
of 30.6.1976,
Section 55
Section 43

The Federal Commission for Protection against Radiation, which comes under the authority of the Federal Department of the Interior, has been given the task of advising the Department on radiation protection matters. It is also consulted by the Federal Departments mentioned above in respect of the adoption of protection measures for patients when radiation is used for medical purposes, and also when, for health reasons, a person should no longer be exposed to radiation in the course of his work.

Section 21
as amended by
Fed. Ordin. of
28.11.1983

The Radiation Protection Section of the Federal Office of Public Health (which comes under the Federal Department of the Interior), and the Swiss National Accident Insurance Office, which comes under the Federal Office of Social

Fed. Council Ordin.
of 30.8.1978,
Section 2

Insurance, have, each in its own area of competence, been given supervisory responsibility with regard to the protection of persons. In establishments which are governed by the Federal Insurance Act, such supervision is the responsibility of the Swiss National Accident Insurance Office or of any body to which it has delegated such responsibility. The Federal Factory Inspectorate is called on to assist the National Insurance Office with the supervision of factories. In other cases the Radiation Protection Section or the body designated by it, carries out radiation protection controls subject to the special provisions laid down for nuclear installations. In addition, instruction on radiation protection in Switzerland is organised by the Federal Office of Public Health with the assistance of the Federal Services and professional organisations concerned.

Fed. Council Ordin.
of 30.6.1976,
Section 45

Fed. Council Order
(unpublished) of
6.2.1959

Radioactivity in the environment is monitored by the Federal Commission for the Monitoring of Radioactivity which reports regularly to the Federal Council on the results obtained, and, in the event of an increase in radioactivity, proposes measures to be taken to ensure the protection of the population.

Ordin. of 9.9.1966
amended on 29.4.1981
(RS 732.32) and also
by Ordin. of 28.11.1983
(RS 732.33)

Should an alarming increase in radioactivity be detected, a warning organisation will be required to take action. This organisation will follow developments in the situation, and propose or recommend any measures it deems necessary. A Committee on Radioactive Emergencies, under the Federal Department of the Interior, heads the warning organisation.

To this effect, the Federal Department of Transport, Communications and Energy must determine, in consultation with the Federal Department of the Interior and the cantons concerned, two areas around the nuclear installation. Area 1 surrounding the installation delineates the area within which a serious incident in the installation could cause a hazard for the population requiring speedy protection measures. Area 2, contiguous to Area 1, covers approximately 20 km, divided into sectors.

According to the circumstances, a simple warning, a general warning or a radioactive warning may be set off.

The nuclear operator must plan the appropriate emergency regulations for his installations; he must set up the necessary equipment and co-operate with the warning organisation.

In general, radiation protection measures taken by the Confederation are based on the recommendations of the International Commission on Radiological Protection (ICRP), and on the standards adopted by the OECD Nuclear Energy Agency.

4. NUCLEAR INSTALLATIONS[3]

Act of 23.12.1959,
Section 4
Fed. Order of
6.10.1978,
Section 1

The basic regulations presently in force were passed under the Federal Act of 1959 on Atomic Energy which provides for a system of licensing for the construction and operation of nuclear installations. However, the Federal Order of 6th October 1978 concerning the above Act amended the licensing procedure by requiring nuclear operators first of all to obtain a so-called general licence determining the site and the outline of the project. A "need requirement" has been attached to this licence which will not be granted unless it is shown that the planned nuclear installation meets a real need in the country.

Section 3
Section 12(2)
Fed. Council Ordin.
of 11.7.1979
(RS 732.011)

Apart from this formal additional obligation imposed by the Order, the construction and operating licences required by the Federal Act of 23rd December 1959 were not in practice granted till after a procedure during which the site proposed for the installation was approved. That is why Swiss legislation has, on a temporary basis, introduced a simplified procedure for the granting of the general licence in the case of operators who have already been authorised to locate their installations on a given site. The details of this simplified procedure are contained in a Federal Council Ordinance of 1979 specifying the procedure applicable to general licences for atomic installations with regard to holders of a site licence.

a) Granting of general licences

Fed. Order of
6.10.1978,
Section 1
Fed. Council Ordin.
of 11.7.1979,
Section 4

The Federal Council is the body which decides upon applications for general licences. Its decision is then submitted to the Federal Assembly for approval. General licences are granted after an enquiry procedure organised by the Federal Council during which, in particular, the opinion of the cantons and communes concerned, together with that of the Federal Services specialised in the field, are sought and referred for comment to the Energy Commission and other experts.

Fed. Order of
6.10.1978,
Section 1

The general licence determines the site to be selected for the installation and the general outline of the project.

b) Granting of technical licences

Fed. Council
18.1.1984,
Section 6

These licences are now granted by the Federal Council.

3. For further details see: "Description of Licensing Systems and Inspection of Nuclear Installations", OECD/NEA, 1980.

Act of 23.12.1959,
Section 7

Fed. Council Ordin.
of 18.1.1984,
Section 4

Act of 13.3.1964,
Sections 1 and 8
(RS 822.11)

Act of 23.12.1959,
Section 4(3)

The applications considered by the Federal Energy Office are sent to the cantons concerned for their opinion; the Office also consults the national specialised bodies. It should be noted that the nuclear installation licensing regime does not apply to installations in which it is intended solely to store or render harmless nuclear fuels or radioactive waste whose total activity is less than one curie. By virtue of the Federal Work Act, nuclear industrial enterprises are required in addition to obtain specific nuclear licences, approval of plans and a special licence. In all cases, it is the cantonal authorities who remain competent to grant licences in respect of building, and fire and water regulations.

c) Technical advisory and supervisory bodies

Ordin. of
14.3.1983
(RS 732.21)

The principal Nuclear Safety Division (DSN) of the Federal Energy Office (Federal Department of Transport, Communications and Energy) gives an expert opinion on safety reports. The Federal Commission for the Safety of Nuclear Installations (CSA) draws up in parallel an opinion on certain particular aspects of the project. This CSA report completes and, in principle, confirms the opinion of the DSN. On the basis of these documents, the Federal Council takes a decision as to the licences. The Federal Energy Office is responsible for putting in hand licensing procedures for nuclear installations.

Act of 23.12.1959,
Sections 8 and 39

Ordin. of
14.3.1983
(RS 732.22)

Nuclear installations are supervised by the Confederation. To this end, the Federal Council and the bodies designated by it, may lay down and follow the implementation of measures to protect persons, property and important rights, and to assure Switzerland's external security and guarantee that its international commitments will be fulfilled. In practice, it is the principal Nuclear Safety Division (DSN) which carries out most technical inspections of installations although the DSN may call on experts from outside the Federal Administration.

The Federal Commission for the Safety of Nuclear Installations and the DSN advise the Federal Energy Office on, and suggest, measures that are necessary for the technical safety of installations.

d) Decommissioning of nuclear installations

Fed. Order of
6.10.1978,
Section 11

Ordin. of 5.12.1983
(RS 732.013)

Act of 23.12.1959,
Section 37

To meet the expenses of the dismantling of nuclear installations which are no longer to be operated, a *Fund for the decommissioning of nuclear installations* has been set up under the responsibility of the Federal Council to collect the necessary payments from the operators of nuclear installations. The necessary capital may be advanced to the Fund by the Federal Council which also lays down the detailed rules on the working of the Fund and, in general, the implementing provisions relating to nuclear installations. Similarly, it is the Federal Council which sets up the administrative bodies necessary.

5. RADIOACTIVE WASTE MANAGEMENT

Act of 23.12.1959, Sections 1 and 4

Ordin. of 18.1.1984, Section 2

Section 3

It should be pointed out in this context that in Swiss regulations, the term *résidus* is used for a particular category of materials. The 1984 Ordinance on definitions and licences in the atomic energy field stipulates that *résidus* (residues) are the radioactive materials (including activation products) whose activity is higher than one curie and which are formed from nuclear fuels after the nuclear transmutation process. The Federal Council may also include in this category, by assimilation, integral parts of nuclear installations which have become radioactive during atomic energy production. The term "radioactive waste" applies to radioactive materials and articles contaminated by such materials which will not be used again. In practice radioactive waste (*déchets*) is mainly material resulting from the use of radioisotopes.

Fed. Council Ordin. of 30.6.1976, Section 102 *et seq.,* Appendix 1 No. 11

Such radioactive waste results from the handling of radioactive sources of all kinds; it broadly includes waste produced as a result of industrial, medical, research, and educational uses.

In fact, Swiss regulations do not always make this distinction and, for convenience, the term waste has been used in this section. When residues are concerned this is indicated in brackets.

a) Waste from nuclear installations

–   *Licensing system*

Act of 23.12.1959, Sections 4 and 9

The 1959 Federal Atomic Energy Act dealt with the question of radioactive waste (residues) only from the viewpoint of a licence, or the revocation of a licence, for its possession and transport.

Fed. Order of 6.10.1978, Sections 1 and 10

Fed. Council Ordin. of 24.10.1979 (RS 732.012)

Provisions dealing with the question of waste are now included in the Federal Order of 6th October 1978 concerning the Atomic Energy Act, and a Federal Council Ordinance of 1979 contains details as to the implementation of the licensing procedure provided for in Section 10 of the Federal Order of 1978, for the taking of preparatory steps to set up a repository for radioactive waste.

Act of 23.12.1959, Section 4

The Federal Council lays down implementing provisions and designates the relevant administrative bodies and the commissions responsible for studying nuclear energy questions. The possession, transport, import and export of radioactive waste (residues) require a licence from the Confederation.

Fed. Order of
6.10.1978,
Section 1

Ordin. of 18.1.1984,
Section 6

The licensing regime applicable to radioactive waste repositories follows the same procedure and makes use of the same authorities as those involved in the licensing of nuclear installations (general licences). The general licence which fixes the site and the general outline of the project also determines the storage capacity, the categories of waste as well as the structure of the underground or surface constructions. Before granting a licence, the Federal Council consults the local communities concerned and the services of the Confederation specialised in the field.

Ordin. of 14.3.193,
Section 2

Act of 23.12.1959,
Section 9

The Federal Energy Office is responsible for implementing the procedure for licences for installations for the disposal of nuclear waste after consultation with the Federal Commission for the Safety of Nuclear Installations. The latter gives its opinion after having seen the first safety assessment reports by the principal Nuclear Safety Division of the Federal Energy Office. Should a licence to possess radioactive waste (residues) be revoked, the waste is transferred either to another licence-holder or to the Confederation.

Section 8

Sections 9 and 39

Fed. Order of
6.10.1978,
Section 10

The Confederation is responsible, as it is for nuclear installations, for supervising the possession of radioactive waste (residues), and this task is carried out by the principal Nuclear Safety Division of the Federal Energy Office. The supervisory bodies are empowered to have any radioactive waste which constitutes a radiation protection hazard seized or disposed of, at the producer's expense.

Act of 23.12.1959,
Section 4

Ordin. of 18.1.1984,
Section 9

A licence is also required for the transport or possession of waste (residues). The granting of such licences is the responsibility of the Federal Energy Office. The task of supervising these activities is carried out by the principal Nuclear Safety Division.

– *Storage and disposal of waste*

Fed. Order of
6.10.1978

As provided for by the Federal Order of 6th October 1978 concerning the Atomic Energy Act, the following principles apply to the management and disposal of radioactive waste:

– producers of waste are responsible for its safe disposal, the Confederation retaining the right, if necessary, to have the waste disposed of at the producer's expense;
– the Federal Council may grant permission under a special procedure for the taking of preparatory steps

Section 3

for the construction of a radioactive waste repository;

- the Federal Council may require waste producers to become members of a public body and to pay equitable contributions so that the costs of waste disposal may be covered;
- general licences for nuclear power plants will only be granted on condition that the permanent and safe storage of the radioactive waste can be guaranteed (transitory provisions have been made for installations in operation or being built).

It is clear from this that the future use of nuclear energy in Switzerland is dependent on it being possible to establish that radioactive waste can be permanently disposed of in a satisfactory manner.

Repositories must conform to the safety conditions and technical criteria laid down by the Federal Commission for the Safety of Nuclear Installations and the Federal Energy Office in Directives R-21 of October 1980.

With regard to operating licences for nuclear power plants which, because already in operation or being built, are not covered by the provisions of the Federal Order of 6th October 1978, the Federal Department of Transport, Communications and Energy has made the continuing validity of such licences after 1985 conditional on it being shown that there is a satisfactory method for disposing of the waste produced. The electricity companies concerned are therefore obliged to submit a proposal containing such a guarantee to the Federal Council before 31st December 1985 (although this time-limit may be put back to a later date).

A Confederation Inter-Agency Working Group on radioactive waste management (AGNEB) was set up by the Federal Council on 15th February 1978. This Group is responsible for following the work carried out in this sector by other bodies, and for preparing the technical elements necessary for making an evaluation and which will serve as an aid to the Federal Council and the Federal Department of Transport, Communications and Energy when taking decisions in this field. It makes sure that the Confederation keeps to the time-limits prescribed for licensing procedures and reports once a year to the Department.

In 1972, the producers of radioactive waste, including the Confederation, formed a private company – the National Corporation for the Disposal of Radioactive Waste (CEDRA) – which has the task of managing the radioactive waste for which the waste producers are responsible.

Fed. Council Ordin.
of 24.10.1979,
Sections 1 and 18

Over and above the licences required for nuclear installations, a special licence is needed in the case of waste repositories, to take preparatory steps to set up such a repository. The Federal Council is the competent authority to grant such licences by virtue of an instruction entrusted to the Federal Department of Transport, Communications and Energy; the cantons concerned and the specialised services of the Confederation are invited to make known their observations. Supervision of the preparatory and follow-up measures and work is carried out jointly by the specialised services of the Confederation designated by the Federal Council, and by the cantons concerned. The Federal Order of 6th October 1978 gave the Federal Council a compulsory purchase power for the setting up of repositories, and this power may transferred to the beneficiary of the compulsory purchase.

Section 14 et seq.
Section 19
Section 20

b) Waste from industrial, research, medical and educational uses

These types of waste are governed by the Radiation Protection Ordinance of 1976, and detailed regulations as to their collection and shipment are contained in a Federal Department of the Interior Ordinance of 1977.

Fed. Council Ordin. of 30.6.1976, Sections 102 to 107 Fed. Dept. of the Interior Ordin. of 18.3.1977 (RS 814.557)

In accordance with the Radiation Protection Ordinance, all radioactive waste producers must make provision for the temporary storage of waste at the site of production, and submit details of their proposal for approval either to the Swiss National Accident Insurance Office in the case of enterprises subject to the Federal Accident Insurance Act, or to the Federal Office of Public Health in all other cases, before the Insurance Office or the Federal Office of Public Health can take a decision as to the licences for the possession and use of radioactive substances, and equipment containing such substances.

Fed. Council Ordin. of 30.6.1976, Sections 10 and 106
Fed. Act of 20.3.1981 (RS 832.21)
Radiation Protection Ordin. (amendment) 28.11.1983 (RS 814.50)

The Confederation is responsible for collecting all radioactive waste produced by institutes and enterprises situated in Switzerland. A list of waste producers is drawn up for this purpose by the Radiation Protection Section of the Federal Office of Public Health which keeps waste producers informed of the date of the annual collection exercise. Waste collection is organised jointly by the Federal Office of Public Health and the Federal Institute for Reactor Research (IFR). The waste is transported to collecting centres designated by the public authorities, and is either stored in facilities set up under the responsibility of the Federal Department of the Interior, or else disposed of. No waste may be sent for treatment to the Federal Institute for Reactor Research without its agreement.

Federal Department of the Interior Ordin. of 18.3.1977 Section 14
Fed. Council Ordin. of 30.6.1976, Sections 106 and 111
Fed. Dept. of the Interior Ordin. of 18.3.1977, Section 14, Appendix 1

The Federal Department of the Interior is the regulatory authority responsible for making any implementing provisions required for radioactive waste management.

Fed. Council Ordin. of 30.6.1976, Sections 106 and 111

6. NUCLEAR THIRD PARTY LIABILITY

Switzerland has signed the Paris Convention of 29th July 1960 on Third Party Liability in the Field of Nuclear Energy, and the Brussels Supplementary Convention of 31st January 1963, but has not ratified them.

Act of 23.12.1959

Fed. Council Ordin. of 13.6.1960 (RS 732.41) (repealed)

Fed. Council Order of 19.12.1960 (RS 732.42) (repealed)

Provisions relating to nuclear third party liability were originally contained in the Federal Act of 1959. These provisions had been followed on 13th June and 19th December 1960 by a Federal Council Ordinance and Order respectively, whose purpose was to regulate the working of the Fund for Delayed Atomic Damage provided for under Section 19 of the 1959 Federal Act.

Fed. Council Ordin. of 30.11.1981 (RS 732.44) (repealed)

Act of 23.12.1959, Section 1

In terms of a Federal Council Ordinance of 30th November 1981 on cover for third party liability, nuclear power plant operators were obliged to cover their liability up to a ceiling of 300 million Swiss francs. However, the Federal Council decided to exempt operators of nuclear installations, the activity of whose nuclear fuel and waste is less than one curie, from the legal provisions on third party liability and mandatory insurance.

Act of 18.3.1983 (RS 732.44)

Section 3

A new Act on Third Party Liability in the Nuclear Field (LRCN) came into force on 1st January 1984. This Act abides by the two basic principles, mainly those of causal liability and the chanelling of liability to the operator of a nuclear installation. On the other hand, the LRCN rejects the principle of third party liability limited in amount and provides that the person liable must commit himself for an unlimited amount. Such liability is covered as follows:

Section 11

– by private insurance up to three hundred million francs for each nuclear installation (50 million for each transport operation);

Section 12

– by the Confederation up to one thousand million francs when the damage exceeds the amount covered by private insurance;

– by all the assets of the person liable; and

– according to the special procedures with regard to "catastrophies".

Sections 14 and 15

The Fund for Delayed Atomic Damage has been changed into the Fund for Nuclear Damage. Fees are to be levied from nuclear operators and holders of transport licences so as to cover the contributions made by the Confederation.

Ordin. of 5.12.1983 (RS 732.441)

A Federal Council Ordinance, which entered into force on the same day as the Act, specifies the scope, insurance conditions, the coverage of costs by the Confederation and the management of the Fund for Nuclear Damage set up by the Act. The Fund, which is within the Finance Administration, is not a legal entity but is financially independent. The

Ordinance also provides for the assignment of the costs of preventive measures taken by the appropriate authorities.

7. NUCLEAR SECURITY

The Swiss Confederation has committed itself internationally to co-operate in the fight against the spread of nuclear weapons. It ratified the Treaty on the Non-Proliferation of Nuclear Weapons (NPT) on 9th March 1977, and has undertaken to observe the Guidelines of the nuclear supplier countries (the London Club) on nuclear transfers (IAEA Doc. INFCIRC/254), subject to the provisions on the transfer of nuclear technology.

There is no legislation dealing specifically with nuclear security. However, special provisions have been included in nuclear enactments adopted by the Confederation.

Fed. Order of
6.10.1978

Section 3

Section 6
Act of 23.12.1959,
Section 5

The general licence required for the operation of a nuclear power plant is granted only to Swiss citizens domiciled in Switzerland. As for corporations, they must be governed by Swiss law, have their headquarters in Switzerland and be under Swiss control. In addition, licenses for nuclear installations may be refused or made conditional upon particular conditions being observed when this is necessary for safeguarding Switzerland's external security, for the fulfilment of its international commitments or for the protection of persons, property and important rights.

Section 8

Section 39

Section 40
Fed. Council Ordin.
of 30.6.1976,
Sections 23 to 25

In supervising nuclear installations and the possession of nuclear fuels, the Federal Council or the body appointed by it takes all steps which may be necessary for the external security of the country and for the fulfilment of its international commitments. Generally, those responsible for inspections in the nuclear field have wide investigatory powers and are bound by professional secrecy. When the national defence is at stake, the supervisory authorities in the radiation protection field have the power to waive health requirements.

Act of 23.12.1959
Section 5

The export of nuclear energy is forbidden when it is contrary to the public interest.

Fed. Council Ordin.
of 17.5.1978,
Section 10

Section 11

Section 7

The granting of licences for the export of sensitive nuclear equipment and materials is assessed by the competent Swiss authorities in the light of the London Club Guidelines on nuclear transfers, subject to the rules on the transfer of technology. The export of fissile material and nuclear equipment must be authorised twice over: first by the import and export branch of the Trade Division of the Federal Department of Public Economy, and secondly, a joint authorisation from the Federal Energy Office, the Federal

Political Department and the Federal Office of External Economic Affairs.

Act of 23.12.1959, Section 29 *et seq.* Section 34

The 1959 Atomic Energy Act provides for penal sanctions which, generally speaking, are applicable to persons who intentionally transgress provisions laid down in the field of nuclear energy. In the present context, the betrayal of secrets concerning the peaceful use of atomic energy is judged more or less severely depending on whether the secrets were or were not passed on to a foreign body or undertaking.

8. TRANSPORT[4]

The transport of radioactive materials in Switzerland is governed by a number of different regulations each dealing with a particular form of transport. In general, these enactments implement in Switzerland the international regulations in this field.

Fed. Council Ordin. of 24.5.1972 (updated 1.1.1979) (RS 741.621) Section 1-4 ADR of 30.9.1957 (revised version 1.10.1978) (RS 0.741.621)

Thus, for road transport, the basic text is the Federal Council Ordinance of 24th May 1972 relating to the transport of dangerous goods by road (SDR). The Ordinance provides that foreign vehicles which do not fully satisfy the technical norms which it prescribes shall nevertheless be allowed into Switzerland provided that they meet the standards laid down in the European Agreement of 30th September 1957 concerning the International Carriage of Dangerous Goods by Road (ADR).

Transport Regulations of 2.10.1967 (updated 1.10.1978) (RS 742.401)

For transport by rail, the legislation in force is contained in the Regulations concerning transport by rail and by water, known as the Transport Regulations, of 2nd October 1967, whose Annex I incorporates the International Regulations concerning the Carriage of Dangerous Goods by Rail (RID). This Annex is itself entitled the Swiss International Regulations concerning the Carriage of Dangerous Goods by Rail (RID/RSD).

Ordin. of 28.10.1976 (RS 747.224.141.1)

The transport of radioactive or fissile materials by inland waterway is governed by the above-mentioned Transport Regulations (RID/RSD), and if on the Rhine, is subject to the Regulations for the Transport of Dangerous Goods on the River Rhine (ADNR) of 29th April 1970.

Air Transport Regulations of 3.10.1952, Sections 13 and 14,

The Air Transport Regulations of 3rd October 1952 apply to the transport by air of radioactive or fissile materials authorised by the Federal Air Office on condition that the

---

4. For further details see Analytical Study in the same series: "Regulations Governing the Transport of Radioactive Materials", OECD/NEA, 1980.

approved by
Fed. Order of 16.12.1952
(RS 748.411)
Decision of 1.7.1963,
Section 1-1

Ordin. of 1.9.1967
as amended
(RS 783.01)

Transport Regulations
of 2.10.1967,
Section 1bis

Air Transport
Regulations
of 3.10.1952,
Section 14

Decision of 1.7.1963,
Section 1

Fed. Council Ordin.
of 24.5.1972,
Section 18

Section 13

Section 36

RID/RSD
(RS 742.401)
Marginal 15

Act of 23.12.1959,
Section 4(b) and (c)

Fed. Council Ordin.
of 18.1.1984

transport is carried out in accordance with the regulations laid down by the International Air Transport Association (IATA) concerning the transport of restricted articles by air.

The sending by post of radioactive or fissile materials whose specific activity does not exceed 0.002 microcuries per gramme is governed by the Federal Council Ordinance of 1st September 1967 as amended on 21st November 1979, which amends Implementing Ordinance I of the Post Office Act. In cases where the specific activity of the materials exceeds this figure, it is the Transport Regulations (RID/RSD) which apply.

The Federal Department of Transport, Communications and Energy is responsible for transport by road, rail and inland waterway. This Department has the task, along with the other bodies concerned, of drawing up regulations in the field of the transport of radioactive and fissile materials. In the case of air transport, the Federal Air Office may impose additional requirements to be observed during transport operations, as long as these do not contradict the regulations laid down in this field by IATA. As for sea transport, the relevant international regulations are applied directly.

The Confederation ensures that drivers of lorries carrying dangerous goods are properly trained. In this connection, the Federal Department of Justice and Police may issue directives specifying the training that must be given by firms specialised in transport. The cantonal authorities are responsible for ensuring compliance with provisions on packaging, labelling, loading and unloading of road vehicles, although these authorities may request the assistance of experts designated by the Federal Department of Justice and Police. In general, this Department, or the Federal Police Office to which it may delegate its powers, may issue all kinds of directives relating to the implementation of the SDR.

For transport by road, rail and inland waterway, the principal Nuclear Safety Division of the Federal Energy Office is given the task of approving requests for despatch and the prior notifications required in the case of the despatch of certain types of package, and is responsible for the technical supervision of transport operations. The Federal Office of Public Health or the Federal Institute for Reactor Research must be informed of any accident occurring to the packages of radioactive materials during transport by road, rail or inland waterway, so that they may take any measures that may be necessary.

The regulations which have been mentioned so far govern the transport of radioactive materials. It should be noted, however, that the transport of nuclear fuels and radioactive waste is also regulated by the 1959 Atomic Energy Act which, in particular, requires a licence granted by the Federal Energy Office for such transport. Transports abroad of nuclear fuels and radioactive waste that are of particular political or economic significance are licensed jointly by the Federal Energy Office, the Federal Political Department and the Trade Division of the Federal Department of Public Economy.

9. PATENTS

Act of 25.6.1954
(RS 232.14) and
Implementing Ordin.
of 19.10.1977
(RS 232.141)

Swiss law contains no regulations dealing specifically with nuclear industrial property. This being so, the ordinary law of patents applies in the nuclear field.

II. INSTITUTIONAL FRAMEWORK

Fed. Constitution,
Article 24 *quinquies*

Act of 23.12.1959,
Section 2

Sections 3 and 5

Since 24th November 1957, when Article 24 *quinquies* was inserted in the Swiss Constitution, nuclear energy has been declared to be the responsibility of the Federal legislature. Thus the Confederation supervises nuclear activities and is very active in structuring and developing them. The Confederation also plays an important role in the field of research and the training of nuclear specialists. Finally, it may acquire the nuclear materials necessary or forbid the export of such materials (although it is normally the electricity companies which acquire and possess nuclear fuels, with the authorisation of the Confederation).

The Federal Council has the necessary regulatory and administrative powers for adopting the regulations required for the development of the use of nuclear energy and for radiation protection. The Federal Department of Transport, Communications and Energy, and the Federal Department of the Interior are responsible for implementing the provisions adopted by the Federal Council in the field of the use of atomic energy, and the field of protection against ionizing radiation respectively. Various commissions study questions relating to the use of atomic energy, each in the field in which it has been made competent.

Ordin. of 7.9.1977
(RS 424.2)

Apart from the Federal Departments and the specialised services of the Confederation, the public sector is also represented by two public bodies, the Federal Institute for Reactor Research and the Swiss Institute for Nuclear Research.

1. REGULATORY AND SUPERVISORY AUTHORITIES

a) Federal Council

The Federal Council, which represents the executive branch of government in Switzerland at Federal level, takes a large part in the organisation and carrying on of nuclear activities.

Act of 23.12.1959,
Sections 11 and 37

Section 4(2)

Section 1(4)

In the first place, the Federal Council assists in the development of regulations in the atomic energy field, and ensures their implementation. More particularly, the Federal Council has the power to broaden the category of activities for which a licence is required. On the other hand, it may also waive the rules on licences, third party liability and insurance, in the case of activities which give rise to only a very low risk of radiotoxicity.

Fed. Order of
6.10.1978,
Sections 1, and 5 to 8
Fed. Council Ordin.
of 11.7.1979,
Sections 3 and 4

Fed. Order of 6.10.1978,
Section 10
Fed. Council Ordin.
of 24.10.1979,
Section 1

On an administrative level, the Federal Council has been made responsible for investigating and deciding on applications for general licences for nuclear installations, prior to construction and operating licences. The Federal Council also grants licences for taking preparatory steps for the setting up of a radioactive waste repository.

Act of 23.12.1959,
Section 8

Ordin. of 18.1.1984,
Section 6

In general, the Federal Council licenses and supervises nuclear installations and materials, and may take any measures necessary for the protection of persons, property and important rights, as well as for Switzerland's external security and fulfilment of its international commitments.

Act of 23.12.1959,
Sections 37 and 38

In general, the Federal Council sets up the necessary administrative bodies, and the commissions responsible for studying questions relating to the use of nuclear energy and to radiation protection.

For purposes of promoting nuclear research, the Federal Council is authorised to give financial assistance to research agencies. In particular, subsidies are granted to the Swiss National Scientific Research Fund, a body which manages part of the funds intended for research and the training of specialists in the field of nuclear science in Switzerland.

The Federal Council appoints the director(s) of the Federal Institute for Reactor Research, as well as the members of its advisory commission.

b) Federal Assembly

Fed. Order of
6.10.1978,
Sections 1 and 8
Fed. Council Ordin.
of 11.7.1979,
Section 4

The Federal Assembly, Switzerland's parliament, is involved in the nuclear field in approving the Federal Council's decisions as to general licences for nuclear installations.

Act of 18.3.1983,

Section 29

Ordin. of 5.12.1983,
Section 4

The Assembly is also competent in respect of third party liability and insurance. Thus, in the case of catastrophes, the Federal Assembly is empowered to draw up indemnification rules determining the general principles of compensation for victims. A special independent body may be set up by the Federal Assembly to ensure that these principles are implemented.

c) Federal Department of Transport, Communications and Energy

Fed. Council Ordin.
of 9.5.1979,
(RS 172.010.15)

Fed. Council Ordin.
of 30.6.1976,
Section 20

The general task of the Federal Department of Transport, Communications and Energy (DFTE) is to prepare legislation on the use of nuclear energy. In conjunction with the Federal Department of the Interior, and after having consulted the competent supervisory bodies, it lays down guidelines on the supervisory measures which should be taken to protect the population, and on co-ordinating the work of the bodies responsible for supervision.

Fed. Council Ordin.
of 24.10.1979,
Sections 6, 14 *et seq.*

The Federal Department has the task of following the licensing procedure in the case of applications for licences to take preparatory steps for studying sites with a view to setting up radioactive waste repositories.

Ordin. of 9.5.1979,
(RS 172.010.15)

Finally, the Federal Department is the authority to whom the Federal Commission for the Safety of Nuclear Installations is responsible.

d) Federal Energy Office

Fed. Council Order
of 23.12.1968,
Section 5

Fed. Act of 19.9.1978
on the organisation of
the Administration
(RS 172.010)

Ordin. of 9.5.1979
(RS 172.010.15)

Under the Order of the Federal Council of 23rd December 1968 on the reorganisation of Swiss administrative authorities, the Federal Energy Office, which forms part of the Federal Department of Transport, Communications and Energy, was given the powers which previously belonged to the Delegate for Atomic Energy Questions except for those which were expressly conferred on the Science and Research Division.

Fed. Council Ordin.
of 18.1.1984

The Federal Energy Office therefore is competent to prepare and implement legislation in the field of nuclear energy, and also to prepare, in conjunction with the Federal Political Department, international nuclear treaties and to ensure that they are properly carried out. The Office also has the task of examining and co-ordinating studies carried out in the field of nuclear energy. The Federal Energy Office is responsible for investigating applications for the construction, operation or modification of nuclear installations, and in the case of nuclear installations which do not produce electricity, also grant the licences.

Section 9

Further, the Office is the competent authority for licensing the transport, import and export of nuclear materials and equipment, and for the storage of nuclear fuels and radioactive waste.

Ordin. of 14.3.1983
(RS 732.21)
Section 11

The Federal Energy Office includes the principal Nuclear Safety Division (DSN). The principal Nuclear Safety Division is called upon to give an expert opinion on the technical safety reports relating to the various licences required under Swiss nuclear law: general licences and licences for the construction and operation of nuclear installations, licences for the transport and marketing of nuclear materials and equipment, and licences in the field of radioactive waste management. The Division also ensures that technical checks are carried out on nuclear installations, and concentrates on measures to be taken to prevent nuclear catastrophes.

e) Federal Department of the Interior

The Federal Department of the Interior has, in the nuclear field, been given regulatory and administrative powers in the area of radiation protection. It is also competent with regard to nuclear research questions and co-ordinates activities with the universities and Federal *Ecoles polytechniques* (see under Federal Institute for Reactor Research).

Fed. Council
Ordin. of
30.6.1976,
Section 111

Section 20

With regard to its regulatory powers, the Federal Department of the Interior has a general responsibility for radiation protection questions. It has the task of laying down the necessary rules for applying the measures enacted by the Federal Council for protection against ionizing radiation. In particular, the Federal Department of the Interior, with the assistance of the Federal Department of Transport, Communications and Energy, and after consulting the competent supervisory bodies, lays down guidelines for the supervisory activities to be carried out in the radiation protection field.

Section 55

Section 46

In addition, the Federal Department of the Interior, in agreement with the Federal Commission for Protection against Radiation, lays down guidelines on measures to be adopted for the protection of persons exposed to radiation for

111

medical purposes. With regard to foodstuffs, it is the Federal Department of the Interior which determines the maximum concentrations of radionuclides which may be incorporated in food products.

Fed. Council Ordin.
of 30.8.1978
(RS 814.532.1),
Section 2

Sections 1 and 5

Fed. Council Ordin.
of 30.6.1976,
Section 31

Moreover, the Federal Department of the Interior determines the training programme, the method of examination, and rights in relation to the training and refresher courses offered by the Confederation in the field of radiation protection. Courses given by private institutions must first be recognised by the Federal Department, or the competent supervisory body, if they are to benefit from subsidies which will be fixed by the Federal Department of the Interior. In any event, no one may use in the course of his work radioactive materials or equipment generating ionizing radiation without having received training recognised by the Federal Department of the Interior or the competent supervisory body.

Section 20

By reason of its administrative powers, the Federal Department of the Interior, with the assistance of the Federal Department of Transport, Communications and Energy, co-ordinates the activities of the nuclear supervisory bodies.

Sections 39 and 40

The Federal Department of the Interior also has the power to impose any necessary measures with regard to the medical supervision of persons exposed to ionizing radiation at work.

Section 106

In the radioactive waste management field, the Federal Department of the Interior ensures the disposal by suitable bodies of radioactive waste other than that coming from electricity-producing nuclear installations and installations for the reprocessing of spent fuel.

Fed. Council Order
of 23.12.1968
(RS 1, 243),
Section 1

Fed. Council Ordin.
of 30.6. 1976,
Section 108

Finally, the Federal Department of the Interior has under its authority the Federal Office of Public Health and the Office of Education and Science, and it may hear appeals from decisions made by the Federal Office of Public Health.

f) Federal Office of Public Health

Through the agency of its Radiation Protection Section, the Federal Office of Public Health enjoys wide administrative and supervisory powers in the field of protection against radiation.

– Administrative powers

Sections 4 and 13

Section 11
amended by Ordin.
of 28.11.1983

The Office is the competent authority for the granting or revocation of licences for the production, use, possession, disposal, import and export of radioactive substances – except in the case of nuclear installations, nuclear fuels and

Ordin. of 30.6.1976,
Section 14

Section 15

Section 16

Section 17

radioactive waste – and for nuclear equipment, whether used for industrial, scientific, medical or agricultural purposes. If, however, a negative opinion is given by the Swiss National Accident Insurance Office, which considers applications from enterprises subject to the Federal Act on Accident Insurance, then the Federal Office is bound by this opinion. Persons possessing radioactive substances or equipment emitting ionizing radiation for which no licence is required because the quantity or activity of nuclear material concerned is below a given threshold, must make declarations to the Federal Office. Persons manufacturing or trading in such substances or equipment which are not freely available or are for restricted use, must submit each year to the Federal Office a report on their activities. The Office may allow certain types of radioactive substances and equipment emitting ionizing radiation or containing radioactive substances to be used generally or for specific purposes. It is the Office which grants the necessary licence for the restricted use of substances and equipment and which receives the declarations of persons possessing substances or equipment available for general use, unless it waives such formalities.

Section 87

Section 91

The Federal Office of Public Health, in consultation with a panel of experts representing various interests, is also the competent authority for approving radioactive substances intended to be used for medical purposes. It must authorise any work which a company wishes to carry out outside its own premises and which involves unsealed radioactive sources.

– *Supervisory powers*

Section 58

Section 59

An expert designated by the Federal Office of Public Health checks those parts of equipment used for therapy which determine the dose given, every time the equipment is modified in such a way that this dose could be affected and in any event at least once a year. The licence-holder keeps a record of the results of these tests. The Federal Office may require that equipment used for diagnosis be checked annually over a period of four weeks in normal working conditions. A record is kept of the number and location of radiographic and radioscopic examinations carried out during this period, as well as of the conditions in which they took place.

Section 20

In general, the Office advises the Federal Department of the Interior and that of Transport, Communications and Energy on the rules to be adopted with regard to the carrying out of inspections.

Section 21 amended
by Fed. Ordin. of
28.11.1983

Section 22

The principal Nuclear Safety Division on the other hand is responsible for inspecting the safety of nuclear installations which are not subject to the Federal Act on Accident Insurance. It also supervises the import and export of radioactive substances and equipment containing such substances.

– Other powers

Fed. Dept. of the
Interior Ordin. of
18.3.1977,
Section 14

The Radiation Protection Section of the Federal Office of Public Health is responsible for the collection and despatch of industrial, research and medical radioactive waste, and sends a circular to waste producers who are listed, to warn them that waste will be collected from the centre which will already have been indicated to them. The Office works in co-operation with the Federal Institute for Reactor Research with respect to the collection and conditioning of this waste. The Office represents the central administration responsible for collecting radioactive waste other than that from nuclear installations, within the National Corporation for the Disposal of Radioactive Waste – CEDRA.

Ordin. of 30.8.1978,
Section 2
Section 6

The Office also organises, along with other Federal services and non-governmental organisations, training and refresher courses in radiation protection. It is entrusted with paying over the subsidies allocated by the Confederation to private institutions organising such courses.

g) Federal Office of Education and Science

The Federal Office of Education and Science (OFES), set up in 1968, replaced the Delegate for Atomic Energy Questions. It comes under the Federal Department of the Interior and deals with matters relating to the co-ordination of scientific activities in the atomic energy field.

The OFES has general powers to study and co-ordinate all scientific and university policy questions in the field of nuclear energy, and for this purpose, collects national and international documentation and scientific information. As for research, the OFES studies questions relating to the promotion and development of nuclear research.

The OFES co-ordinates research activities carried out in university circles, the private sector, and by government authorities. It represents the Government in bodies carrying out basic and applied research. It assists in the work of, *inter alia,* the National Research Council, the Board of the National Society for the Promotion of Industrial Atomic Technology, and the Advisory Commission of the Federal Institute for Reactor Research. It also deals with research into thermonuclear fusion, and high and medium- energy nuclear physics.

h) Other authorities

Other Federal Departments are called on to regulate questions falling within the nuclear energy field, and in particular: the Federal Department of Justice and Police, for the transport by road of dangerous goods, and in the framework of the peacetime protection of the population; the Federal Political Department and the Federal Office of External Economic Affairs for the export of nuclear materials of particular significance; the Federal Military Department for radiation protection on behalf of the army; and the Federal Finance Department with respect to legislation on nuclear units of measure.

2. ADVISORY BODIES

a) Federal Commission for the Safety of Nuclear Installations

i) Legal status

Fed. Council Ordin. of 13.6.1960

Section 1

The Federal Commission for the Safety of Nuclear Installations (CSA) was set up by Ordinance of the Federal Council dated 13th June 1960. The Commission, which comes under the Federal Energy Office acts as an advisory body to the Federal Council and the Federal Department of Transport, Communications and Energy.

ii) Responsibilities

Ordin. of 14.3.1983 (RS 732.21)

The Commission's functions were recently redefined by a Federal Council Ordinance of 14th March 1983 which repealed the provisions of the Ordinance of 1960. It is henceforth less involved with operational aspects.

Section 2

The Commission gives its opinion with regard to applications for general licences as well as for licences for the construction, putting into operation, operation and modification of nuclear installations.

In particular, it stipulates whether, in view of experience gained and the state of the art of science and technology, all necessary measures which can reasonably be required have been taken to protect man and the environment from ionizing radiation. The Commission may restrict itself to dealing with basic nuclear safety questions, or with points on which a project diverges from solutions which have proved satisfactory in other cases.

With regard to the protection of installations against aggression by third parties, it gives its opinion on the technical

115

aspects of conception and operation inasmuch as they are connected with nuclear safety.

It comments on the expert reports prepared on this topic by the principal Nuclear Safety Division (DSN) and by other Federal services.

Section 3

The Commission follows the operation of nuclear installations in Switzerland and abroad from the viewpoint of the basic aspects of nuclear safety. It suggests the measures it considers necessary and which may reasonably be required in the light of experience and the current state of science and technology.

Section 4

The Commission gives its comments when nuclear safety legislation is being drawn up or amended.

It follows the development of regulatory requirements concerning nuclear safety. It may recommend the adoption or amendment of requirements applying to nuclear power plants, and may participate in any work of this kind carried out by other bodies.

Section 5

The Commission analyses the basic nuclear safety questions concerning installations themselves, and studies the general difficulties involved in assessing their degree of safety. It may recommend measures to increase the safety of installations, and improvements to the licensing procedure and to the supervision of the operation of installations.

It follows nuclear safety research at home and abroad, and proposes relevant research that could be carried out in Switzerland, or suggests that Switzerland be involved on a bilateral or multilateral basis in the carrying-out of projects.

Section 6

The Federal Department of Transport, Communications and Energy, and the Federal Office may submit other nuclear safety questions to the Commission for consideration.

iii) Structure

Section 7
Section 8

The Federal Commission for the Safety of Nuclear Installations comprises a maximum of thirteen nuclear experts, proposed by the Federal Department of Transport, Communications and Energy, and nominated by the Federal Council. The Chairman of the Federal Commission is appointed by the Federal Council on the proposal of the said Department. Members of the Commission carry out their duties as private individuals, and not as part of their main professional activities. They are not bound by any instructions and may not be replaced.

Section 9
Section 10

In order to carry out its duties properly, the Federal Commission may set up internal permanent sub-commissions and specialised groups of experts. If necessary, it may, with permission of the Federal Energy Office, invite external experts to assist with its work.

Sections 10 and 11

Representatives of the principal Nuclear Safety Division (DSN) may attend meetings and inspections of the Federal Commission.

Section 13

The quorum for discussions within the Federal Commission is fixed at two-thirds of its members, and its decisions are taken on a straight majority basis. Should there be an equal number of votes on each side, the Chairman of the Federal Commission has the casting vote.

Section 17

The Federal Commission's work is confidential and an obligation of professional secrecy is imposed on experts. However, the Chairman of the Federal Commission can, with the permission of the Federal Department of Transport, Communications and Energy, send inspection results to the competent cantonal or local authorities, and to the insurers of the installation involved. The Federal Commission for the Safety of Nuclear Installations is served by a secretariat attached to the principal Nuclear Safety Division.

b) Federal Commission for Protection against Radiation

Act of 23.12.1959,
Section 38
Commission Regulation
(unpublished) of
19.12.1966

The Federal Commission for Protection against Radiation was set up and attached to the Federal Department of the Interior under Section 38 of the Federal Act.

i) Responsibilities

Ordin. of 19.4.1963
repealed by Ordin.
of 30.6.1976
Section 111

The Commission is responsible for giving general advice to the Federal Department of the Interior on questions relating to the protection of the population against hazards from ionizing radiation. Thus the Commission is consulted in particular on any changes or additions to be made to maximum permissible dose definitions for persons exposed to radiation, on guideline activity levels and surface contamination in the environment.

Section 43

If there are medical grounds for prohibiting, whether temporarily or permanently, a person occupationally exposed to ionizing radiation from suffering further exposure, the Federal Department of the Interior must ask for the Federal Commission's opinion on the matter.

Section 55

Guidelines relating to requirements for the protection from radiation of patients being medically examined are adopted by the Federal Department of the Interior after agreement has been given by the Federal Commission for Protection against Radiation.

ii) Structure

Members of the Federal Commission come from university and medical circles and from the Administration.

c) Federal Commission for the Monitoring of Radioactivity

Fed. Council Order
(unpublished) of
6.2.1959

Fed. Council Ordin.
of 30.6.1976,
Section 45

Section 91

The Federal Commission for the Monitoring of Radioactivity, which comes under the authority of the Federal Department of the Interior, keeps a permanent check on radioactivity in the environment. It regularly informs the Federal Council of the results of its monitoring activities, and prepares for it information to be given to the public and guidelines as to what should be done in the event of an increase in the level of ambient radioactivity. If necessary, the Federal Commission may propose to the Federal Council the measures that should be taken to ensure the protection of the population. Work using unsealed radioactive sources and being carried on outside a firm's premises, must be notified to the Federal Commission by the Federal Office of Public Health when there is a risk of contamination of the environment.

Members of the Federal Commission for the Monitoring of Radioactivity include experts from university circles and from the Federal *Ecole polytechnique*.

d) Organisation for giving warning of any increase in radioactivity

Fed. Council Order
(unpublished)
of 17.2.1964

Fed. Council Order
of 9.9.1966 as
amended on 7.7.1981
(RS 732.32) and by
Ordin. of 28.11.1983
(RS 732.33)

In the event of a dangerous increase in radioactivity, an organisation for giving warning of any increase in radioactivity is called upon to follow developments in the situation and to propose or recommend appropriate protection measures. It is headed by a Committee on Radioactive Emergencies which comes under the Federal Department of the Interior. This Committee has at its disposal, amongst other resources, an alarm post and a monitoring centre.

The Committee is composed of representatives of Federal Departments, branches of the Administration, the Federal Commission for the Monitoring of Radioactivity, the Federal Institute for Reactor Research, and other organisations. There is a maximum of fifteen members, and each member has at least one substitute.

e) Technical Commission for the Practical Application of Ionizing Radiation

The Technical Commission for the Practical Application of Ionizing Radiation comes under the Federal Department of Transport, Communications and Energy. It has the task of giving advice to the Confederation and interested firms on the subject of Swiss participation in national or international projects concerning the use of ionizing radiation.

3. PUBLIC AND SEMI-PUBLIC AGENCIES

a) Federal Institute for Reactor Research

i) Legal status

Fed. Order of
14.3.1960

Ordin. of 11.10.1971
(RS 424.3)

By Federal Order of 14th March 1960, the Swiss Federal Assembly approved the contract entered into between the Swiss Confederation and the company *Société Réacteur S.A.* of Würenlingen, set up in 1955, to transfer the company's installations to the Federal Institute for Reactor Research (IFR), a public body coming under the authority of the Federal *Ecole polytechnique* of Zurich. The Institute is organised and operates in accordance with the provisions of a 1971 Ordinance.

ii) Responsibilities

Section 2

Fed. Dept. of the
Interior Ordin. of
18.3.1977

Section 14

Appendix 1,
Section 14

Following the transfer, on 1st May 1960, of the *Réacteur* company's installations to the IFR, and in accordance with clause 2 of the contract dated 12th February 1960 between the Swiss Confederation and the company *Société Réacteur S.A.*, the Federal Institute for Reactor Research carried on the work of its predecessor, namely research in the nuclear and reactor technology fields. Thus the IFR is responsible for constructing and operating research reactors which, it is hoped, will then make it possible for nuclear reactors to be built and operated industrially. The IFR may also manufacture radioactive substances intended for various uses, particularly in the medical, agricultural and chemical fields. Further, the IFR studies processes for ensuring protection against ionizing radiation, and also deals with radioactive waste management and processing. Thus, the Institute organises, along with the Federal Office of Public Health, the annual collection of waste produced in industry, medicine, research and education. This waste, together with certain categories of low and medium-level waste from installations, is conditioned by the IFR. Organic and beta/gamma waste from the industrial, medical, research and educational sectors, together with inflammable low-level waste from nuclear power plants, are to be burned in the Federal Institute's incinerator.

Furthermore, the IFR carries out research into the management of active waste, either on its own account or under contract to an association of waste producers, the National Corporation for the Disposal of Radioactive Waste (CEDRA). Thus, since 1976, the IFR, in conjunction with CEDRA, has developed research programmes relating to low and medium-level radioactive waste packaging and conditioning, and to the retention capacity of certain rocks. Since 1978, the IFR has, with the assistance of CEDRA and the

119

Federal authorities concerned, been studying an enlarged nuclear management project with a view to finding solutions to the problems raised by the disposal of waste produced within Switzerland as a whole.

iii) Structure

The following authorities are responsible for running the Federal Institute for Reactor Research:

- the Federal *École polytechnique* Council
- an Advisory Commission
- the Institute's Management Board.

The Federal Ecole polytechnique Council: It is the Council's task to direct and generally supervise the IFR, and its installations. To do this, it draws up internal rules and lays down relevant instructions for the proper working of the Federal Institute.

For important matters connected with the extension and use of installations, the Council consults the Advisory Commission. The Council has the power to delegate some of its technical functions.

After consulting the Advisory Commission, the Council of the *Ecole* approves the annual programme of work prepared by the Institute's Management Board and submits the corresponding budgetary arrangements to the Federal Council. After consulting the Advisory Commission, the Council of the *Ecole* puts forward the name(s) of the director(s) of the Federal Institute for nomination by the Federal Council.

The Advisory Commission. The Advisory Commission assists the Federal *Ecole polytechnique* Council with regard to major issues concerning the use and extension of the Federal Institute's installations. It examines the budget and gives its opinion on the programmes of work and expansion prepared by the Institute's Management Board and presented to the Council of the *Ecole*. Finally, the Advisory Commission may submit to the Council, proposals for the designation of the director(s) of the Federal Institute. The Chairman of the *Ecole polytechnique* Council, together with the directors invited by the Federal Institute, may attend meetings of the Advisory Commission.

The Advisory Commission is composed of a Chairman and fifteen members, appointed by the Federal Council for four years. Ten of the members are appointed on the recommendation of organisations: the Union of Swiss Electricity Power Stations, the Industry Committee, the Swiss Chemical Industries Society, the Swiss Bankers' Association, the Swiss Insurers' Association, the Swiss Machine Makers' Society and the Swiss Union of Trade and Industry. Three members are proposed by the *École polytechnique* Council, and represent the teaching bodies of the Federal *École polytechnique*, the Lausanne *École polytechnique* et *universitaire* and the Swiss universities, respectively. Finally, two members are chosen by the Federal Council from within the Federal Administration.

The Federal Institute's Management Board: The day-to-day running of the Federal Institute is carried out by one or more directors appointed by the Federal Council on the proposal of the Federal *École polytechnique* Council, after consulting the Advisory Commission.

iv) Financing

The expenses of running the IFR, as well as the cost of its own scientific research, are borne by the Swiss confederation. Third parties for whom the IFR carries out research work must make an appropriate financial contribution to the outlays incurred. The Federal Council fixes the annual budget of the Federal Institute, submitted to it by the Federal *École polytechnique* Council after consideration by the Advisory Commission, on the basis of the programme of work established by the Institute's Management Board.

b) Fund for the Decommissioning of Nuclear Installations

i) Legal status

Fed. Order of
6.10.1978
Ordin. of 5.12.1983
(RS 732.013)

Provision was made in the Federal Order of 6th October 1978 concerning the Atomic Energy Act for the setting up of a Fund for financing the decommissioning and possible dismantling of nuclear installations no longer in service. This Fund was set up on 1st January 1984 and is managed under the supervision of the Federal Council and has been given legal personality.

ii) Responsibilities

The Fund was set up to manage the mandatory contributions made by the owners of nuclear installations and which are used to meet the cost of dismantling nuclear installations no longer in use.

iii) Structure

Section 11

The Fund is administered by a Commission composed by eleven members appointed by the Federal Council

iv) Financing

Section 2
Section 13

The Fund's resources will be constituted by the contributions paid by the owners of nuclear installations. The Commission of the Fund will fix the amount due by each owner according to his means. If necessary, the Federal Council will make any loans required.

c) National Corporation for the Disposal of Radioactive Waste (CEDRA)

i) Legal status

CEDRA is a private co-operative company set up in 1972 by the waste producers (the Confederation and six electricity companies), to undertake, at national level, the study and final disposal of the various categories of radioactive wastes.

ii) Responsibilities

CEDRA has the task of looking for, preparing and operating sites suitable for the storage of radioactive waste.

In conjunction with the competent Federal authorities and the IFR, CEDRA undertakes research programmes aimed at the actual setting up of new permanent repositories for waste storage. It is particularly concerned with studying the physico-chemical properties of the geologic formations envisaged as potential storage sites, solidified waste safety, packaging material, proposed repositories, the organisation of storage sites, and the working out of new ideas for the safe disposal of waste.

To ensure the exchange of information and to promote co-operation in the field of waste management, CEDRA maintains contact with similar organisations in foreign countries.

iii) Structure

All Swiss producers of waste of nuclear origin, including the Confederation represented by the Federal Office of Public Health, are members of CEDRA. The Confederation participates on two counts, first as a producer of waste from research reactors and from the processing of radioactive materials, and secondly as the collector of waste produced in the fields of industry, research, medicine and education.

The Board of Directors of CEDRA is composed of persons from Ministerial Departments and from the world of industry concerned with the disposal of active waste. Particular responsibility for studying the technical and safety aspects of waste processing has been given to a technical commission made up of specialists in the nuclear energy field. To accomplish its task, the Commission may call on external experts.

iv) Financing

CEDRA is a non-profit making organisation. Expenses are paid out of capital and members' subscriptions. The cost of radioactive waste disposal is borne entirely by the producers of the waste concerned.

TURKEY

TABLE OF CONTENTS

I. GENERAL REGULATORY REGIME

Act No. 2960 of
9.7.1982 (RG[1] No. 17753
of 13.7.1982)

In Turkey there is no general Nuclear Energy Act and apart from legislation relating to the Turkish Atomic Energy Authority (TAEA), the applicable law chiefly covers protection against ionizing radiation and the licensing of nuclear installations.

1. MINING REGIME

Act No. 6309 of 3.3.1954
(RG No. 8655 of
11.3.1954)
amended by Act No. 271
of 11.7.1963
(RG No. 11459 of
20.7.1963)

Turkish legislation regulating mining activities specifies that, in principle, the prospecting and mining of radioactive ores, even where deposits are located on private land, is a State monopoly but that the State may grant prospecting and mining licences to applicants for such licences.

Under the Turkish mining regime, the Mineral Research and Exploration Institute (MTA) is responsible for the exploration of radioactive minerals and for related technological research. ETIBANK is responsible for mining and milling of radioactive minerals. (see Part II below for further details).

2. RADIOACTIVE SUBSTANCES, NUCLEAR FUELS AND EQUIPMENT

Decree No. 7/9038 of
12.11.1974
(RG No. 15078 of
30.11.1974)

Regulation published in
RG No. 15372 of
30.9.1975

Regulations governing the use in general of radioactive substances, fissile materials and equipment emitting ionizing radiation are laid down in the 1974 Decree on protection against radiation, which supersedes a 1967 Decree. In accordance with the provisions of the 1974 Decree, a Regulation was issued in 1975 containing provisions relating to the system of registering and licensing such materials and equipment.

---

1. RG: *Resmi Gazete = Official Gazette.*

3. PROTECTION OF WORKERS AND THE PUBLIC AGAINST IONIZING RADIATION

Decree No. 7/9038
Regulation No. 15372

General standards concerning protection of the public and workers against ionizing radiation are laid down in the 1974 Decree. The 1975 Regulation contains provisions relating to radiation protection rules concerning persons handling X-ray equipment in industry and in the medical field, the use of X-rays and sealed radioactive sources for medical purposes and the use of particle accelerators.

Decree No. 7/6174 of
29.3.1973
(RG No. 14502 of
9.4.1973)

In 1973, the Ministry of Labour also issued a Decree on dangerous activities. The dangerous activities listed in the Decree include operations involving the use of X-rays, radioactive substances and equipment emitting ionizing radiation. For the purpose of protecting workers against radiation, the Decree lays down the safety rules to be complied with in the handling of such substances and equipment.

Decree No. 7/6229 of
5.4.1973
(RG No. 14511 of
18.4.1973),
amended by Decree
No. 7/8761 of 15.7.1974

Again in 1973, the Ministry of Health and Social Assistance published a Decree which covers the protection of workers in radiology and nuclear medicine. The Turkish Atomic Energy Authority, and in particular its Nuclear Safety and Radiation Protection Department, is responsible for drawing up and enforcing the implementing regulations.

4. NUCLEAR INSTALLATIONS[2]

Decree No. 83/7405 of
18.11.1983
(RG No. 18256 of
19.12.1983)

Regulations No. 3, 4, 5,
and 6 published in 1978
by TAEA

Regulation No. 7
(RG No. 16675 of
23.6.1979)

Regulation No. 7
(RG No. 16394 of
1.9.1978)

Turkish licensing regulations for nuclear installations are laid down in a Decree made on 18th November 1983. This Decree, which entered into force on 19th December 1983, supersedes a similar Decree (Decree No. 7/9141 of 5th December 1974) while maintaining in essence the same licensing procedure. This Decree amended in 1980. Various other technical regulations adapted from the Codes of practice of the International Atomic Energy Agency (IAEA) applicable to the overall design and to the safety criteria to be met in the design and construction of reactors have also been published. In addition, a Regulation on the licensing of operating staff for nuclear installations was issued in 1978.

---

2. For further details see "Description of Licensing Systems and Inspection of Nuclear Installations", OECD/NEA, 1980.

Decree No. 83/7405

The licensing procedure is divided into three main stages:

- site licence
- construction licence
- operating licence.

Any application for a licence concerning a reactor or any other category of nuclear installation must be submitted to the Turkish Atomic Energy Authority. In the case of a power reactor, the applicant is usually the Turkish Electricity Authority.

The Turkish Atomic Energy Authority is responsible for examining licence applications and for granting licences.

The Authority's appropriate departments are also responsible for inspecting operating nuclear installations.

5. RADIOACTIVE WASTE MANAGEMENT

Decree No. 83/7405,

Radioactive waste processing installations are classified as nuclear installations and as such, are covered by the 1983 Decree on the licensing of nuclear installations.

Regulation No. 15372

Measures for protecting workers and the public against radioactive waste hazards are laid down in the 1975 Regulation relating to radiation protection and safety.

Detailed regulations relating to radioactive waste management are currently being drawn up by the Turkish Atomic Energy Authority.

6. NUCLEAR THIRD PARTY LIABILITY

Act No. 299 of 8.5.1961
(RG No. 10806 of
13.5.1961)
Act No. 878 of 1.6.1967
(RG No. 12620 of
13.6.1967)

Although Turkey became a Contracting Party to the Paris Convention in 1968, it does not yet have any special legislation in this field. However, there is a requirement that any operator of a nuclear installation within the meaning of the Convention must have an insurance policy or some other suitable form of financial security, approved by the Turkish Atomic Energy Authority, to cover his liability.

7. NUCLEAR SECURITY

Nuclear installations in Turkey are covered by the IAEA safeguards under an agreement transferring safeguards to

IAEA signed on 30th September 1968 by the IAEA, Turkey and the United States.

Decree No. 8/3527 of
20.8.1981
(RG No. 17490 of
20.10.1981)

Regulation No. 8
published
in RG No. 16702 of
20.7.1979

Turkey has also ratified the Treaty on the Non-Proliferation of Nuclear Weapons and on 30th June 1981, it signed the relevant Safeguards Agreement with IAEA, which entered into force on 1st September 1981. In addition, a Code of Practice was brought out in 1979 on physical protection requirements for special nuclear materials. The Code is based on the IAEA Recommendations on the subject (INF-CIRC/225/Rev. 1).

8. TRANSPORT[3]

At the moment there are no special regulations on the transport of radioactive materials. Nevertheless the Turkish authorities apply the technical provisions laid down in the regulations published by the appropriate international organisations in this field and, more specifically, those in the IAEA Regulations for the Safe Transport of Radioactive Materials, 1973 Edition.

Decree No. 7/9038

The Turkish Atomic Energy Authority is also responsible in general for licensing and supervising the transport of radioactive substances as well as their import and export.

Regulation published in
RG No. 15742 of
22.10.1976
Decree No. 8/522 of
6.3.1980
(RG No. 16998 of
25.5.1980)

As regards international agreements relating to the safe transport of dangerous goods, Turkey applies the International Regulations concerning the Carriage of Dangerous Goods by Rail (RID), those in the European Agreement concerning the International Carriage of Dangerous Goods by Road (ADR) and the international regulations issued by the International Air Transport Association (IATA) and the International Maritime Organisation (IMO) to this effect.

9. PATENTS

Turkish law does not contain any provisions specific to nuclear patents.

---

3. For further details, see Analytical Study in the same series: "Regulations Governing the Transport of Radioactive Materials", OECD/NEA, 1980.

II. INSTITUTIONAL FRAMEWORK

1. REGULATORY AND SUPERVISORY AUTHORITIES

a) Prime Minister

Act No. 6821 of 27.8.1956 setting up the Commission now superseded by Act No. 2690 of 9.7.1982

In Turkey, nuclear activities were, at the outset, put under the authority of the Prime Minister. More specifically, the Atomic Energy Commission (now the Authority) was made responsible to him and administratively attached to the office of the Head of the Government.

For a while this responsibility was delegated to the Minister of Energy and Natural Resources but in 1966 the Commission was again brought under the direct authority of the Prime Minister and this is still so following the recent reorganisation of the Commission into the Authority (see below for further details).

b) Minister of Energy and Natural Resources

The above Minister is the supervisory authority of the Mineral Research and Exploration Institute and of ETI-BANK (see below).

2. PUBLIC AND SEMI-PUBLIC AGENCIES

a) Turkish Atomic Energy Authority

Act No. 2690 of 9.7.1982

The former Commission was recently reorganised to give it greater operational independence and broaden its field of responsibility and has been renamed the Turkish Atomic Energy Authority (TAEA).

i) Legal status

Section 3

To enable it to carry out the new programme assigned to it, the Authority, while still supervised by the Prime Minister, is now a legal entity.

ii) Responsibilities

Section 1

The Authority's general objective is to promote the peaceful uses of nuclear energy under the energy development plans approved by the Turkish Government and the application of nuclear techniques. Its task is to provide the framework in which the basic principles and policies relating to nuclear energy may be formulated and scientific, technical and administrative research in this field carried out and supervised.

Section 4

More specifically, the Authority is responsible for the following:

- formulating general policy and relevant programmes on the peaceful uses of nuclear energy and submitting them to the Prime Minister for approval;
- carrying out or co-ordinating research on nuclear energy applications in the context of Turkey's scientific, technical and economic development;
- planning, advising on and participating in the exploration, mining, processing and distribution of nuclear raw materials and other related activities, and the import, export and marketing of such substances (this also covers fissile and other materials of strategic importance);
- constructing and operating research centres, laboratories and pilot plants;
- conducting research with a view to giving industry access to nuclear technology and know-how;
- creating and operating installations for the production and distribution of radioisotopes;
- issuing licences to private and State enterprises conducting the various activities involving radioactive materials, supervising such enterprises from the radiological safety standpoint, and ensuring that licensing conditions are complied with;
- issuing licences and permits with regard to site approval, construction and operation, and environmental protection for power and experimental reactors and other large nuclear installations;
- taking the necessary steps to arrange for the transport, processing, storage and disposal of radioactive waste produced by nuclear installations and radioisotope laboratories;
- training the staff required in the nuclear sector;
- supplying all necessary information in this field.

iii) Structure

Section 5

The Authority is headed by a President appointed by the Government. The President is the Authority's official representative and is responsible for implementating its programme. He is assisted by three Vice-Presidents.

Section 3

The Turkish Atomic Energy Authority has a Commission, an Advisory Committee, several specialised technical and administrative departments and affiliated research centres.

Section 6   The members of the *Commission*, which is headed by the President, consist of the Vice-Presidents, three representatives from various ministries and four representatives from universities. Representatives of ministries and universities are appointed for four-year terms by the Prime Minister. The Commission determines the working principles and programmes of the TAEA, approves its draft budget and submits it to the Prime Minister. The Commission is responsible for the preparation of the decrees and regulations in its field.

Section 7   The members of the *Advisory Committee* are appointed for three-year terms from among the representatives of universities and experts in various governmental bodies. The Committee studies matters submitted to it by the Commission and makes recommendations.

Section 8   Under three Vice-Presidents, the five specialised Departments empowered to implement the legal responsibilities of the TAEA are the following:

- Nuclear Safety Department;
- Radiation Protection Department;
- Research, Development and Co-ordination Department;
- Technology Department; and
- Administration and Finance Department.

iv) Financing

One outcome of the structural reorganisation is that the Authority now has its own budget. Its financial resources are derived from:

- payments out of the general budget of the government;
- local and foreign aids, donations etc.,
- income for services provided, production of goods and sale of publications.

b) Cekmece Nuclear Research and Training Centre

The Cekmece Centre (CNAEM) was founded in 1962 near Istanbul and is affiliated to the Turkish Atomic Energy Authority. It is a governmental research centre and, as such, is open to universities and other scientific and research institutes for purposes of co-operation in the development and application of nuclear science and technology in various fields.

The programme of work of the CNAEM is prepared and implemented according to the national nuclear programme, in support of the national economy. This work covers, in particular, post-graduate research, application and training.

130

The CNAEM constructed a 1 megawatt thermal power reactor (TR-1) in 1959 for research and isotope production for industrial and medical purposes and was operational from 1962 to 1977. It has now been dismantled and will be used for research. A 5 megawatt TR-2 reactor has been constructed and has begun operating for irradiation purposes.

The Centre is run by a Director, assisted by a Co-ordination Committee and a Security Committee. Three Deputy Directors each responsible for technical, research and training and administrative matters respectively direct the different departments involved.

c) Ankara Nuclear Research and Training Centre

The above Centre (ANAEM) was established in 1966, under the supervision of the Turkish Atomic Energy Authority, to carry out applied and fundamental research studies.

ANEAM performs its work in collaboration with universities and other governmental organisations and provides assistance with training programmes in the nuclear field.

Like the Cekmece Centre, the Centre is run by a Director, also assisted by two Committees and three Deputy Directors.

d) Lalahan Nuclear Research Institute in Veterinary Medicine and Animal Science

This Institute was set up in 1981 and is located by the Ministry of Agriculture's Zootechnical Research Institute near Ankara.

The Institute performs research and studies the application of nuclear techniques in animal health and breeding.

It is run by a Director, assisted by two Deputy Directors, responsible for administration and R and D respectively.

e) Mineral Research and Exploration Institute

Act No. 2804 of 14.6.1935 (RG No. 3035 of 22.6.1935) Act No. 6309 Act No. 271

The above Institute (MTA) was set up on 22nd June 1935 to explore the ore deposits in Turkey. MTA is a governmental organisation under the supervision of the Ministry of Energy and Natural Resources

The Institute, which is headed by a Director General appointed by the Government, undertakes explorations to determine the areas of mineral and raw material deposits and carries out scientific and geological investigations as well as chemical analyses and technological tests. The duties assigned to the Institute by the Act setting it up and Act No. 6309 include exploration for radioactive ores and related technological research.

f) ETIBANK

Act No. 2805 of
14.6.1935
(RG No. 3035 of
22.6.1935)

ETIBANK was set up in 1935 to carry out activities related to mining, metallurgy, chemicals and commercial banking. ETIBANK is a state economic enterprise under the supervision of the Ministry of Energy and Natural Resources.

ETIBANK is run by a General Manager appointed by the Government. Its tasks include the mining of radioactive ores explored by MTA as well as yellowcake production.

g) Turkish Electricity Authority

Act No. 1312 of
15.7.1970
(RG No. 13559 of
25.7.1970)

The Turkish Electricity Authority (TEK) was established in 1970 to produce, under its own monopoly, transmit, distribute and commercially dispose of the electrical energy needed by the country.

i) Legal status

TEK is a state economic enterprise under the supervision of the Ministry of Energy and Natural resources and is a legal entity.

ii) Responsibilities

In addition to general duties concerning electrical energy, TEK is also responsible for planning, surveying, constructing, commissioning and operating nuclear power plants in Turkey.

iii) Structure

The Turkish Electricity Authority consists of a General Manager, six Assistant General Managers and a Board. The duties related to nuclear energy fields are carried out by the *Nuclear Power Plant Division* which is supervised by a Director and two Deputy Directors. The Division consists of nine technical sections and has one site manager and one project manager.

iv) Financing

The capital stock of TEK is assigned by the Government. Additionally, the financial requirements of TEK can be met from the following sources:

- payments from the general budget of the Government;
- annual profits from the energy sales;
- various local and foreign credits.

132

UNITED KINGDOM

Table of contents

I. GENERAL REGULATORY REGIME

Atomic Energy Act, 1946
Nuclear Installations
Act, 1965

In the United Kingdom, legislation dealing specifically with nuclear energy was introduced in 1946, in step with the development of the uses of this type of energy for peaceful purposes. In discussing nuclear legislation, a rough division is sometimes made between Acts primarily directed at the protection of people such as the Radioactive Substances Act, 1960, the Factories Act, 1961 and the Health and Safety at Work etc. Act, 1974, and legislation dealing with nuclear installations primarily concerned with licensing and controlling the safe operation of nuclear plants and also dealing with third party liability for damage.

The purpose of this Chapter is to provide an overall picture of the law governing all nuclear activities in the United Kingdom. The following Chapter will deal in greater detail with the Acts, Order and Regulations mentioned below, which provide the institutional framework for such activities.

1. MINING REGIME

Atomic Energy Act,
1946,
Sections 6 and 7

There are no mining activities connected with uranium extraction in the United Kingdom. However, the Secretary of State for Energy is empowered to search for and work minerals and acquire property for this purpose and may authorise other persons to do the same on his behalf. He is also empowered to provide for the compulsory vesting of the right to work minerals either in himself or in the United Kingdom Atomic Energy Authority (UKAEA).

2. RADIOACTIVE SUBSTANCES, NUCLEAR FUELS AND EQUIPMENT

The possession of and trade in radioactive substances and nuclear fuels is governed mainly by the Radioactive Substances Act, 1948.

Radioactive Substances
Act, 1948, Section 1 as
applied by the Atomic
Energy Authority Act,
1954, Section 2(1)

Under the 1948 Act, the United Kingdom Atomic Energy Authority (UKAEA) has power to manufacture, buy or otherwise acquire, treat, store and transport any radioactive substances. The Act also provides for the control of import and export of such substances. The Radioactive Substances

Radioactive Substances Act, 1948, Sections 2 and 3
Radioactive Substances Act, 1960, Section 1
Section 2
S.I.[1], 1954, No. 23 as amended
S.I. 1981, No. 1641 as amended by S.I. 982, No. 1446

Act of 1960 regulates the keeping and use of radioactive material and lays down general provisions for registration of users of radioactive material for the purposes of an undertaking carried on by them and exemptions from registration, in particular as respects the UKAEA and licensees of nuclear installations. In addition, a licence is required from the Secretary of State for Trade for the import and export of certain radioactive substances, and atomic equipment.

Nuclear Installations Act, 1965, Section 1 as amended by the Nuclear Installations Act, 1965 etc. (Repeals and Modifications) Regulations, 1974 (S.I. 1974, No. 2056)
S.I. 1971, No. 381

The construction and operation of any installation for the manufacture, storage or processing of nuclear fuel by any person other than the Crown or the UKAEA requires a licence from the Health and Safety Executive. The Nuclear Installations Regulations, 1971, made under the 1965 Act, prescribe as licensable various classes of installations where a nuclear hazard could arise, those being, *inter alia,* installations in which nuclear fuel is manufactured, in which enriched uranium is produced and in which plutonium or uranium is extracted from irradiated matter. Also covered are installations in which isotopes ready for use for industrial, chemical, agricultural, medical or scientific purposes, are produced from nuclear matter.

3. PROTECTION OF WORKERS AND THE PUBLIC AGAINST IONIZING RADIATION[2]

Medicines (Radioactive Substances) Order, 1978 (S.I. 1978, No. 1004)
Medicines (Committee on Radiation from Radioactive Medicinal Products) Order, 1978 (S.I. 1978, No. 1005)
Medicines (Administration of Radioactive Substances) Regulations, 1978 (S.I. 1978, No. 1006)
S.I. 1969, No. 808
S.I. 1968, No. 780
Health and Safety at Work Act, 1974, Section 11

The health protection of workers and the public against the hazards of ionizing radiation is regulated by the Radioactive Substances Act, 1960, the Medicines Act, 1968, the Health and Safety at Work Act, 1974, as well as by the Factories Act, 1961 under which regulations have been made governing the use of sealed sources and unsealed radioactive substances. The Health Ministers (i.e. those respectively responsible for health in England, Scotland, Wales and Northern Ireland) are the authorities with overall responsibility for all aspects of health protection. Direct responsibility for such protection is vested in the Health and Safety Commission and the Health and Safety Executive. The safety of workers in nuclear installations is also regulated by conditions attached to nuclear site licences.

---

1. S.I.: Statutory Instrument.
2. For further details see Analytical Study in the same series: "Regulations Governing Nuclear Installations and Radiation Protection", OECD/NEA, 1972.

Radioactive Substances Act, 1960, Sections 6, 7, 8 and 10

Radiological Protection Act, 1970, as amended, Section 1

The Radioactive Substances Act, 1960 regulates the keeping and use of radioactive material. The Radiological Protection Act, 1970, as amended by the Health and Safety at Work etc. Act, 1974, provides for the setting up of a National Radiological Protection Board with functions and powers concerning the advancement of knowledge, the provision of information and advice, including advice to Government departments, and the provision of technical services. The Health and Safety at Work etc. Act, 1974, is a general Act, providing for health, safety and welfare in connection with work, including the nuclear field.

4. NUCLEAR INSTALLATIONS[3]

S.I. 1971, No. 381

The Nuclear Installations Act, 1965 and the Nuclear Installations Regulations, 1971 govern the construction and operation of nuclear installations in the United Kingdom, and health protection at such installations is regulated by the Health and Safety at Work etc. Act, 1974.

Nuclear Installations Act, 1965, Section 1 as amended by S.I. 1974, No. 2056

The competent authority for the licensing of nuclear installations is the Health and Safety Executive which is responsible through the Health and Safety Commission to the Secretary of State for Energy for nuclear safety questions, and to the Secretary of State for Employment, through the Health and Safety Commission, for nuclear health and safety protection questions.

Nuclear Installations Act, 1965

S.I. 1971, No. 381

The 1965 Act makes provision for the licensing of nuclear installations other than those operated by a Government Department or the UKAEA by means of a nuclear site licence, which sanctions the use of a particular site for a specific reactor type or plant. The 1971 Regulations made under the Act prescribe as licensable various classes of establishment in the nuclear field where nuclear hazards could arise. The 1965 Act is listed in Schedule 1 of the Health and Safety at Work etc. Act, 1974 and is thus a *relevant* statutory provision within the meaning of Part 1 of that Act. This provides the basis for the control of activities involving ionizing radiations.

Nuclear Installations Act, 1965, Section 2 as amended by the Atomic Energy Authority Act, 1971, Section 17

Finally, Section 2 of the 1965 Act provides that a permit granted by the UKAEA or a Government Department is required in addition to a nuclear site licence (where that is required), for the use of any site by any person other than the UKAEA or a Government Department for any treatment of

---

3.   For further details see: "Description of Licensing Systems and Inspection of Nuclear Installations", OECD/NEA, 1980.

irradiated matter involving the extraction of plutonium or uranium or the enrichment of uranium. Permits granted by the UKAEA are limited to work for the purpose of research and development. They may be revoked or surrendered.

5. RADIOACTIVE WASTE MANAGEMENT

Radioactive Substances Act, 1960, Sections 6, 7 and 8

Sections 9, 10 and 11

The Radioactive Substances Act, 1960 governs the disposal and accumulation of radioactive waste in the United Kingdom. Such activities may not be undertaken without an authorisation granted by the Secretary of State for the Environment. Disposal from licensed sites and UKAEA premises must be authorised by the Secretary of State and the Minister of Agriculture, Fisheries and Food.

Control of Pollution Act, 1974, Sections 30(5) and 36(6)

S.I. 1976, No. 959

S.I. 1980, No. 1709

Regulations may also be made concerning control of pollution including pollution of water by radioactive waste as provided under the Control of Pollution (Radioactive Waste) Regulations, 1976. Radioactive waste which is also toxic is controlled under the Control of Pollution (Special Waste) Regulations, 1980.

Also, a Nuclear Industry Radioactive Waste Executive (NIREX) has been set up for the purpose of centralising activities in the radioactive waste management field (see Chapter II).

6. NUCLEAR THIRD PARTY LIABILITY[4]

The basic legislation on nuclear third party liability in the United Kingdom is contained in the Nuclear Installations Act, 1965, which implements the provisions of the 1960 Paris Convention on Third Party Liability in the Field of Nuclear Energy and the 1963 Brussels Convention Supplementary to the Paris Convention.

The Nuclear Installations Act, 1965 was amended by the Energy Act, 1983. Part II of the 1983 Act, which was brought into force on 1st September 1983, is concerned with nuclear installations and has for its main purpose the amendment of the third party liability provisions of the Nuclear Installations Act, 1965 to give effect to the provisions of two 1982 Protocols to amend the above-mentioned Paris and Brussels

---

4. For further details see Analytical Study in the same series: "Nuclear Third Party Liability", OECD/NEA, 1976.

Conventions. The provisions of Part II of the 1983 Act increase the sums available to meet claims for nuclear damage.

The Energy Act, 1983, Section 27

The 1983 Act amends Section 16 of the 1965 Act to increase the liability limit for operators of licensed sites from £5 million to £20 million per incident. The lower limit of £5 million is retained in the case of certain small *prescribed* sites (see below). There is also provision for these two limits to be increased by order; thus there will be no need for further primary legislation if the liability limits in the Paris Convention are increased at some future time. There are consequential amendments which require licensees to provide cover for their liabilities under the 1965 Act – they must provide cover up to £20 million per incident – and to notify the competent authority if claims against them exceed the specified proportion of the maximum liability.

Section 28

The 1965 Act is further amended to increase the total amount of public funds available to meet claims from £50 million to the Sterling equivalent of 300 milion Special Drawing Rights. The Act also provides for reciprocity with other countries, to cover any period when the United Kingdom has, but the country in which the occurrence has happened has not, given effect to the new Protocols.

Section 29

Finally, the 1965 Act is amended to express in Special Drawing Rights, in place of Sterling, the minimum amount which must be left available (in an incident involving nuclear material in the course of carriage) for general claims as opposed to claims in respect of damage to the means of transport. The minimum is set at 5 million Special Drawing Rights which may be increased by order.

The Nuclear Installations (Prescribed Sites) Regulations, 1983 S.I. 1983, No. 919 Regulation 3 Regulation 4 Regulation 5

A new set of Regulations prescribes the sites whose licensees are subject to a lower limit of liability per incident under Section 16(1) of the Nuclear Installations Act, 1965 as amended by the Energy Act, 1983. Essentially, the sites prescribed are the sites of small installations. They are prescribed by reference to the type and designed thermal power output of any nuclear reactor with its associated fuel, and by reference to the activity of other radionuclides which may also be present. The Regulations also provide for cases where nuclear material of different levels of activity is present as well as for overall limits of mass for fissile material.

Nuclear Installations Act, 1965, as amended, Section 7(1) Sections 8 and 9 Congenital Disabilities (Civil Liability) Act, 1976, Sections 3 and 4

Under the 1965 Act, nuclear site licensees are under an absolute duty, and are liable for breach of this duty, to ensure that no occurrences involving nuclear matter on their sites cause personal injury or damage to property and are under a similar duty as regards ionizing radiations emitted on or from their sites. The same duty lies upon the UKAEA and the Crown. Moreover, the Congenital Disabilities (Civil Liability) Act, 1976 provides that if a child is born disabled as the result of an injury to either parent caused by a breach of such a duty, the child's disabilities are to be regarded for the purposes of the 1965 Act as injuries caused on the same occasion as those caused to the parent.

7. NUCLEAR SECURITY

The Atomic Energy Act, 1946, the Radioactive Substances Act, 1948 and the Nuclear Installations Act, 1965 (as amended by the Atomic Energy Authority Act, 1971) confer wide powers on the Secretary of State for Energy to prevent any improper use of fissionable materials.

In connection with security control, the Nuclear Safeguards and Electricity (Finance) Act, 1978 provides for giving effect to an international agreement of 6th September 1976 for application of safeguards in the United Kingdom related to the Non-Proliferation Treaty.

The Official Secrets Acts, 1911-1920 make provision for the security of certain Crown property by declaring that certain activities in relation to any such property shall be a criminal offence. They also provide that certain activities by Crown servants and those who have contact with the Crown shall be offences.

S.I. 1975, No. 182

Section 3 of the 1911 Act provides that particular premises may be declared to be *prohibited places* for the purpose of those Acts. Section 6(3) of the Atomic Energy Authority Act, 1954 brings *any place belonging to or used for the purposes of the UKAEA* within the definition of places which may be declared to be as *prohibited places*. An order was made in 1975 declaring certain of the Authority's premises to be such *prohibited places*.

Further provision is made by Section 2 of the Nuclear Installations Act, 1965, as amended by Section 17 of the Atomic Energy Authority Act, 1971. This allows the Secretary of State to make orders applying the Schedule to the 1965 Act (which was added by the 1971 Act) to any premises in respect of which a permit under Section 2 of the 1965 Act has been granted for purposes other than research and development only. In particular, paragraph 3 of the Schedule brings any such site within the definition of places which may be declared to be *prohibited places*.

Section 19 of the 1971 Act further provides that paragraphs 2 and 4-6 of the Schedule shall apply to any company registered in the United Kingdom and formed for the purposes of the Treaty of Almelo (relating to the gas centrifuge enrichment process).

These paragraphs have the additional effect of bringing any office, employment or contract with a body to which they apply within Section 2 of the Official Secrets Act, 1911, extending the powers of special constables in relation to those premises allowing the Secretary of State to give directions for the security and safety of the site and restricting the termination of employment on certain grounds.

S.I. 1971, No. 569
S.I. 1975, No. 182
S.I. 1973, No. 17

Orders have been made applying the Schedule to British Nuclear Fuels Ltd. (BNFL), declaring certain premises of the UKAEA and of BNFL to be *prohibited places* and designating Urenco Ltd. and Centec Centrifuge Techniques Ltd. for the purpose of Section 19.

8. TRANSPORT[5]

The transport of radioactive materials is governed by different regulations, depending on the mode of transport used. Essentially, however, all the modal regulations reflect the IAEA Regulations for the Safe Transport of Radioactive Materials, 1973 Edition (as amended in 1979).

S.I. 1974, No. 1735
S.I. 1970, No. 1827 as amended by S.I. 1975, No. 1522
S.I. 1981 No. 1747
S.I. 1980, No. 1965

Rail transport of radioactive materials is governed by the British Railways Board Publication *List of Dangerous Goods and Conditions of Acceptance,* BR 22426, Class 7; transport by road is regulated by the Radioactive Substances (Carriage by Road) (Great Britain) Regulations, 1974 and the Radioactive Substances (Road Transport Workers) (Great Britain) Regulations; the rules applying to maritime transport are the Merchant Shipping (Dangerous Goods) Regulations, 1981; finally, the Air Navigation Order, 1980 regulates *inter alia* the carriage by air of radioactive materials.

9. PATENTS

Atomic Energy Act, 1946,
Section 12 as amended by Patents Act, 1949
Patents Act, 1977,
Sections 55 to 59
and Schedule 4

It should be noted here that until the passing of the Patents Act 1977, Section 12 of the Atomic Energy Act, 1946, as amended by the Patents Act, 1949, conferred certain rights on the Secretary of State for Energy in relation to atomic energy patents. It was however repealed by the 1977 Act. Schedule 4 of the 1977 Act contains provisions relating to things done under the provisions of earlier Acts. Sections 55-59 of the 1977 Act now contain provisions relating to the Secretary of State's rights in relation to patents generally.

---

5. For further details see Analytical Study in the same series: "Regulations Governing the Transport of Radioactive Materials", OECD/NEA, 1980.

II. INSTITUTIONAL FRAMEWORK

Atomic Energy Act,
1946,
Section 1

Radioactive Substances
Act, 1948

S.I. 1953, No. 1673
S.I. 1957, No. 561
S.I. 1959, No. 1826
S.I. 1964, No. 490
S.I. 1964, No. 2048
S.I. 1970, No. 1537
S.I. 1974, No. 692

As mentioned in the preceding Chapter, nuclear legislation was introduced in the United Kingdom with the Atomic Energy Act, 1946. The responsibility for the development and control of nuclear activities was entrusted to the Minister of Supply, and further detailed in 1948, with provision made for the *appropriate Minister* to regulate for health and safety. In parallel with the development of nuclear energy, this responsibility was successively transferred to the Lord President of the Council in 1953, to the Prime Minister in 1957, to the Minister for Science in 1959, to the Secretary of State for Education and Science in 1964, to the Minister of Technology in 1965.

Between 1970 and 1974 these duties were discharged by the Secretary of State for Trade and Industry, and since 1974 by the Secretary of State for Energy, though responsiblity for the control of radioactive substances is now undertaken by the Secretary of State for the Environment.

Atomic Energy Authority
Act, 1954

Health and Safety at
Work etc. Act, 1974

The United Kingdom Atomic Energy Authority (UKAEA) was set up in 1954 and is the statutory body responsible, subject to the Secretary of State's overall duty in that respect, for the general development of nuclear energy in the United Kingdom, while the Health and Safety Commission and the Health and Safety Executive were established in 1974 as bodies corporate, generally responsible, *inter alia,* for the control of hazardous activities, including ionizing radiation.

In 1970, a review was undertaken of governmental functions in the United Kingdom, which covered departmental boundaries as well as the central mechanism of public policy making. Following the review, a reorganisation of central government took place with a view to improving the efficiency of government. This entailed changes both in the methods of operation between government departments and within departmental organisation itself, and consequently, had a direct effect on the general regime governing nuclear activities.

S.I. 1970, No. 1537

As a consequence of this review, certain functions in the nuclear field, formerly discharged by several Ministries, were unified. In particular, the Department of Trade and Industry was formed to take over the responsibilities for general industrial policy and administration, which were previously divided between the Board of Trade and the Ministry of Technology. The Secretary of State for Trade and Industry was given responsibility for atomic energy and most of the various functions related thereto under the Atomic Energy

141

Act, 1946, the Atomic Energy Authority Act, 1954, and the Nuclear Installations Act, 1965. The Secretary of State for Energy has now taken over these functions.

S.I. 1970, No. 1681
Radioactive
Substances Act, 1960

Major changes were made in those parts of the Government machine dealing with the environment, in particular, the Ministries of Housing and Local Government, of Public Building and Works and Transport were merged into a Department of the Environment, under a Secretary of State for the Environment, with responsibility for questions involving protection against the hazards of ionizing radiation, radioactive substances and waste. The Department of Transport was later separated from the Department of the Environment in 1976.

1. REGULATORY AND SUPERVISORY AUTHORITIES

No single authority has overall responsibility for nuclear energy in the United Kingdom. While the Secretaries of State for Energy and for the Environment are competent for the development and the health and safety aspects of nuclear energy respectively, they share those powers in certain instances with other Ministers when nuclear energy questions come within the latter Ministers' sphere of competence. In Scotland, Wales and Northern Ireland, many of the functions carried out by different Ministers in England are exercised by the corresponding Ministers in these countries. (This should be assumed to be the case in the following text unless otherwise stated.)

a) Secretary of State for Energy

Atomic Energy Act,
1946,
Section 1
Section 10

Sections 4, 5 and 6

Sections 8 and 9

Section 12(8) as amended
by Section 106(3) of
the Patents Act, 1977

Under the Atomic Energy Act, 1946, the Secretary of State for Energy has a duty to promote and control the development of atomic energy. He may, by order, although no such order has been made, prohibit various activities relating to atomic energy except under his licence. The Act also gives the Secretary of State powers to obtain information on materials, plant and processes; to enter and inspect certain premises; to search for and to authorise other persons to search for certain minerals; and to acquire compulsorily substances, minerals and plant which are for the production or use of atomic energy or research into matters connected therewith, and rights under contracts. He is also given certain rights relating to the use of atomic energy patents, as mentioned in the preceding Chapter.

Atomic Energy Authority
Act, 1954

Sections 1 and 3

The 1954 Act which set up the United Kingdom Atomic Energy Authority (UKAEA) and transferred to it certain activities previously carried on by the Secretary of State's predecessor, provides that the Secretary of State has the general duty of ensuring that the UKAEA attach proper degrees of importance to the various applications of atomic energy and may give directions to the Authority. He exercises general control over it, but generally does not intervene in the details of its work. He appoints the Chairman and members of the Authority and lays before Parliament an annual report on its activities.

b) Secretary of State for the Environment

Radioactive Substances
Act, 1948, as amended,
Section 5

Health and Safety at
Work etc. Act, 1974,
Section 15

S.I. 1974, No. 1821

The Radioactive Substances Act, 1948, as amended by the Atomic Energy Authority Act, 1954, provides for the control of radioactive substances and certain apparatus producing radiation, in the interest of health and safety. It enables safety regulations to be made by the appropriate Minister as respects premises or places in which radioactive substances are manufactured, produced, treated, stored, etc., for the purpose, among others, of preventing injury being caused by ionizing radiation to workers and the population. Furthermore, power to make regulations for safety purposes is now included in the powers contained in the Health and Safety at Work etc. Act, 1974 (see below for further details), and the Radioactive Substances Act, 1948 (Modification) Regulations, 1974, amend Section 5 of the 1948 Act, so that in its application to Great Britain, that Act no longer contains such powers, which are now vested in the Secretary of State for the Environment by the 1974 Act.

Radioactive Substances
Act, 1960, Sections 6,
7 and 8

The Radioactive Substances Act, 1960 regulates by way of compulsory registration the keeping and use of radioactive substances on premises used for the purpose of an undertaking, and similar control is exercised on mobile radioactive sources. Radioactive waste disposal and storage may not be undertaken without an authorisation granted by the Secretary of State for the Environment. Disposals from licensed sites and UKAEA premises require authorisation of the Secretary of State and the Minister of Agriculture, Fisheries and Food.

Control of Pollution
Act, 1974, Sections 30(5)
and 36(6)

S.I. 1976 No. 959

S.I. 1980, No. 1709

The Secretary of State may also make regulations concerning control of pollution of water by radioactive waste as provided under the Control of Pollution (Radioactive Waste) Regulations, 1976. These Regulations give the same powers to the Secretary of State for Wales as respects Wales. The Control of Pollution (Special Waste) Regulations 1980 confer similar powers on the Secretaries of State for the Environment in Wales and Scotland.

143

c) Minister of Agriculture, Fisheries and Food

Radioactive Substances
Act, 1960, Sections 6, 8,
9, 11 and 12
Nuclear
Installations Act,
1965, Schedule 1
as amended
by Section 17
of the Atomic Energy
Authority Act, 1971

The power to grant authorisations for the disposal of radioactive waste on or from any premises used by the UKAEA or any premises in respect of which a nuclear site licence is in force or in respect of which after the revocation or surrender of a nuclear site licence the period of responsibility of the licensee has not come to an end, is exercisable by the Minister of Agriculture, Fisheries and Food and the Secretary of State for the Environment. The Minister is empowered to appoint inspectors who may exercise rights of entry to *prohibited premises* where the officer is so authorised (see Chapter I, *Nuclear security*).

Dumping at Sea Act,
1974

The Minister of Agriculture, Fisheries and Food is a licensing authority for the purpose of the Dumping at Sea Act. This Act enabled the United Kingdom to ratify the Convention for the Prevention of Marine Pollution by Dumping from Ships and Aircraft. It prohibits dumping in the sea except in accordance with a licence granted by the licensing authority and prescribes penalties for breach.

d) Secretary of State for Social Services

Radiological Protection
Act, 1970, Sections 1 and
2

The Secretary of State for Social Services and the other United Kingdom Health Ministers have responsibilities in matters of health, and they are administratively accountable for the National Radiological Protection Board.

e) Secretary of State for Transport

List of Dangerous Goods
and Conditions of
Acceptance
BR22426, Class 7
S.I. 1974, No. 1735

The Secretary of State for Transport has general competence for the purpose of those regulations governing the transport by rail and road of radioactive materials.

f) Secretary of State for Trade

Merchant Shipping
(Dangerous Goods)
Regulations, 1981
S.I. 1981, No. 1747
Air Navigation Order,
1980
S.I. 1980, No. 1965,
Article 42(1)(b)
Merchant Shipping
(Prevention of Pollution)
Intervention Order, 1980,
S.I. 1980, No. 1093

In so far as radioactive materials constitute dangerous goods, the Secretary of State has power to regulate their carriage by sea and air. He may also make provision in relation to marine pollution by radioactive substances, as the result of a shipping casualty.

Air Navigation
(Restriction of Flying)

The Secretary of State also has power to restrict or prohibit flying in the vicinity of specified atomic energy

144

(Atomic Energy
Establishments)
Regulations, 1981,
S.I. 1981, No. 30

establishments by reason of national defence or any other reason affecting the public interest.

S.I. 1954, No. 23
as amended
S.I. 1981, No. 1641
as amended by
S.I. 1982, No. 1446

In addition, the Import of Goods (Control) Order, 1954 and the Export of Goods (Control) Order, 1981, made under the Import, Export and Customs Powers (Defence) Act 1939, provide that a licence is required from the Secretary of State for Trade for the import or export of certain radioactive substances and atomic energy appliances and equipment.

g) Secretary of State for Education and Science

Education Act, 1980
Section 27(1)*(c)*
Education (Schools and
Further Education)
Regulations, 1981
S.I. 1981, No. 1086,
Regulation 6

In the public sector of education, radioactive substances with an activity in excess of 0.002 of a microcurie per gram may not be used in the course of instruction without the approval of the Secretary of State for Education and Science. There is a similar restriction on the use of apparatus (other than a television receiving set or similar apparatus) in which electrons are accelerated by a potential difference of 5 kilovolts or more.

2. ADVISORY BODIES

a) Medical Research Council

Science and Technology
Act, 1965

The Medical Research Council (MRC) is an autonomous body, established by Royal Charter. It is grant-aided through the Secretary of State for Education and Science and its functions include advising the Government and authorities discharging responsibilities in that field on the somatic and genetic effects of ionizing radiations. The Council advises on the biological bases on which radiation protection standards rest, in the light of its own and the latest international findings.

b) National Radiological Protection Board

Radiological Protection
Act, 1970, Section 1
as amended by the
Health and Safety at
Work Act, 1974
Section 77

The National Radiological Protection Board was established by the Radiological Protection Act, 1970. The functions of the Board are: *a)* by means of research and otherwise to advance the acquisition of knowledge about the protection of mankind from radiation hazard; and *b)* to provide information and advice to persons, including Government Departments with responsibilities in the United Kingdom in relation to the protection from radiation hazards, either of the community as a whole or of other particular sections of the community.

S.I. 1974, No. 1230
Radiological Protection
Act, 1970
Section 1(1) and (2)

The functions of the Board were extended by the National Radiological Protection Board (Extension of Functions) Order, 1974, which provided that the Board's existing functions mentioned above should be exercised in respect of dangers of radiation which is electro-magnetic but not ionizing. The Board has power to provide technical services to persons concerned with radiation hazards and to make charges for those services and for providing information and advice.

Radiological Protection
Act, 1970, Section 1(7)

The Health Ministers gave two directions to the Board on 9th August 1977 under the Radiological Protection Act, requiring the Board to advise on radiation protection standards and to specify Emergency Reference Levels of Dose, and guidance on their derivation, for those with responsibilities for the protection of the public in the event of an accident involving, or likely to involve, radiation doses to the public in excess of dose limits.

Section 2 as amended by
the National Radiological
Protection Board
(Constitution
Amendment)
Order, 1980, S.I. 1980,
No. 970

Section 1(4)

Section 1(8)

Section 2(1)

The Board is a body corporate, consisting of a Chairman and not less than seven nor more than twelve other members. The Chairman and members of the Board are appointed by the Health Ministers (the Ministers respectively responsible for health in England, Scotland, Wales and Northern Ireland). In practice, by arrangement between the Health Ministers, appointments are made by the Secretary of State for Social Services after consultation with the Medical Research Council and the UKAEA.

Health and Safety at
Work
Act, 1974, Section 77
amending Section 1 of the
Radiological Protection
Act, 1970

In order to avoid duplication of activities, the Board has assumed responsibility for the Radiological Protection Service of the Medical Research Council and carries on in place of the Atomic Energy Authority activities related to the effect of radiation hazards on health and safety. Section 77 of the Health and Safety at Work Act, 1974 amends Section 1 of the Radiological Protection Act, 1970 by requiring the Board, in carrying out such of its functions as relate to matters to which the functions of the Health and Safety Commission relate, to act in consultation with the Commission and to have regard to its policies. It empowers the Board, on the direction of the Health Ministers, to enter into an agreement with the Commission to carry out such functions of the Commission relating to ionizing or other radiation as may be determined by or in accordance with the direction.

Radiological Protection
Act, 1970, Section
1(2)(b),
Section 3

The Board is financed from receipts from charges it makes for the provision of services and from funds provided by Parliament through the Secretary of State for Social Services.

Radiological Protection
Act, 1970, Section 3(4)

The Board must prepare each year a statement of accounts and other records for submission to the Secretary of State for Social Services, who in turn lays them before Parliament with his own report, after the Statement has been examined and certified by the Comptroller and Auditor General.

The Board carries out pilot studies and research on its own volition in addition to undertaking such work under contract. In 1974 the Medical Research Council and the Board established a Joint Committee on Radiological Protection to improve liaison between two bodies, particularly with regard to research into radiobiology.

c) Advisory Committee on the Safety of Nuclear Installations

In September 1976, the standing Royal Commission on Environmental Pollution, which was set up in 1970, presented to Parliament its Sixth Report, covering nuclear power and the environment. The Royal Commission expressed concern about the *need for a source of independent, expert advice to the Government on technical matters and which are relevant to policy decisions on major and hazardous technological developments, whether nuclear or otherwise ... the Health and Safety Executive have a responsibility to give such advice and ... should develop the capability to do so.*

The Government agreed with this recommendation, and in 1977, an Advisory Committee on the Safety of Nuclear Installations was set up. The Committee consists of a Chairman and fifteen members appointed for a three-year term, drawn from Government departments, scientific and industrial circles.

The Health and Safety Commission appoints the Members of the Advisory Committee on the Safety of Nuclear Installations.

The Committee's mandate is to advise the Health and Safety Commission and make recommendations on major issues affecting the safety of nuclear installations including their design, siting, operation and maintenance which are referred to them or which they consider to require consideration.

d) Radioactive Waste Management Advisory Committee

In its Sixth Report to Parliament, the Royal Commission on Environmental Pollution (see above) took the view that *the responsibility for developing the best strategy for dealing with radioactive wastes is one for the Government, and specifically for a department concerned to protect the environment, not one concerned to promote nuclear power,* and recommended that a Committee be established to advise the responsible Ministers on broad policy issues affecting radioactive waste management.

The Government accepted this recommendation and the Secretary of State for the Environment accordingly set up the Radioactive Waste Management Advisory Committee in 1978 as a non-statutory body, offering independent advice. A majority of the members, including the Chairman, are independent scientists and the other members are drawn from the nuclear and electricity industries and their trade unions. The members are appointed by the Secretary of State for the Environment. The Committee is advised and assisted by representatives of Government departments and public authorities.

The Committee's mandate is to advise the Environment Ministers on major issues relating to the development and implementation of an overall policy for the management of civil radioactive waste, which includes waste management implications of nuclear policy, of nuclear systems design, of research and development, and the environmental aspects of handling and treatment of wastes.

3. PUBLIC AND SEMI-PUBLIC AGENCIES

a) United Kingdom Atomic Energy Authority

i) Legal status

Atomic Energy Authority
Act, 1954, Section 1
Nuclear Installations
Act, 1965, Section 1
Atomic Energy Authority
Act, 1954, Section 5

The United Kingdom Atomic Energy Authority (UKAEA) was set up as a statutory corporation in implementation of the Government's wish that the responsibility for day to day details of the production and use of atomic energy be taken out of Ministerial hands. Therefore, while it is responsible to the Secretary of State for Energy, the UKAEA enjoys a certain degree of autonomy. Furthermore, nuclear installations operated by the Authority are not subject to licensing but observe the same standards of safety as those imposed on licensees. The Authority is also empowered, subject to Ministerial authority, to purchase compulsorily any land required for the performance of its functions.

ii) Responsibilities

Atomic Energy Authority
Act, 1954, Section 2(2)
Science and Technology
Act, 1965, Section 4
Control of Pollution
Act, 1974, Section 101

The functions of the Authority are to produce, use and dispose of atomic energy and to carry out research into related matters; to manufacture, buy or acquire, store and transport any articles which, in its opinion may be required in connection with the production and use of atomic energy; to produce, treat, transport and dispose of radioactive substances; and to disseminate information relating to and train persons in matters connected with atomic energy and radioactive substances. This broad mandate was extended to include non-nuclear research and development activities and to certain activities related to the treatment and disposal of wastes.

Atomic Energy Authority
Act, 1954, Section 3(5)

The Authority must submit to the Secretary of State for Energy a report on its activities as soon as possible after the end of each financial year, and this is laid down before Parliament for information.

iii) Structure

Atomic Energy Authority
Acts, 1954 and 1959,
Section 1

The Authority consists of a Chairman and from seven to fifteen members; all are appointed by the Secretary of State for Energy on a full-time or part-time basis. Three must be persons with extensive knowledge of atomic energy matters, one must be an authority on financial and administrative matters and one must be experienced in labour relations.

Atomic Energy Authority
Act, 1971

Section 1

Section 2

In 1971, the UKAEA's responsibilities in respect of fuel cycle operations were transferred to British Nuclear Fuels Ltd., which was set up for this purpose. Simularly the manufacture of radiochemicals was transferred at the same time to the Radiochemical Centre Ltd. (now Amersham International Ltd.)

In 1977, the UKAEA was reorganised into various management units together with headquarters at its London Office and the Safety and Reliability Directorate which provides an advisory service to government departments and organisations on all aspects of safety and reliability, including transport.

The Authority establishments and their activities are the following:

The London Headquarters co-ordinate with management units policy decisions and relations with Government departments, and other national and international organisations.

The Atomic Energy Research Establishment, Harwell directs its efforts to problems of reactor development and nuclear power generally as well as to work done for industry and the public sector (including Government departments).

The Atomic Energy Establishment, Winfrith is primarily concerned with reactor physics, nuclear data, radiation shielding, reactor safety, control engineering, etc.

The Culham Laboratory is the UKAEA centre for research in nuclear fusion, plasma physics and associated technology.

The Risley Nuclear Power Development Establishment incorporates the Northern Division Headquarters and provides design, procurement and inspection services; technical and economic assessment studies and is concerned with reactor component development.

The Dounreay Nuclear Power Development Establishment is the principal centre for fast reactor development.

The Springfields Nuclear Power Development Laboratories are concerned with fuel and plant development in support of the nuclear fuel cycle.

The Windscale Nuclear Power Development Laboratories are engaged on the development of plutonium fuels for fast reactors.

The Safety and Reliability Directorate, Culcheth mentioned above is concerned with developing technology to establish nuclear plant safety. It carries out R & D work in its field on behalf of the Health and Safety Commission.

iv) Financing

Atomic Energy Authority Act, 1954, Section 4

The UKAEA is financed by Parliamentary grant to an amount determined by the Secretary of State for Energy with the consent of the Treasury, and by income from work carried out under contracts concluded with Government departments for research work and services rendered as well as from commercial operations. Since 1977, funds for work on waste management are provided by the Department of the Environment.

Section 4(3)

The Authority is required to transmit to the Comptroller and Auditor General statements of account in respect of each financial year.

b) Health and Safety Commission and Executive

i) Legal status

Health and Safety at Work etc. Act, 1974, Section 10
Sections 11(3) and 12
Section 10(7)

The Health and Safety *Commission* and the Health and Safety *Executive,* the operational arm of the Commission, were set up as bodies corporate under the general authority of the Secretary of State for Employment (in nuclear safety matters they consult the Secretary of State for Energy). The functions of the Commission and of the Executive and of their officers are performed on behalf of the Crown.

ii) Responsibilities

Section 11

The general functions of the *Commission* and the *Executive* are to undertake activities and make appropriate arrangements respecting health, safety and welfare in connection with work, and control of dangerous substances and certain emissions into the atmosphere. This general mandate extends to all aspects of health protection related to nuclear activities.

Section 13
Section 14
Section 16

The *Commission* is empowered to make agreements with any Government department or person to perform on behalf of the *Commission* or the *Executive* any of their functions. It

150

may also make agreements with any Ministers, Government department or public authority to perform on their behalf functions which are exercisable by them, if the Secretary of State considers it appropriate for the *Commission* to do so. The *Commission* may appoint persons or committees to provide it with advice in connection with its functions (see description of Advisory Committee on the Safety of Nuclear Installations above) and has power to direct investigations and enquiries. It may furthermore approve and issue codes of practice with the consent of the Secretary of State, following consultation with the appropriate body (for example the National Radiological Protection Board as respects a code relating to electro-magnetic radiations).

Nuclear Installations
Act, 1965 etc. (Repeals
and Modifications)
Regulations, 1974
S.I. 1974, No. 2056

Health and Safety at
Work Act, 1974

Section 18

Section 19

The Health and Safety Executive is the authority responsible for the licensing of nuclear installations in the United Kingdom and appoints the Nuclear Installations Inspectorate. The Inspectorate ensures the compliance with all statutory requirements concerning the safety of the work force and the public in nuclear establishments. Certain provisions of the Nuclear Installation Act, 1965, relating to licensing are included in the Health and Safety at Work Act, 1974. The *Executive* has a duty to make adequate arrangements to enforce the health and safety provisions of the 1965 Act and the relevant statutory provisions of the 1965 Act and the relevant statutory provisions of the 1974 Act, and may appoint inspectors to carry into effect the statutory provisions within its field of responsibility.

Schedule 2, Paragraph 14

The *Commission* must submit to the Secretary of State, as soon as possible after the end of each accounting year, a report on its activities.

iii) Structure

Section 10

The *Commission* consists of a Chairman and not less than six nor more than nine members, all appointed by the Secretary of State for Employment. Before appointing the members of the *Commission* (other than the Chairman), the Secretary of State, as to three of them, consults organisations representing employers, as to three others, organisations representing employees, and as to any other members he may appoint, organisations representing local authorities, including professional bodies, the activities of which are pertinent to the purposes of the 1974 Act.

Section 10

The *Executive* consists of a Director and two other members. The *Commission* appoints the Director of the *Executive* with the approval of the Secretary of State; the other two are appointed by the *Commission,* also with his approval after consultation with the Director.

iv) Financing

Section 43

The Secretary of State is empowered, with the consent of the Treasury, to pay the *Commission* such sums as he considers appropriate for the performance of its functions. The *Commission* in turn pays the *Executive* such sums as it considers appropriate for the carrying out of its work.

Schedule 2, Paragraph 14

The *Commission* is required to prepare each year a statement of accounts for the Secretary of State and the Comptroller and Auditor General; the latter examines the statement, certifies it, and lays a copy thereof with his report before Parliament.

c) Central Electricity Generating Board

i) Legal status

Electricity Act, 1957,
Sections 2 and 8
Electric Lighting Act,
1909, Section 2
Electric Lighting
(Clauses)
Act, 1899, Section 10

The Central Electricity Generating Board (CEGB) was set up as a statutory corporation in 1958. The CEGB and Electricity Council together replaced the Central Electricity Authority, which was set up in 1948. The CEGB is responsible for the management of its own affairs, although the Secretary of State for Energy may give the CEGB general directions and he has certain other functions in relation to the CEGB such as the approval of major investment programmes and individual power plant and transmission projects.

ii) Responsibilities

Electricity Act, 1957,
Section 2

The CEGB is responsible for developing and maintaining an efficient co-ordinated and economical system of supply of electricity in bulk for all parts of England and Wales, and for providing bulk supplies of electricity to the area Electricity Boards via the grid transmission network for distribution to consumers.

Electricity (Amendment)
Act, 1961, Section 1

The CEGB operates eight nuclear power plants, and three others are in course of construction. The electricity supply legislation makes no distinction between conventional power plants and nuclear installations, and there are no special provisions for nuclear plants except that since 1961 the CEGB has had power to produce radioactive material at any of its nuclear plants for commercial purposes. The CEGB has to comply with United Kingdom nuclear legislation.

Electricity Act, 1957,
Section 10

An annual report is prepared by the CEGB on their performance policy and programmes each year, which is laid before Parliament by the Secretary of State for Energy.

iii) Structure

Electricity Act, 1957,
Sections 2 and 4

The Secretary of State for Energy appoints the Chairman and between seven and nine other members of the CEGB, including a deputy chairman. All the members must have

152

experience and capacity either in electricity supply, industrial, commercial, or financial matters, applied science, administration or the organisation of workers. The Secretary of State for Energy must ensure that as many of the CEGB members as he considers requisite for the efficient performance of the CEGB duties are appointed as whole-time members.

The Electricity (Central Authority and Area Boards) Regulations, 1947 Electricity Act, 1947, Section 3

Each appointment is for a period of up to five years, and upon such conditions including remuneration as may be decided by the Secretary of State for Energy with the approval of the Treasury.

iv) Financing

Electricity Act, 1947, Section 37

The CEGB receives its income from the Area Electricity Boards in England and Wales, in the form of prices charged for the electricity supplied to them in accordance with a published tariff.

The capital requirements of the CEGB and the Area Electricity Boards are arranged on their behalf by the Electricity Council.

Electricity Act, 1957, Sections 15 and 16 The Electricity (Borrowing Powers) Order, 1974

A large proportion of capital needs are met from internal resources, comprising annual profits after interests and depreciation charges are taken into account. The rest comes from external borrowings by the Electricity Council. Long-term loans take the form of direct advances from the Secretary of State for Energy and stock issues (in each case with the approval of the Treasury), and include loans raised overseas. Temporary loans, from banks and the superannuation funds, provide finance in between the dates of the Exchequer advances, normally fortnightly. Total borrowings may not at any time exceed £6,500 million.

The Electricity Council operates pooled banking arrangements for Electricity Boards in England and Wales.

Electricity Act, 1947, Section 46

The CEGB's statement of accounts is examined by independent professional auditors, and is laid before Parliament by the Secretary of State for Energy with the auditors' report.

d) South of Scotland Electricity Board

i) Legal status

Electricity Reorganisation (Scotland) Act, 1954 Section 2

The South of Scotland Electricity Board (SSEB) was set up on 1st April 1955 under the Electricity Reorganisation (Scotland) Act, 1954, and reports to the Secretary of State for Scotland.

ii) Responsibilities

SSEB is responsible not only for the generation and transmission of electricity in the South of Scotland but also for distribution to some 1,500,000 consumers in a district extending to some 21,000 square kilometres.

SSEB owns and operates two nuclear power plants, both sited at Hunterston, Ayrshire, and a further nuclear power plant is under construction at Torness, East Lothian.

iii) Structure

Electricity (Scotland)
Act, 1979, Schedule 1

The Secretary of State for Scotland appoints the Chairman, Deputy Chairman and up to seven part-time members of the Board. The Chairman and Deputy Chairman are full-time members of the Board and are normally appointed for a period of five years. The part-time members are normally appointed for periods of three to four years.

iv) Financing

Section 29

SSEB's fixed and working capital requirements are financed from internal and external sources, the latter being limited by statutory borrowing powers and Government-set external financing limits (EFL's or cash limits). Internal sources of finance consist of surplus, depreciation and capital receipts; external sources of finance consist of temporary borrowing from banks and other sources, and longer term borrowing from the Government and overseas institutions in the form of interest bearing loans.

Section 30

The SSEB is accountable to the Secretary of State for Scotland to whom its Annual Report and audited Accounts are submitted in accordance with the provisions of the Electricity (Scotland) Act, 1979.

e) Electricity Council

Electricity Act, 1957,
Section 3

The Electricity Council was established by the Electricity Act, 1957. It has a Chairman, two deputy chairmen and not more than three other members appointed by the Secretary of State for Energy from among persons qualified in the same way as those who may be appointed members of the CEGB (see above). In addition, the Chairman of the CEGB and two other persons appointed by it, and the chairmen of the Area Electricity Boards are also members. Among the Electricity Council's duties are advising the Secretary of State on questions affecting the electricity supply industry and promoting and assisting the maintenance and development by the CEGB and Area Electricity Boards in England and Wales of an efficient, co-ordinated and economical system of electricity supply.

f) Area Electricity Boards in England and Wales

Electricity Act, 1947

There are twelve such Boards which were originally constituted by the Electricity Act, 1947 and are responsible for acquiring bulk supplies of electricity from the CEGB and distributing such supplies to the customers in their respective areas.

g) British Nuclear Fuels Limited

i) Legal status

Atomic Energy Authority Act, 1971, Section 1

Section 7

Section 11

British Nuclear Fuels Ltd.
(Transfer of Shares) Order, 1981
S.I. 1981, No. 868

As part of the reorganisation of the UKAEA, British Nuclear Fuels Ltd., (BNFL) was set up as a commercial company to which were transferred the fuel cycle operations previously undertaken by the Production Group of the UKAEA, together with the related property, rights, liabilities and obligations. In consideration of this transfer, shares in BNFL were issued to the UKAEA, although it is entitled to have shareholders in the private sector, so long as the UKAEA and the Secretary of State hold more than 50%. BNFL is responsible to the Secretary of State for Energy who may by order provide for the transfer of shares to himself. The Secretary of State has now transferred to himself all the shares in BNFL held by the UKAEA.

Atomic Energy (Miscellaneous Provisions) Act, 1981, Section 1

The Secretary of State has power to dispose of shares held by him in any nuclear company (including BNFL).

ii) Responsibilities

BNFL is responsible for supplying fuel and other fuel cycle services, notably reprocessing, and works in close co-ordination with the UKAEA in the field of research and development connected with the fuel cycle.

iii) Structure

BNFL is managed by a Board of twelve Directors, appointed in accordance with the Company's Articles of Association, one of whom is the Chairman, another the Managing Director and another the Deputy Managing Director. The Secretary of the Board convenes the Annual General Meeting at the direction of the Board.

The Company is organised into a head office in Risley which controls operations in its three Divisions.

The activities of the three Divisions are the following:

The Fuel Division at Springfields extracts and purifies uranium from imported ore concentrates; in addition, it fabricates fuel elements.

155

The Enrichment Division at Capenhurst operates a gaseous diffusion enrichment plant which provides enriched uranium for the United Kingdom reactor programme. Through a subsidiary company, BNFL is in partnership with organisations in the Netherlands and the Federal Republic of Germany. The partnership operates a centrifuge enrichment plant at Capenhurst which provides enriched uranium for the United Kingdom overseas customers.

The Reprocessing Division at Windscale (now known as Sellafield) is responsible for the reprocessing plant there and for operation of the Calder and Chapelcross nuclear power plants.

iv) Financing

Atomic Energy Authority Act, 1971, Sections 11(4) and 12(1)
Section 13
S.I. 1976, No. 1298
Nuclear Industry (Finance) Act, 1977, Section 1
Section 2
British Nuclear Fuels Ltd. (Financial Limit) Order, 1981
S.I. 1981, No. 487
Nuclear Industry (Finance) Act, 1981, Section 1

The initial capital was subscribed by the Secretary of State with the consent of the Treasury. The Secretary of State and the Authority may also make loans to the Company up to an overall limit. This limit was increased from £50 to £75 million by the British Nuclear Fuels Limited (Payment and Loan Limited) Order, 1976. Under the Nuclear Industry (Finance) Act, 1977, the Secretary of State is empowered, with the consent of the Treasury, to guarantee any loans made to BNFL, including the loan interest. The financial limits of the Company were further raised to £300 million which may be increased to an amount to be specified by order, and in any event not exceeding £500 million. The financial limits of the Company were again raised by the Nuclear Industry (Finance) Act 1981, which extended the limits laid down by the 1977 Act and substituted a new limit of £1,000 million which may be increased to an amount to be specified by order not exceeding £1,500 million.

Atomic Energy Authority Act, 1971, Section 14

After the holding of the General Meeting of the Company where the Directors' and Auditors' Reports and Statement of Accounts are considered, the Secretary of State is required to lay before Parliament a Statement of Accounts which in accordance with the Companies Acts, 1948 to 1980, are laid before the Company at that meeting, together with all relevant documents.

h) Amersham International Limited (formerly the Radiochemical Centre Limited)

Atomic Energy Authority Act, 1971, Section 1
Atomic Energy (Miscellaneous Provisions) Act, 1981, Section 1

Also as part of the reorganisation of the UKAEA, the Radiochemical Centre Limited was set up as a commercial company at the same time as BNFL, to take over the activities previously undertaken by the UKAEA in connection with the production and marketing of radioactive materials. The Company, which has subsidiaries in a number

Amersham International
Ltd.
(Transfer of Shares)
Order, 1981
S.I. 1981, No. 850

of countries including Australia, France, the Federal Republic of Germany, Japan and the United States, was renamed Amersham International Limited in 1981. The Government has powers, which it has since decided to exercise, to divest itself of ownership of the Company. The shares held by the UKAEA in the Company were transferred to the Secretary of State for Energy and were sold by him.

i)   The National Nuclear Corporation Limited

The National Nuclear Corporation Ltd. (NNC) was set up in 1973 as a private limited company whose shareholders are the UKAEA, General Electric Company Ltd. and British Nuclear Associates Ltd. (representing companies engaged in the nuclear construction industry). The NNC is responsible for the design, construction and marketing of nuclear power plants. The issued share capital is £10 million.

Nuclear Industry
(Finance)
Act, 1977, Section 3

In 1977, the Secretary of State for Energy was empowered to incur, with the consent of the Treasury, out of money provided by Parliament, any expenditure necessary for the acquisition for the Crown of shares in the National Nuclear Corporation.

j)   The Nuclear Industry Radioactive Waste Executive

The Nuclear Industry Radioactive Waste Executive (NIREX) was set up in 1982 by British Nuclear Fuels Ltd., the Central Electricity Generating Board, the UKAEA and the South of Scotland Electricity Board. NIREX is not a legal entity.

NIREX was established in order to provide the above bodies with a mechanism by which they can successfully fulfil their own duties in this field and work within a comprehensive plan for waste management. It is envisaged that NIREX will in due course undertake and/or procure the undertaking of activities in connection with the relevant responsibilities and functions of its constituents in the waste management field, and will play an important part in the development, co-ordination and implementation of a plan for waste management.

The Executive will have a Director consisting of senior representatives of BNFL, CEGB, UKAEA and SSEB. The UKAEA has agreed to provide, on a repayment basis, a small staff based at Harwell.

UNITED STATES

TABLE OF CONTENTS

I. GENERAL REGULATORY REGIME

Atomic Energy Act of
1954, as amended
68 Stat. 919
42 USC[1] 2011 *et seq.*[2]

The centerpiece of nuclear legislation in the United States is the *Atomic Energy Act* of 1954, a comprehensive statute which displaced the Atomic Energy Act of 1946.

In the United States, the Federal Government has assumed most responsibility for regulating nuclear energy. For example, federal legislation and administrative regulations govern facility licensing. Usually, the States can regulate a particular entity whenever the Federal Government fails to act; however, in the nuclear field, courts recently have struck down State efforts to regulate nuclear waste disposal and transport of radioactive materials. States can adopt more stringent standards for radioactive air pollutants than federal standards governing the same activities. Sometimes, the States agree to assume control over an activity which normally would be regulated by the Federal Government. In the nuclear sphere, about half of the States, under close federal supervision, draft and enforce laws controlling by-product and source materials as well as small quantities of special nuclear material (see Chapter, below, on *Radioactive Substances, Nuclear Fuels and Equipment*). States are not permitted to license nuclear reactors. This study does not refer to any State laws.

Energy Reorganization
Act of 1974
88 Stat. 1233
42 USC 5801 *et seq.*

Department of Energy
Organization Act of
1977
91 Stat. 565
42 USC 7101 *et seq.*

Congress has enacted a general framework for nuclear energy centered around the Atomic Energy Act of 1954. Initially, the Atomic Energy Commission (AEC) constituted an independent regulatory agency to oversee the peaceful use of atomic energy. Congress subsequently abolished that agency, when it enacted the Energy Reorganization Act of 1974. The Act created the independent administrative agency, the Nuclear Regulatory Commission (NRC), and

---

1. USC = United States Code.
2. In the United States, federal laws generally are cited as ... USC, Section ... which refer to a title and section of the United States Code. American federal legislation is arranged by subject matter; for example Title 42 contains public health and safety laws. Laws are also cited as ... Stat. ... which refers to the Statutes at Large, a chronological compilation of all American legislation without regard to subject matter.

Later in this study, citations to the Code of Federal Regulations (CFR) appear. When an administrative agency promulgates a regulation, it usually publishes the proposed rule in the Federal Register (Fed. Reg). After public comment, the final rule is published in the Register. Citations to the Register appear as ... Fed. Reg. ... meaning volume and page number. It is also included in the Code of Federal Regulations, a frequently updated series. The CFR is arranged into titles which do not correspond numerically to parallel subject areas in the USC; for example, most nuclear regulations can be found in 10 CFR which deals with all aspects of energy law. The CFR is arranged into titles, subdivided into chapters, parts and then into subparts and sections.

This synopsis sometimes refers to Executive Orders handed down by the President. Usually these documents articulate policy, confirm international understandings, or create advisory bodies. They are cited by number and date.

transferred to it all the licensing and related regulatory functions previously assigned to the Atomic Energy Commission. The remainder of the AEC's functions were distributed to the Energy Research and Development Agency (ERDA). The Department of Energy Organization Act of 1977 abolished ERDA and vested the Department of Energy (DOE), a new cabinet-level agency, with power over most other aspects of nuclear energy.

These agencies, and other federal administrative agencies listed in Part II of this study, fill in the interstices of the broad legislative scheme outlined by Congress.

1. MINING REGIME

Despite some active uranium mining in the United States, the Atomic Energy Act of 1954 does not specifically mention mining. Since the early 1950s, the Atomic Energy Commission and its successors have made estimates of American uranium ore reserves and potential uranium supply. Now the DOE supervises the National Uranium Resource Evaluation (NURE) program, begun in 1974 by the AEC in response to concern about the adequacy and availability of domestic uranium.

68 Stat. 919, and
Sections 62111
42 USC 2092 and 2014

The Nuclear Regulatory Commission is responsible for licensing extraction of *source material,* defined as uranium or thorium or any ores containing those materials in such concentration as NRC may determine by regulation. In 1981, 42 uranium recovery facilities were operating pursuant to NRC licenses. (For details of the licensing process, see the Chapter on *Radioactive Substances, Nuclear Fuels and Equipment).*

The Bureau of Mines in the Department of the Interior controls all lands with valuable mineral deposits. Commercial operators can lease the land in order to mine uranium or other minerals, but the land is reserved from sale by the Federal Government. The Department of Energy also issues permits specifically for uranium exploitation.

68 Stat. 919,
Sections 65 to 68
42 USC 2095 to 2098

The Department of Energy can require detailed reports on mining of source material, but not prior to actual removal from its place in nature. Regulations must not discourage independent prospecting for new deposits. The Atomic Energy Act empowers DOE to purchase any real property which might contain deposits of source material. The Department can issue leases or permits to prospect for source materials on federal lands, and, by virtue of an executive order, can allow prospecting in national parks. In concert with permit requirements, no individual partnership or corporation can benefit directly from confidential information learned about mineral deposits while participating in DOE or NRC projects conducted on public land.

2. RADIOACTIVE SUBSTANCES, NUCLEAR FUELS AND EQUIPMENT

68 Stat. 919,
Sections 53, 62 and 81
42 USC 2073, 2092 and 2111

Pursuant to the Atomic Energy Act of 1954, the Nuclear Regulatory Commission (NRC) can issue licenses to transfer or receive, own or possess, and import or export special nuclear material, source material, or by-product material. Although the legislation discusses each category separately, the provisions are similar.

a) Special nuclear material

68 Stat. 919,
Section 11(aa)
42 USC 2014(aa)

68 Stat. 919,
Section 51
42 USC 2071

The term *special nuclear material* means plutonium, uranium enriched in the isotopes 233 or 235 and any other materials which the NRC determines to be special nuclear material. It also includes any material artificially enriched by any of the foregoing substances. In order to add substances to the list, 1) the Nuclear Regulatory Commission must find such material capable of releasing substantial quantities of atomic energy; 2) there must be a determination that the material is in the interest of the common defense; and 3) the President must give written assent. Congress has thirty days to disapprove the action.

68 Stat. 919,
Section 53(a) to (c)
42 USC 2073(a)
to 2073(c)

The NRC can issue licenses to research or medical facilities or to commercial operators, and for any other uses consistent with the purposes of the Act. Guided by the dual criteria of protecting public health and safety and promoting the common defense, the NRC issues general or specific licenses depending on the physical characteristics of the special nuclear material, the quantities to be distributed, and the intended use of the material. Initially, the Atomic Energy Commission (predecessor to the NRC) could distribute material by sale, lease with option to buy, or in return for in-kind services. Now, the Government generally requires facility operators to buy special nuclear material. The DOE itself establishes a reasonable price scale and agrees to repurchase any unused material.

68 Stat. 919,
Section 53(e)
42 USC 2073(e)

The NRC can regulate licensees by forbidding assignment of licenses, explicitly defining all limits of ownership, and ensuring that no licensee will be able to construct an

68 Stat. 919,
Section 53*(f)*
42 USC 2073*(f)*

atomic weapon. Except when provisions of the Price-Anderson Act apply for indemnification against third party liability, licensees must hold the Government and the Commission harmless for any losses resulting from the use or possession of the material. The DOE must allocate sales of such material on the basis of the project's probable contribution to basic research, to the development of peaceful uses of atomic energy, or to the economic and military strength of the United States.

68 Stat. 919,
Section 54*(a)* and *(d)*
42 USC 2074*(a)* and 2074*(d)*

The DOE controls the unlicensed foreign distribution of special nuclear material, while the Commission licenses exports. Many of the export regulations overlap with the provisions of the Nuclear Non-Proliferation Act and this aspect is therefore dealt with in the *Nuclear Security* Chapter, below. Subject to certain price limitations, the Government can purchase special nuclear material produced abroad through use of special nuclear material leased or sold by the United States. There is a statutory exemption for the supply of small amounts of special nuclear material contained in laboratory samples or medical devices to foreign users and a general exemption allowing quick shipment of small amounts in an emergency.

68 Stat. 919,
Sections 55 and 56
42 USC 2075 and 2076

The DOE can purchase special nuclear material without the general bidding procedures applicable to most government contracts. It can establish guaranteed purchase prices for plutonium generated in research reactors and enriched uranium produced by researchers or commercial operators.

68 Stat. 919,
Section 57
42 USC 2077

A person subject to the Atomic Energy Act may engage in the production of special nuclear material outside the United States only if this activity is pursuant to the Nuclear Non-Proliferation Act and agreements negotiated in accordance with its provisions, or if specifically approved by the Secretary of Energy after consultation with the Department of State, Arms Control and Disarmament Agency, the Nuclear Regulatory Commission, the Department of Commerce, and the Department of Defense.

b) Source material

68 Stat. 919,
Section 11*(z)*
42 USC 2014*(z)*

Nuclear source material is defined as uranium, thorium or any other material which the Commission determines to be source material. It also includes ores containing one or more of the foregoing materials in such concentration as the Commission may establish by regulation (see under *Mining regime*). If the Commission seeks to enlarge the definition of source material, it must find that the material is essential to the production of special nuclear material and that its designation as source material is in the interest of the common defense. The President must agree in writing and Congress has an opportunity to review the determination.

68 Stat. 919,
Sections 62 to 64
42 USC 2092 to 2094
10 CFR, Part 40

A person needs a general or specific license to transfer, own, export or import, or extract source materials except that licenses are not required for quantities of source material which, in the opinion of the Commission, are unimportant. Provisions involving foreign and domestic distribution of source material generally parallel those for special nuclear materials. There are, however, special reporting requirements with respect to ownership, possession, extraction, and refining of source materials.

c) By-product material

68 Stat. 919,
Section 11(e)
42 USC 2014(e)

The term *by-product material* means any radioactive material (except special nuclear material) yielded in, or made radioactive by exposure to the radiation incidental to the process of producing or utilizing special nuclear material; it includes the tailings produced when source material is milled.

68 Stat. 919,
Sections 81 and 82
42 USC 2111 and 2112

Licensing requirements similar to those for possession of special nuclear material or source material apply to by-product materials. The Department of Energy is to encourage maximal development of peaceful application for by-product material. To this end, the Government can sell material to potential users, limited only by health and defense considerations. Any price schedule inaugurated by the DOE must not discourage private enterprise from competing with government sources. The NRC can exempt certain users from the necessity of a license, or may decide that, for certain types of by-product material, the strict structure of a licensing scheme is not warranted. The government controls the export of by-product material with a system very similar to that for special and source materials.

68 Stat. 919,
Section 83
42 USC 2113
68 Stat. 919,
Section 83(b)
42 USC 2113(b)

Licenses for ownership of by-product material must contain conditions to ensure that the licensee will comply with decontamination or decommissioning requirements. Ownership of by-product material at sites where ores were processed primarily for their source material content and where such by-product material is deposited reverts to the Federal Government or to the States if they have exercised an option to acquire following termination of the license. There is an outline of these requirements in the *Radioactive Waste Management* Chapter of this Study. The Nuclear Regulatory Commission is responsible for overseeing compliance with decontamination and decommissioning requirements. When land or by-product ownership passes to the United States, the Department of Energy becomes the competent authority to monitor the facilities in conjunction with State agencies.

The NRC administers over 9 000 by-product material licenses, and 26 States handle an additional 12 000 licenses as part of co-operative agreements with NRC. As part of this responsibility, NRC regulates radiography, gas chromatography, well logging, and other industrial applications of atomic energy. The NRC issues a small number of general and specific licenses for consumer products containing radioactive material; for example, smoke detectors, ceramics and watches and signs containing tritium.

d) Trade

68 Stat. 919,
Section 123
42 USC 2153
68 Stat. 919,
Section 127
42 USC 2156

Any agreement for nuclear co-operation between the United States and another nation must contain assurances that the co-operating party will undertake safeguards to protect special nuclear material purchased or produced under the agreement, so long as the material is in the possession or under the jurisdiction of the co-operating party, regardless of the duration of the agreement.

68 Stat. 919,
Sections 126 and 127
42 USC 2155 and 2156
68 Stat. 919,
Sections 128 and 130
42 USC 2157 and 2159

The NRC cannot issue export licenses or exemptions unless it makes certain findings and until it is notified by the Secretary of State that in the judgment of the executive branch the proposed action will not be inimical to the common defense and security. The Secretaries of Energy, Commerce, and Defense, the Director of the Arms Control and Disarmament Agency and the Nuclear Regulatory Commission co-operate to complete this executive branch judgment. Whenever there are several contracts involving one nation, the Commission may render a single opinion as regards compliance with the statutory criteria if there are no materially changed circumstances from the terms of a preceeding contract. Such a decision is not subject to judicial review. With Congressional approval, the President can overrule an NRC decision not to permit export.

68 Stat. 919,
Sections 127 to 129
42 USC 2156 to 2158

The International Atomic Energy Agency (IAEA) safeguards govern all important nuclear exports. Some minor components are not covered. Foreign governments cannot transfer United States-origin special nuclear materials to other nations unless the United States approves the action. Prior approval must be obtained from the United States for any reprocessing of nuclear material originating in the United States.

3. PROTECTION OF WORKERS AND THE PUBLIC AGAINST IONIZING RADIATION

a) Protection of workers

10 CFR Part 19
10 CFR 19.2

Worker protection requirements apply to all NRC licensees. The regulatory goal is to keep workers informed about

10 CFR 19.1 *et seq.*
10 CFR 19.3

the health protection problems associated with exposures to radiation, methods of minimizing exposures and actual radiation exposure received and to encourage workers to bring matters regarding occupational radiation protection to the attention of Commission inspectors. Licensees must post various documents including operating procedures and any notice of violation. Workers are to be instructed in health protection procedures, and appropriate responses to warnings of exposure. Individual workers must receive notification and reports in writing containing information on annual exposure. At the time of termination, licensees must supply workers with written reports on exposures received during the worker's period of employment.

10 CFR 19.4 to 9.7

NRC inspects facilities to ensure compliance with the Commission's radiological health and safety standards. Representatives of workers and the licensee accompany the inspectors. If there are fears of non-compliance at a particular facility, a worker or worker's representative can request an unscheduled inspection, but NRC can decide that an inspection is unwarranted if an informal review reveals no reasonable grounds to believe a violation has occurred.

10 CFR Part 20
10 CFR 20.101
10 CFR 20.102
10 CFR 20.201 to 20.206

Permissible radiation dosages, the calculation of which is explicitly described in this section, are measured by both calendar quarter and accumulated occupational dose. Before a licensee may permit a worker to undertake assignments in restricted areas, he must obtain information about the worker's prior occupational exposure. Each licensee must take various preventive measures such as radiation protection equipment, surveys of hazards, personnel monitoring, and display of signs, labels, and signals. Each licensee must train employees in precautionary techniques.

Licensees must also comply with applicable requirements of the Occupational Health and Safety Act, administered by the Occupational Safety and Health Administration within the Department of Labor, as well as applicable State health and safety laws.

b) **Protection of the public**

68 Stat. 919,
Sections 3, 31, 33, 83 and 84
42 USC 2013, 2051, 2053,
2113 and 2114
National Environmental Policy Act of 1969, as amended
83 Stat. 852
91 Stat. 685,
Section 112

All phases of nuclear facility construction and operation as well as the regulation of nuclear materials are subject to public health, safety and environmental constraints. Under the National Environmental Policy Act of 1969, environmental impact statements must be prepared before the NRC may issue a construction permit or operating license for a nuclear reactor. In the case of NRC, environmental factors are most visible in licensing and waste disposal decisions (see those chapters of this study). Licensees must also comply with all applicable environmental laws, including the Federal Water Pollution Control Act of 1972 and the Clean Air Act of

1974, as amended. Under the latter statute, radioactive emissions are by definition classified as "hazardous pollutants." The Department of Transportation and the Environmental Protection Agency (EPA) either develop or assist in developing standards. In addition to meeting existing regulatory criteria, licensees must predict emission levels during various postulated accident situations. During each license review, NRC completes a biological assessment of facility impact pursuant to the Endangered Species Act. NRC also reviews the socio-economic impacts of siting decisions.

Executive Order 12114
(4.1.1979)

An Executive Order requires NRC to consider the environmental effects abroad of licensing the export of power reactors.

Radiation Control for
Health and Safety Act
of 1968
82 Stat. 1179,
Section 355

82 Stat. 1179,
Section 357

The Radiation Control for Health and Safety Act of 1968 amends the Public Health Services Act. This statute inaugurates authority for the Federal Government to promulgate standards to control emission from electronic products. Regulation extends to ionizing or non-ionizing electromagnetic radiation as well as particle, sonic, infrasonic and ultrasonic radiation.

82 Stat. 1179
Section 358
21 CFR Part 1000
82 Stat. 1179,
Section 359

The regulations promulgated under this Act are performance standards. They apply, in some instances, to warnings, labels, and instructions. In promulgating regulations, the Department of Health and Human Services (DHHS) must consult a Technical Electronic Product Radiation Standards Committee, consisting of five representatives each from government and industry as well as four persons chosen from the public and one from labor. Manufacturers must notify the Government, distributor and consumer of any danger with reasonable promptness, disclosing as much information as possible about adverse effects without compromising trade secrets.

NRC licenses hospitals and physicians contemplating use of radioactive materials in diagnosis and treatment. NRC reviews facilities, personnel, program controls, and equipment described in each application to ensure safety of the public and occupationally exposed workers. In the United States, however, most authority to regulate non-radiological health and safety matters rests with individual States.

4. NUCLEAR INSTALLATIONS[3]

a) Licensing[4]

88 Stat. 1233,
Sections 2, 203 and 204
42 USC 5801, 5843
and 5844

With a few exceptions, such as Department of Energy or Department of Defense reactors, the Nuclear Regulatory Commission (NRC) licenses all nuclear installations in the United States pursuant to authority conferred by the Energy Reorganization Act of 1974. Within NRC, the Office of Nuclear Material Safety and Safeguards licenses fuel cycle facilities and the Office of Nuclear Reactor Regulation processes reactor licenses.

When a utility company decides to build a nuclear power plant, it first seeks a construction permit or limited work authorization pending issuance of the permit. The formal licensing process begins with filing the application, usually comprising ten or more large volumes of materials addressing safety, environmental, safeguards, and antitrust issues. Once the utility has gathered all data required by the Standard Review Plan (an agency guideline for evaluating completeness of applications), NRC accepts the application by formally docketing it. NRC distributes relevant documents to the press, local, State and federal officials, and publishes a notice of docketing in the Federal Register.

68 Stat. 919,
Section 29
42 USC 2039

The NRC staff undertakes a safety review in accordance with the Standard Review Plan for Light Water Reactors, a constantly updated guide containing requirements for each system, component, and structure important for safety. Once the staff finishes the Safety Evaluation Report, the Advisory Committee on Reactor Safeguards (ACRS), a statutorily-created committee which advises the Commission with regard to the hazards of existing or proposed reactor facilities and the adequacy of proposed reactor safety standards, completes its review and meets with NRC staff and the applicant. It then submits a letter report to the NRC presenting the results of its independent analysis and recommending whether NRC should issue a construction permit.

A public hearing can be held on the safety aspects of the application. The Atomic Safety Licensing Board (ASLB) presides at the hearing conducted in an adversary manner when intervenors contest. A public hearing is mandatory in the case of construction permit proceedings even if the

---

3.   This Chapter concerns power reactors as opposed to research reactors, waste disposal sites, uranium mills, storage centres, burial sites, or other installations requiring an NRC licence. For these, see Chapters 1, 2, 5 and 8 of this study dealing with mining, possession and trade, waste disposal, and transport, respectively.

4.   For further details, see "Description of Licensing Systems and Inspection of Nuclear Installations", OECD/NEA, 1980.

application is uncontested. After a public hearing, the three member panel reaches an initial decision as to whether a construction permit should be granted. The ruling can be appealed to the Atomic Safety and Licensing Appeal Board (ASLAB,) and to the Commissioners. Following final Commission action, an appellant can petition for review by the appropriate Federal Court of Appeals.

The environment review is parallel to, yet separate from, consideration of safety aspects of the application. The staff review, public comment, and hearing procedures are similar. In appropriate cases, hearings on safety and environmental issues can be combined.

When the Attorney General completes an antitrust report, the NRC publishes the Attorney General's advice, and upon petition by the Attorney General or other interested parties, an anti-trust hearing will be held.

NRC can issue a Limited Work Authorization in advance of the final decision on a construction permit, approving preparatory steps once all environmental and site selection issues have been resolved and the ASLB concludes that there is reasonable assurance that the proposed site would be suitable from the standpoint of radiological health and safety for a reactor of the general size and type proposed. Installation of the structural foundations may be authorized prior to issuance of the construction permit if, in addition to the findings described above, the ASLB determines there are no unresolved safety issues relating to such work which would justify withholding the authorization.

46 Fed Reg. 28639 (1981)

Two or three years before the scheduled completion of construction, the applicant files for an operating license. The entire process is repeated. A public hearing is not mandatory, but may be conducted on petition by the NRC or interested parties. In order to streamline the licensing process, NRC recently promulgated a new rule mandating that alternative sites must be considered during the construction permit stage, but no longer need be reconsidered during the request for an operating license.

Each operating license contains detailed provisions relating to safety and environmental protection. The licensed facility undergoes periodic inspection during its operating life. The NRC, as part of its Systematic Evaluation Program (SEP), may require backfitting of a licensed plant to meet new safety and environmental requirements.

NRC currently is attempting to simplify the lengthy licensing process in order to reduce the present fourteen year lapse between filing of the initial application and issuance of the operating permit to six or eight years.

46 Fed. Reg. 28533 (1981)

After extensive public comment, NRC issued a "Statement of Policy on Conduct of Licensing Proceedings". This

169

47 Fed. Reg. 13750
(1982)
47 Fed. Reg. 12940
(1982)

guide recommends adherence to reasonable time schedules, consolidation of intervention proceedings, inauguration of mandatory negotiation to solve procedural and substantive disputes, and better management of discovery by accelerated rulings on critical or dispositive issues. The Commission recently amended its regulations to omit review of financial responsibility prior to issuance of a permit or operating license and to eliminate the requirement in operating license proceedings, to consider the need for more electrical power and alternative energy supplies. The Commission is also considering other proposals for regulatory reform.

b) Operation

NRC currently is emphasizing human factors in planning revisions of operating guidelines. After public hearings, NRC published new guidelines for control room design which utilities must implement.

The NRC licenses both operators and senior operators and has introduced stricter criteria for experience, training and qualifications.

Much of NRC's operational activities concern safety. Using a Standard Safety Review Plan, NRC is trying to implement improvements which have been developed as a result of the Three Mile Island accident.

88 Stat. 1233,
Section 210
42 USC 5850
68 Stat. 919,
Section 11*(j)* and *(q)*
42 USC 2014

In 1983, NRC augmented this review process with a National Reliability Evaluation Program (NREP) stressing interactions between various plant systems. NRC licensees must report unplanned occurrences which have safety implications; in 1980 reporting requirements were made more stringent. NRC analyses each abnormal occurrence to ascertain whether the operator violated regulations, and, if a problem is widespread, NRC can take appropriate enforcement action.

NRC undertakes regular inspection and enforcement activities. Inspections cover preconstruction through decommissioning, and NRC maintains resident inspectors at each reactor site. NRC's investigative program also responds to information gained from inspectors or the general public. Investigators work with federal, State, and local law enforcement personnel to probe allegations ranging from faulty reactor operation or construction to loss or theft of licensed material, overexposure of personnel, and sabotage.

5. RADIOACTIVE WASTE MANAGEMENT

Three agencies share responsibility for the United States' waste management policy. The NRC must formulate and implement regulations ensuring that disposal methods are safe for long-term waste management. DOE has the "lead responsibility" for developing technologies and programs for handling, treatment, storage, transport and disposal of commercial spent nuclear fuel, high level waste, and all defense-generated waste. The EPA must establish the maximum allowable release of radionuclides to the biosphere.

a) High-level waste

Nuclear Waste Policy
Act of 1982
96 Stat. 2201
42 USC 10101 *et seq.*

On 7th January 1983 the United States Congress enacted the Nuclear Waste Policy Act of 1982 (NWPA). The NWPA establishes the Federal Government's responsibility for the permanent disposal of high-level radioactive waste and spent nuclear fuel and authorizes the Secretary of the DOE to construct a repository for their disposal. The NWPA requires that the repository be ready to receive high-level radioactive waste and spent nuclear fuel for disposal by 1998.

The repository will be financed by fees paid by owners and generators of high-level waste and spent nuclear fuel under a standard disposal contract that was published as a final rule in the Federal Register on 18th April 1983.

96 Stat. 2201
42 USC 10101

The NWPA also provides for a Federal Government interim storage program for up to 1 900 metric tons of spent nuclear fuel. In addition, the NWPA requires DOE to submit a proposal for a Monitored Retrievable Storage Facility, authorizes a Test and Evaluation Facility, and provides for a DOE/utility demonstration program for the dry storage of spent nuclear fuel and a co-operative program for spent nuclear fuel rod consolidation in existing power reactor water storage basins.

10 CFR Part 60,
Section 60.10 to 60.73
48 Fed. Reg. 28194
(1983)

In 1981, NRC published a final rule outlining procedures which it will follow in considering applications for a repository license from DOE. These procedures are being reviewed to determine whether revisions are necessary in light of the NWPA. In addition, the NRC recently published its final technical criteria governing high-level waste disposal as required by Section 121 of the NWPA. The rule contains siting, design, and performance criteria, as well as criteria for monitoring and testing programs. The rule adopts a multi-barrier approach, and concerns the waste package itself, the engineered repository structure, and the site and its environs.

West Valley
Demonstration
Project Act
94 Stat. 1347
42 USC 2021*(a)*

In order to demonstrate the solidification of liquid high-level wastes, Congress passed the West Valley Demonstration Project Act, authorizing a high-level waste project in West Valley, New York. This project, at the first commercial fuel reprocessing site, will demonstrate solidification of waste by vitrification or other technology. DOE has primary responsibility for the facility, with NRC monitoring activities.

b) Low-level waste

Low-level Radioactive
Waste Policy Act
94 Stat. 3347
42 USC 2021*(b)* to *(d)*

The Low-level Radioactive Waste Policy Act announced a broad federal policy for disposal of low-level nuclear waste, defining "disposal" as isolation of the material pursuant to NRC requirements. Each state is responsible for providing capacity for disposal of low-level nuclear waste generated within its borders, but the Federal Government controls waste from DOE defense installations or federal research and development projects. Congress perceives management of low-level waste as a regional problem, requiring States to enter into compacts to funnel wastes to regional disposal centers. After 1st January 1986, member States of a regional compact can exclude waste originating outside their region, if the compact is consented to by Congress.

96 Stat. 2201
42 USC 10101 *et seq.*

The Nuclear Waste Policy Act of 1982 provides that DOE may take title and custody of closed commercial low-level nuclear waste facilities if NRC finds that certain requirements are met, including decommissioning and closure requirements, as well as long-term financial arrangements.

10 CFR, Part 61

NRC regulations divide low-level waste management into an operational and post-operational phase. The rules aim to protect individuals against inadvertent exposure, protect the public from general releases into the environment, and maintain stability of the disposal site. The regulations include classification of waste, procedural criteria for licensing and technical criteria for sites. NRC has licensed disposal of special nuclear material at two commercial burial sites, and is closing one exhausted site. The NRC is assisting some 26 States which are co-operating with it.

c) Disposal at sea

Marine Protection
Research, and
Sanctuaries
Act of 1972
88 Stat. 50,
Section 2

Congress adopted a policy regulating dumping of all material which could adversely affect human health, welfare, the marine environment, or the economic potential of the sea by passing the Marine Protection Research and Sanctuaries Act of 1972. The Act applies to United States registered vessels or aircraft, or foreign craft dumping materials in territorial waters. The Act specifically identifies radioactive waste as a controlled substance, regardless of whether it is generated by a civilian or military source: no-one can dump high-level waste. In specific instances, NRC may allow dumping of low-level waste if disposal would not unreasonably endanger human health or the marine environment or its economic potential. In reviewing applications, NRC considers the volume and concentration of the material to be dumped, the projected disposal site, disposal method, and the persistence of any permanent adverse effects.

96 Stat. 2165

On 6th January 1983, Congress enacted a two-year moratorium on ocean disposal of low-level radioactive waste except for small amounts to be disposed of for research or demonstration purposes.

d) Uranium mill tailings

Uranium Mill Tailings
Radiation Control
Act of 1978
92 Stat. 3021
42 USC 7901 *et seq.*

In passing the Uranium Mill Tailings Radiation Control Act of 1978, Congress found that mill tailings at active and inactive uranium milling operations may pose a significant health hazard, especially through potential radon diffusion into the environment. In co-operation with interested States, Indian tribes, and site users, the Act provides for assessment and remedial action at inactive sites and, where appropriate, for reprocessing tailings to extract any remaining uranium or unstable materials. The Act also establishes a program to regulate mill tailings during uranium or thorium ore processing at active mill operations and after termination of such operations in order to stabilize and control such tailings in a safe and environmentally sound manner, and to minimize or eliminate radiation health hazards to the public.

92 Stat. 3021,
Section 102
42 USC 7912

The DOE is directed to designate inactive uranium processing sites for remedial action, and to complete any remedial action at such locations.

92 Stat. 3021,
Section 106
42 USC 7916

Relying on the advice of EPA, DOE develops remedial action priorities at each site. When appropriate, DOE can require States to purchase real property for disposal sites. If a property owner voluntarily undertook remedial action prior to the date of enactment of the Act, he may ask for reimbursement. When necessary, DOE can purchase lands for potential disposal sites, and in some cases can utilize land owned by the Department of the Interior.

92 Stat. 3021,
Section 108
42 USC 7918

DOE, after promulgation of health and safety standards by EPA, can solicit proposals from private parties who want to reprocess mill tailings. Then DOE must decide whether recovery of residual minerals at each site is practical, depending upon source material concentration remaining in the residue. A person allowed to recover any mineral must remit a share of the resulting profit to the DOE in order to

173

repay DOE for any remedial actions in rehabilitating the site. At present, DOE is planning remedial actions at 24 inactive uranium mill processing sites.

6. NUCLEAR THIRD PARTY LIABILITY[5]

68 Stat. 919,
Sections 2*(i)* and 170
42 USC 2012 and 2210

The Price-Anderson Act, passed in 1957 as an amendment to the Atomic Energy Act of 1954, provides a source of funds to pay public liability claims resulting from a nuclear incident.

68 Stat. 919,
Section 11*(q)*
42 USC 2014*(q)*

A *nuclear incident* is any occurrence within the United States, causing personal injury or property damage inside or outside the United States, resulting from hazardous properties of special nuclear, source or by-produce materials.

As originally passed, the Act limited total liability for any single nuclear accident to $500 million in government funds plus the amount of liability insurance available in the private market – $60 million at the time. The Act provided that if damages from a nuclear accident exceeded the amount of private insurance coverage ($60 million), the Federal Government would indemnify the utility licensees in an amount not to exceed $500 million. The obligation by the government to provide funds once private insurance has been exhausted is referred to as "government indemnity". The total ceiling on liability was therefore the sum of private insurance coverage plus government indemnity that amounted to $560 million in 1957.

Originally promulgated for a period of ten years, the Price-Anderson Act was amended several times. In 1967, it was extended for a further ten-year period and in 1975 it was again extended until 1st August 1987.

10 CFR, Part 140

The ensuing legislation, as implemented by NRC's regulations, provides a three-layered system to meet public liability claims in the event of a nuclear incident causing personal injury or property damage. The first layer of this system requires all licensees of commercial nuclear power plants rated at 100 electrical megawatts or more to provide proof of financial protection in an amount equal to the maximum liability insurance available from private sources. Currently, this level is $160 million.

The second layer consists of a deferred premium plan, developed through consultation between the Government and

---

5. For further details, see the Analytical Study in the same series: "Nuclear Third Party Liability", OECD/NEA, 1976.

insurers and enacted into law. Under this retrospective premium system, nuclear power utilities would share liability for any damage exceeding $160 million that results from a nuclear incident. Each commercial reactor licensee would be assessed a pro rata share of damages up to the statutory maximum of $5 million per reactor per incident. This amount cannot exceed $10 million per reactor annually if there are successive incidents.

Until recently, the Government contributed the difference between $560 million and the sum of the first and second layers. That sum has now reached $560 million [$160 million (first stage) + $400 million (second stage)]. Government indemnity has therefore been phased out. The Government collected fees for these indemnity agreements, which decreased as the Government's potential contribution was phased out. Henceforth, the limit of liability for a single nuclear incident will increase without limit in increments of $5 million for each new commercial reactor licensed.

68 Stat. 919,
Section 170*(i)*
42 USC 2210*(i)*

If a nuclear incident occurring in the United States is of such magnitude that anticipated damage awards exceed $560 million, Congress, taking into consideration a report prepared by NRC on the incident's causes and effects, must review the incident, and may take whatever action is necessary and appropriate to protect the public.

Although the Price-Anderson Act extends through 1987, the Nuclear Regulatory Commission has meanwhile submitted a report to Congress recommending the measures to be taken in its respect. (NUREG-0957, 1st August 1983).

7. NUCLEAR SECURITY[6]

a) Information and restricted data

68 Stat. 919,
Section 11*(y)*
42 USC 2014
68 Stat. 919,
Sections 141 and 142
42 USC 2161 and 2162
68 Stat. 919,
Sections 142*(e)* and 143
42 USC 2163

A major component of the national domestic safeguards system is the control and declassification of restricted data. The term *Restricted Data* means all data concerning 1) design, manufacture or utilization of atomic weapons; 2) the production of special nuclear material; 3) the use of special nuclear material in the production of energy. DOE reviews restricted data and declassifies as much as possible in order to enlarge public understanding and disseminate technical information. The Department of Defense participates in this

---

6. This study does not describe detailed United States regulations related to defense and emergency preparedness.

175

68 Stat. 919,
Section 144
42 USC 2164

process, and the Central Intelligence Agency participates when the information to be reviewed for declassification involves the atomic energy programs of other nations. The energy agencies can divulge restricted data to other nations when authorized by an international agreement, but cannot reveal information about design and fabrication of nuclear weapons. In co-operation with regional defense organizations, the United States may share certain types of weapons information.

68 Stat. 919,
Section 145
42 USC 2165

10 CFR Parts 10 and 11

The Office of Personnel Management can supervise security checks on licensees or persons holding government contracts. There are elaborate criteria for determining employee access to restricted data, and appellate procedures under the aegis of a Personnel Security Board. When necessary, the President can involve the Federal Bureau of Investigation (FBI) in security checks.

10 CFR 9.100
10 CFR 9.3

In concert with the foregoing regulations, NRC and DOE participate in a wider information disclosure system. First, there are rules mandating public hearings conducted according to standards outlined in the "Sunshine Act." Both agencies also process requests under the Freedom of Information Act. Most inquiries usually concern generic health and safety issues about the construction and operation of nuclear plants, and transport of spent fuel.

68 Stat. 919,
Section 147
42 USC 2167

Through rulemaking, including appropriate notice and comment procedures, the NRC can safeguard information about the licensee's security measures and material accounting procedures if disclosure would endanger public health or the common defense by increasing the likelihood of theft, diversion or sabotage.

b) Domestic safeguards

NRC takes measures to deter, prevent and respond to the unauthorized possession or use of special nuclear material, and to the sabotage of nuclear facilities. In general, safeguards for fuel facilities emphasize protection against theft or diversion of special nuclear material, while those for power reactors stress protection against radiological sabotage.

10 CFR 73.26

Less than one-fourth of the licensed fuel cycle facilities must meet the stringent requirements for physical protection required of facilities having formula quantities of materials. Formula quantities consist of over 5 kg of highly enriched uranium, or more than 2 kg of plutonium.

10 CFR 73.67
10 CFR 73.55
10 CFR Part 75

Most fuel cycle facilities are subject to rules on licensee fixed site and in-transit requirements for physical protection of special nuclear material of moderate and low strategic significance. These rules control access to plants by mandating various detection systems. Entry controls and constant surveillance ensure security. Only authorized material place-ment and movement occur. Isolation zones permit security personnel to seal off potential threats. Regulations stipulate special training for guards and provide for communication with central alarm facilities. Frequent emergency testing maintains system efficiency. In the case of radiological sabotage, plants must establish special communications with local law enforcement officials. Security guards have authority to use deadly force if they reasonably believe it necessary for their own self defense or the defense of others. These domestic safeguards are in concert with regulations published in 1980 implementing the US-IAEA safeguards agreement.

Another aspect of domestic safeguards concerns accounting and inventory control to detect losses of nuclear material. The physical inventory method is time-consuming and reasons for discrepancies are often difficult to ascertain. NRC is currently working to reform and amend this procedure.

c) Export of nuclear equipment and technology[7]

Nuclear Non-Proliferation Act of 1978 92 Stat. 120 22 USC 3201

Trade in nuclear materials and technology involves several agencies. The NRC licenses exports of nuclear facilities, materials and components, while the DOE controls technology exports and bilateral and multilateral technical exchange agreements. DOE also assumes primary responsi-bility for "subsequent arrangements" pursuant to co-opera-tion agreements; for example, approval of reprocessing of United States-supplied nuclear materials or re-transfer of United States-supplied materials between foreign nations. The Department of Commerce licenses exports of dual-use equipment and the balance of plant items related to nuclear facilities. Procedures for executive branch judgments on exports involve the Departments of State, Defense, Energy, and Commerce and the Arms Control and Disarmament Agency, as well as the Nuclear Regulatory Commission under the Nuclear Non-Proliferation Act of 1978.

The NRC licenses exports of reactors, isotope separation plants, reprocessing plants, heavy water production facilities, plants for fabrication of nuclear reactor fuel elements, some components for the above facilities, special nuclear material, source material, by-product material, deuterium and nuclear grade graphite. Technical know-how, design, fabrication, and operation of such facilities are also subject to special rules

---

7. Major publications of DOE and NRC treat export and import as part of nuclear non-proliferation policy. Therefore, this information appears here rather than in Chapter 2 concerning radioactive substances, nuclear fuels and equipment.

implemented by DOE. Technical data includes information of any kind such as a model, prototype, blueprint, or operating manual as well as intangible technical services. To decide whether to grant a license, DOE and the Department of Commerce consider the stated end use and significance of the commodity or technical data, availability from non-United States sources, guarantees against use for explosive purposes or proliferation, the country's participation in international energy agencies and intelligence data on a country's nuclear intentions and activities. The exporter, while responsible for the license application, must ask the manufacturer for relevant data when deciding whether an application is necessary.

92 Stat. 120,
Section 403
68 Stat. 919,
Section 123
42 USC 2153
92 Stat. 120,
Sections 201 to 203
22 USC 3241 to 3243

The Nuclear Non-Proliferation Act requires the President to initiate discussions with supplier and receiver nations to develop new international approaches to nuclear energy. Working in co-ordination with the IAEA, DOE will initiate training for foreigners to disseminate new safeguards techniques.

68 Stat. 919,
Section 126
42 USC 2155
Foreign Assistance
Act of 1961
75 Stat. 424,
Section 669
22 USC 2429
75 Stat. 424,
Section 670
22 USC 2429 and 2751

The Foreign Assistance Act of 1961, as amended, precludes economic assistance to countries which deliver nuclear enrichment equipment or technology to other countries, unless the recipient country co-operates with multilateral and international safeguards agreements. A receiving country subject to the Act cannot obtain such materials from third countries without placing them under multinational control subject to IAEA safeguards. The President, nevertheless, can furnish assistance otherwise prohibited if termination would be seriously prejudicial to the achievement of the Government's non-proliferation objectives, and provided that the receiving nation transmits reliable assurances that it will not acquire or develop nuclear weapons.

8. TRANSPORT[8]

49 CFR 173.393(b)

The Federal Government regulates the transport of radioactive materials primarily through the NRC and Department of Transportation (DOT). States also regulate transport under certain circumstances, and monitor shipments of hazardous materials in conjunction with NRC and

8. For further details see Analytical Study in the same series: "Regulations Governing the Transport of Radioactive Materials", OECD/NEA, 1980.

DOT. NRC and DOT partition their regulatory responsibilities through a "Memorandum of Understanding" which helps to avoid duplication. For international shipments, DOT is the designated authority for implementing IAEA safeguards, but NRC advises DOT on technical matters. In practice, the NRC reviews and approves all package designs of American origin for Type B and/or fissile materials in the case of domestic shipments.

68 Stat. 919,
Sections 57, 69 and 81
42 USC 2077, 2099
and 2111

The Atomic Energy Act of 1954 requires a general or specific license to possess or transfer source material, special nuclear material, or by-product material. Licensing decisions depend on the physical characteristics and quantities of material as well as upon the intended use.

10 CFR 30.13, 40.12
and 70.12

Subject to certain restrictions, NRC regulations in 10 CFR, Part 71 grant to specific licensees a general license to transfer radioactive material to a carrier for transport. Common and contract carriers, warehousemen, freight forwarders, and the United States Postal Service are specifically exempt from NRC licensing.

Transportation Safety
Act of 1974
88 Stat. 2156,
Sections 104 and 105
49 USC 1803 and 1804

The Transportation Safety Act of 1974, incorporating the Hazardous Materials Transportation Act, specifically designated radioactive material as hazardous. Transport regulations cover not only carriage (DOT), but also packing, handling, and re-handling (NRC).

88 Stat. 2156,
Section 112
49 USC 1811

Within the DOT, the Federal Highway Administration, Federal Railroad Administration, United States Coast Guard, and Federal Aviation Administration monitor and enforce multimodal regulations promulgated by the Materials Transportation Bureau (MTB), Office of Hazardous Materials Regulation. Each agency within DOT also makes its own rules for whichever transport modality it governs. States regulate transport of small quantities of source, by-product, and special nuclear material too small to form a critical mass; in general, however, State regulations cannot be inconsistent with federal guidelines.

68 Stat. 919,
Section 147
42 USC 2167

10 CFR Part 73

The Commission publicly discloses all routes and quantities of material transported. Such disclosures are made ten days after shipment. NRC teams conduct field studies of proposed routes, working closely with licensees and State and local law enforcement personnel. In 1981, the NRC published a final rule providing for advance notice to State authorities for shipments of nuclear waste (including spent nuclear fuel) to, through, or across the boundaries of a State. Notice is not required where the waste shipment does not pose a potentially significant hazard to the health and safety of the public. Of the estimated 400 000 packages of radioactive waste and spent fuel shipped each year, only a few hundred require such notification. Strict physical protection requirements control the transport of quantities which exceed a threshold value of special nuclear material content. The Government can require approved route plans, armed escort, vehicle immobilization, communication equipment, constant surveillance, and periodic reporting.

89 Stat. 413,
Section 201

An amendment to the Energy Reorganization Act of 1974 forbids the NRC to license any air shipment of plutonium except for medical use, without safe containers. Two packages, certified in 1978 and 1981, now are in use, and are able to withstand the crash of a high speed jet aircraft as well as crushing, puncturing, slashing, fire, and deep underwater immersion.

49 CFR 174.89,
174.14,
174.700 and
174.715

If the shipper selects rail transport, he must place the radioactive packages away from explosives or cars occupied by railroad personnel. DOT regulations limit the amount of material which may be transported at any one time. Special tables incorporated into the regulations dictate the minimum distance which may exist between packages and people, animals, or other radioactive parcels if the packages are stored in a warehouse, depot, or rail car. Special decontamination requirements apply when rolling stock is used to transport radioactive materials.

49 CFR 177.834 and
177.870

When the shipper plans to transport material by road, special precautions in the DOT regulations govern storage and loading of packages and the gross weight to be carried. In addition, the NRC imposes special handling and surveillance requirements similar to those outlined for rail transport. There are also DOT spatial limitations on shipment placement within vehicles and special reporting requirements in case of an accident.

The Coast Guard, as assisted by the National Cargo Bureau, Inc., inspects cargo stowed for shipment on inland waterways or the high seas. If a foreign ship does not enter internal waters of the United States, it may transit the territorial sea without meeting complex American packaging requirements as long as the shipment is in compliance with the International Maritime Organization (IMO) Code.

DOT, the Federal Emergency Management Agency, and representatives of industry and State governments are developing a model emergency response planning program for use by shippers and carriers. These agencies, assisted by DOT, DOE, EPA, and the Food and Drug Administration (FDA), published guidelines for State and local governments.

9. PATENTS

68 Stat. 919,
Section 31

When an inventor seeks to patent an invention impinging on some facet of nuclear energy, all usual federal procedural

42 USC 2051
10 CFR Part 81

and substantive patent laws apply. In addition, NRC and DOE each have special statutes, regulations, procedures, and requirements. A description of the NRC model follows; a model for DOE would be essentially similar. NRC conducts significant research and development programs through grants, loans, contracts, and other types of arrangements. These endeavours result in scientific discoveries which can be the subject of patent applications.

68 Stat. 919,
Section 155
42 USC 2185

The fact that the invention or discovery was known or used before shall be a bar to the patenting of such invention or discovery even though such prior knowledge or use was under secrecy classification within the atomic energy program of the United States.

68 Stat. 919,
Section 152
42 USC 2182

Any invention or discovery made or conceived in the course of or under any contract or other arrangement entered into with, or for, the benefit of the NRC shall be vested in, and be the property of, the NRC, except that the NRC may waive its claim to any such invention or discovery. If there is a disagreement between the applicant for a patent and the NRC as to whether or not an invention or discovery was made or conceived under such a contract or other arrangement, the applicant may request a hearing before a Board of Patent Interferences. The Board shall follow the rules and procedures established for interference cases and either the applicant or the NRC may appeal its final order to the Court of Appeals for the Federal Circuit.

68 Stat. 919,
Section 153
42 USC 2183
68 Stat. 919,
Sections 154, 156
and 157
42 USC 2184, 2186
and 2187

In addition, after a hearing, NRC can declare any patent to be "affected with the public interest" if 1) the invention or discovery covered by the patent is of primary importance in the production or utilization of special nuclear material or atomic energy; and 2) the licensing of such invention or discovery is of primary importance to effectuate the policies and purposes of the Atomic Energy Act. Provided that appropriate hearings are held, the NRC can use the patent itself, or grant licenses if the discovery is of sufficient importance to the conduct of an activity by such licensee. The NRC has standard specifications which serve as the basis for granting a patent license. Once NRC issues a license, no court can grant injunctive relief prohibiting disclosure and use. The inventor's recourse is to file for royalties. In determining a reasonable royalty fee, the NRC shall take into consideration a) the advice of the Patent Compensation Board; b) any defense, general or special, that might be pleaded by a defendant in an action for infringement; c) the extent to which, if any, such patent was developed through federally financed research; and d) the degree of utility, novelty, and importance of the invention or discovery. The NRC may consider the cost to the patent owner of developing such invention, or discovery, or acquiring such patent.

10 CFR 81.11

The inventions covered by U.S. patents, and patent applications vested in the Government of the United States as represented by NRC, normally will best serve the public interest when they are developed to the point of practical application and made available to the public in the shortest time possible. NRC generally prefers to issue non-exclusive licenses to all interested parties. Whenever the NRC deems it appropriate to grant an exclusive license, the license is negotiated on terms and conditions most favourable to the interests of the public and the Government. In considering the request for such a license, due weight will be given to assisting small business and minority business enterprises, as well as economically depressed, low income and labor surplus areas within the United States.

10 CFR 81.30 and 81.31

NRC does issue limited exclusive licenses if the NRC determines that 1) the invention may be brought to the point of practical application in certain fields of use or in certain geographical locations by exclusive licensing; 2) the desired practical application has not been achieved under any non-exclusive license granted on the invention; and 3) the desired practical application is not likely to be achieved expeditiously under a non-exclusive license or as a result of further government-funded research or development. Third parties can oppose exclusivity. The determination of exclusive licensees depends on the capacity of the applicant to further technology and market development, the efficacy of his development plan, the projected impact on competition, and the benefit to the government. In addition, the NRC considers whether the applicant is a small or minority businessman or from economically depressed, low income or labor surplus areas, and whether the applicant is a United States citizen or corporation.

10 CFR 81.52 and 81.53

In accordance with NRC procedures, an applicant for a license, a licensee or a third party shall have the right to appeal any decision of the NRC concerning the grant, denial, interpretation, modification, or revocation of a license. The NRC will designate an Invention Licensing Appeal Board to decide such an appeal on the record and evidence submitted by the appellant and the NRC to the Board. The Board shall make findings of fact and reach a conclusion with respect to the propriety of the decision of the NRC, which conclusion shall constitute the NRC's final action on the license.

II. INSTITUTIONAL FRAMEWORK

Various governmental and non-governmental, Federal and State bodies contribute to United States nuclear regulation, power production, and research. The following Part will, however, concentrate on national regulatory and advisory bodies, and public and semi-public agencies. This introductory section will provide an overview to explain the interrelationships among these bodies.

68 Stat. 919
42 USC 2011 *et seq.*

The Federal Government assumes primary responsibility for regulating nuclear energy; moreover, federal grants and contracts fund a major portion of academic and private research and development. Until 1974, the Atomic Energy Commission (AEC) served as the umbrella agency charged with responsibility for all civilian and military projects involving atomic energy. It was an independent agency, with Commissioners appointed by the President. Once confirmed by the Senate, the President could not remove appointees at will; therefore, AEC was to a large extent insulated from the political process.

88 Stat. 1233
42 USC 5801 *et seq.*

91 Stat. 565
42 USC 7101 *et seq.*

88 Stat. 1233,
Section 201
42 USC 5841

91 Stat. 565,
Section 201
42 USC 7101 *et seq.*

In 1974, in order to separate regulatory activities from the promotion of nuclear energy, Congress split AEC's functions, setting up the Nuclear Regulatory Commission (NRC) to license most commercial use of nuclear materials, and the Energy Research and Development Administration (ERDA) to take over all other AEC responsibilities. Then in 1977, Congress abolished ERDA, incorporating its functions into a new Department of Energy. The NRC, like the AEC, is an independent administrative agency headed by Commissioners who cannot be removed except for malfeasance in office. On the other hand, the Secretary of Energy, is appointed by the President with the advice and consent of the Senate, and serves at his pleasure.

5 USC, Appendix I

Various advisory bodies assist federal agencies. Under the Federal Advisory Committee Act, most advisory bodies must be fairly balanced in terms of points of view represented and the functions to be performed; the meetings must be open to the public. Usually these committees consist of experts or officials who advise on technical matters or policy issues. In some instances, special working groups composed of representatives from many Government agencies work together as planning groups, serving in an advisory capacity.

State governments also regulate aspects of nuclear energy. There is now a *Model State Radiation Control Act.*

States take major responsibility for emergency planning. A wide range of state and local government agencies ranging from law enforcement to public health and environmental agencies participate in nuclear energy policy (see Part I).

The United States academic community also plays a major role in nuclear research and development. There are public institutions of higher learning funded by State governments, and private colleges and universities which depend on private philanthropy. These institutions receive grants and contracts from federal agencies to finance research. A few actually assume total responsibility for operating government-owned laboratories.

Many public and semi-public bodies aid in recommending policy alternatives. There are numerous societies of scientists and engineers which also set up working groups to study nuclear policy, and publish journals and informative reports. Some, such as the National Academy of Sciences or the American Nuclear Society, can be influential in policy formation.

Environmentalist and consumer groups can present oral and written testimony at hearings to consider proposed legislation and regulation. They often intervene in the licensing process, and initiate litigation.

Finally, private industry plays an important role in the energy field. Public utilities individually and as consortiums lobby for legislative proposals. The private sector has set up research groups such as the Electric Power Research Institute (EPRI) which conduct research on a non-profit basis. Some corporations operate government-owned laboratories under contract.

All of the foregoing groups help shape United States nuclear policy; however an exhaustive listing of the non-governmental entities concerned would be outside the scope of this study.

1. REGULATORY AND SUPERVISORY AUTHORITIES

As mentioned previously, NRC and DOE share most authority over nuclear affairs. The following paragraphs outline the role and structure of those agencies. A list of other federal agencies having oversight functions are arranged by the cabinet-level department to which they belong; for instance, the United States Geological Survey (USGS) is a part of the Department of the Interior.

a) Nuclear Regulatory Commission

i) Legal status

88 Stat. 1233,
Sections 2 and 201
42 USC 5801 and 5841

In 1974, Congress passed the Energy Reorganization Act creating the Nuclear Regulatory Commission (NRC) to assume the licensing function of the AEC. This independent regulatory body enjoys its own legal personality. While the Commission is responsible to the President, it exercises considerable independence in regulatory matters.

ii) Responsibilities

68 Stat. 919
42 USC 2011 *et seq.*
83 Stat. 852

The NRC is responsible for licensing and regulating nuclear materials and facilities, and for conducting research in support of the licensing and regulatory process as mandated by the Atomic Energy Act of 1954 (as amended) and other applicable statutes. These responsibilities include protecting the environment, safeguarding materials and plants in the interest of national security, and assuring conformity with antitrust laws. The Commission acts through standards setting and rulemaking, technical reviews and studies, issuance of licenses, permits and authorization, inspection, investigation, and enforcement, evaluations of operating experience, and undertaking of research and development.

68 Stat. 919,
Sections 53, 62, 83, 84
42 USC 2073, 2092,
2113 and 2114
68 Stat. 919,
Sections 103 and 104
42 USC 2133 and 2134

88 Stat. 1233
Sections 202 and 203
42 USC 5842 and 5843

The Commission issues licenses for transfer, delivery, acquisition, ownership, possession, or import of special nuclear material, source material, and by-product material. It licenses medical and academic facilities as well as commercial power reactors. NRC also licenses research projects such as breeder reactors. Licensing extends to both construction and operation of facilities and includes licensing of operating personnel (see Part I).

88 Stat. 1233,
Section 208
42 USC 5848
88 Stat. 1233,
Sections 210 and 205
42 USC 5848
88 Stat. 1233,
Sections 210 and 205
42 USC 5850 and 5845

As part of its safety program, NRC reviews the operating safety and security safeguards at each facility which it licenses. It monitors, tests, and recommends upgrading of all systems which can present a health or safety hazard, and evaluates transport and waste storage technologies to prevent radiation hazards to the general public. In conjunction with DOE, NRC develops contingency plans to deal with sabotage, threats, and thefts relating to special nuclear material, high-level waste and nuclear facilities. These programs depend on analysis of operating experience, including reports of abnormal occurrences. Additionally, NRC identifies unresolved safety issues arising during the application process or operation of facilities, and then recommends research strategies to correct deficiencies (see Part I).

68 Stat. 919,
Sections 221 to 236
42 USC 2271 to 2284

NRC maintains an active inspection and enforcement program. It can investigate violations and initiate enforcement proceedings by pursuing negotiations or holding administrative hearings and, as a last resort, by involving the federal

185

court system. NRC can seek judicial remedies such as injunctions, and can assess fines and penalties. These enforcement powers extend not only to technical violations occurring during operation, but to trespass on NRC installations, photographing of facilities, and communication of restricted data. Enforcement also involves checks on emergency preparedness and compliance with transport regulations (see Part I).

68 Stat. 919,
Sections 141 to 160
42 USC 2161 to 2190

The Energy Reorganization Act of 1974 and the Atomic Energy Act of 1954 vest NRC with additional powers to control classified or restricted data and assist the Patent Office in patenting designs or inventions related to nuclear energy. NRC itself can issue licenses to use inventions.

68 Stat. 919,
Section 274
42 USC 2021
and 2152

The NRC enters into co-operative agreements with States to help them assume the responsibility for regulating certain aspects of nuclear energy, such as medical applications and transport. The co-operating State assumes responsibilities for narrowly circumscribed facets of the regulatory function, normally assigned to NRC (see Part I).

68 Stat. 919,
Section 170
42 USC 2210

Under the Price-Anderson Act, NRC enters into indemnification agreements with nuclear reactor licensees for liability arising out of a nuclear incident. It investigates the causes of major incidents and reports to Congress.

iii) Structure

88 Stat. 1233,
Section 201
42 USC 5841

The Energy Reorganization Act of 1974 established NRC as an independent regulatory agency with five Commissioners, of whom no more than three may be members of the same political party. The President, with the advice and consent of the Senate, appoints the Commissioners, who must be United States citizens. Each Commissioner serves for five years and, during that time, may not engage in any other business or vocation. The President may remove a Commissioner only for neglect of duty, inefficiency, or malfeasance in office. Each Commissioner enjoys equal access to all data relating to Commission duties, and each has equal authority and responsibility in decision-making. In order for the Commission to act, a majority of members present must concur; however, a quorum requires the presence of three Commissioners.

88 Stat. 1233,
Section 201
42 USC 5841
and 5801

The President appoints one of the five Commissioners as Chairman who acts as the principal executive officer and the official spokesman of the Commission. The Chairman is responsible for preparing policy planning and guidance for Commission consideration, and for conducting the administrative, organisational, budgetary and certain personnel functions of the NRC.

The NRC structure consists of several offices, some of which are legislatively established in the Energy Reorganization Act of 1974. Others exist through internal organizational decisions. In the following paragraphs, appropriate references indicate which offices are established by statute.

– Commission Staff Offices

Seven offices fulfill staff functions for the Commission. Two of these, the Office of Public Affairs and the Office of Congressional Affairs, report directly to the Chairman. The other five offices report to the Commission.

The Office of Public Affairs plans and administers NRC's program to inform the public and the news media of agency policies, programs, and activities. This office also serves as a conduit between the public and the Commission, helping to communicate public concerns to Commissioners.

The Office of Congressional Affairs advises and assists the Commission and senior staff on Congressional matters. It co-ordinates NRC relations with Congress, maintaining a liaison with Congressional committees as well as with individual legislators. It also participates in planning and developing the NRC's legislative program.

The Office of the Secretary provides secretariat services for the conduct of Commission business and implementation of decisions, including planning meetings, recording deliberations, managing staff paperwork, monitoring the status of various actions and maintaining official records. This office also processes institutional correspondence, controls the service of documents in Commission proceedings, and supervises the NRC Public Document Room, where members of the public may obtain access to various Commission documents.

The Office of the General Counsel performs legal functions by assisting in the review of Appeal Board decisions, petitions seeking direct Commission relief and rulemaking proceedings. This Office drafts legal documents necessary to execute Commission decisions. The General Counsel analyses proposed legislation which would affect the Commission's functions. In addition, the Office assists in drafting legislation and preparing testimony for Congressional and administrative hearings. In conjunction with the Department of Justice, this Office represents the Commission in court proceedings.

The Office of Policy Evaluation independently reviews positions developed by the NRC staff which require policy determinations by the Commission. This office conducts analysis and projects which are self-generated or requested by the Commission.

The Office of Inspector and Auditor conducts internal audits and investigations of NRC operations, allegations of NRC employee misconduct, equal employment and civil rights complaints, and claims for personal property loss or damage. It hears employees' concerns about Commission activities. It develops policies to govern the financial and management audit program, and is the agency contact with the General Accounting Office (GAO), the agency primarily responsible for oversight and auditing of federal agencies and programs.

The Office of Investigations is a new office that assumed part of the former duties of the Office of Inspector and Auditor. It is responsible for the conduct, supervision, and quality control of investigations of licensees, applicants, contractors or vendors, including the investigation of allegations of wrong-doing by those other than NRC employees and contractors. It advises and assists the Office of Inspector and Auditor in appropriate referrals of criminal matters to the Department of Justice.

– Other Offices

Several other offices advise and assist the Commission in its licensing and regulatory responsibilities.

68 Stat. 919,
Section 29
42 USC 2039

The Advisory Committee on Reactor Safeguards (ACRS) consists of fifteen scientists and engineers who advise the Commission on safety aspects of nuclear facilities and standards. It undertakes continuous study of reactor safety research, and examines potential hazards of proposed or existing production, utilization and research facilities. It reviews certain safety issues in connection with requests for pre-application site approval, and for standard plant design approvals. The ACRS also makes recommendations on applications for construction permits and operating licenses. It must submit an annual report to Congress on the NRC Safety Research Program. The Committee's activities include providing testimony for Congressional hearings, as well as answering to specific questions posed by Congress, the NRC or individual Commissioners, and conducting site visits. It also advises DOE upon request.

The Atomic Safety Licensing Board provides a pool of hearing officers for licensing and regulatory matters. From this panel composed of lawyers and technical experts, the Commission draws three-member licensing boards. These boards conduct public hearings and render appropriate initial decisions regarding granting, suspension, renewal or amendments to NRC licenses. Those initial decisions may be appealed to the Atomic Safety and Licensing Appeal Board.

The Atomic Safety and Licensing Appeal Board also consists of lawyers and technical experts from which three-member appeal boards are selected. These appeal boards hear appeals from licensing board decisions and review those decisions on their own initiative if no appeals are filed. Appeal board decisions are reviewable by the Commission.

– *Operational Offices*

All of the other agency offices report to the Commission through the Executive Director for Operations (EDO). The EDO directs and controls the Commission's operational and administrative activities, allocating responsibilities among staff offices. He co-ordinates the development of policy options for Commission consideration, and supervises day to day operations. As the chief executive officer, he reports directly to the Chairman.

Seven offices based near Washington D.C., plus five regional offices, provide administrative support.

The Office of Administration directs agency programs for organization and personnel management. It classifies information, administers the NRC security program, and controls technical information and documents. It collects license fees and manages contracts and procurement. The office also administers the Freedom of Information Act (FOIA) and Privacy Act responsibilities of the Agency and provides various services in connection with rules, proceedings, and documents. The office co-ordinates staff development and training services, and administers agency transport and housekeeping needs.

The Office of the Executive Legal Director provides legal advice and services to the Executive Director for Operations and staff, including representation of the NRC in administrative hearings involving licensing of nuclear materials or facilities. It enforces license conditions and administrative regulations. The office provides counsel on matters of nuclear safeguards, contracts, security, patents, research, administration and personnel and drafts or reviews administrative regulations necessary to implement new statutory enactments.

The Office of Small and Disadvantaged Business Utilization and Civil Rights develops equal employment policies, recommending improvements or corrections in compliance with federal law, and monitors the agency's affirmative action program. The Office works to implement legislation to assist small businesses and businesses owned by socially or economically disadvantaged persons. It helps to channel contract awards to firms located in labor surplus areas.

The Office of Resource Management develops and maintains NRC financial and manpower management programs including accounting, budgeting, cost analysis, resource planning and analysis and data processing systems development and support. It develops management information for NRC offices, and assists the EDO in the budget review process. It also maintains a liaison with the Office of Management and Budget, other government agencies, Congressional committees, and industry.

The Office for Analysis and Evaluation of Operational Data co-ordinates collection, storage and retrieval of operational data associated with licensed activities. It then analyses and evaluates that operational experience and provides feedback to NRC activities involving licensing, standards and inspection.

It also interacts with the Advisory Committee on Reactor Safeguards and industry groups which conduct operational safety data analysis and evaluation.

The Office of International Programs plans and implements programs of international nuclear safety co-operation, creating and maintaining relationships with foreign regulatory agencies and international organizations. It co-ordinates NRC export-import and international safeguards policies, issues export and import licenses, and co-ordinates NRC responses to other agencies concerning export-import matters.

The Office of State Programs helps States implement nuclear regulatory programmes. It co-ordinates relationships with State governments and interstate bodies. It manages State co-operative agreement programs and administers the indemnification program for licensees. In addition, the Office reviews the financial qualifications of licensees and verifies that applicants are not in violation of the antitrust laws.

– Technical services

Four departments reporting to the Commission through the Executive Director for Operations are responsible for more technical aspects of the NRC's activities.

88 Stat. 1233,
Section 204
42 USC 5844

The Office of Nuclear Material Safety and Safeguards consists of three divisions: Division of Safeguards, Division of Fuel Cycle and Material Safety, and Division of Waste Management. It licenses and regulates facilities and materials associated with the processing, transport and handling of nuclear materials and disposal of nuclear waste. It regulates uranium recovery facilities. It reviews and assesses safeguards against threats, theft and sabotage for licensed facilities.

88 Stat. 1233,
Section 203
42 USC 5843

The five divisions of the Office of Nuclear Reactor Regulation are: Licensing; Engineering; Systems Integration; Safety Technology; and Human Factors Safety. The office licenses nuclear power, test, and research reactors. It reviews applications for construction permits and operating licenses so that each facility can be built and operated without undue risk to human health and safety and with minimal impact on the environment. Throughout the lifetime of a facility, the office monitors operating reactors to ensure their safe operation. It also oversees decommissioning activities.

88 Stat. 1233,
Section 205
42 USC 5845

The Office of Nuclear Regulatory Research is divided into divisions of Engineering Technology; Accident Evaluation; Risk Analysis; Facility Operations; and Health, Siting and Waste Management. Each division undertakes research necessary for the performance of the Commission's licensing and regulatory functions. The Office also analyses the effectiveness of regulations.

The Office of Inspection and Enforcement has five divisions: Fuel Facilities; Materials and Safeguards; Reactor Programs; Engineering and Quality Assurance; and Emergency Preparedness. Personnel assigned to this Office perform inspections of all licensed facilities and materials to ensure compliance with regulations. The Office identifies potentially harmful factors or conditions that may adversely affect nuclear security, the environment or human health and safety. After conducting investigations, it recommends appropriate action, such as modification, renewal, or denial of licenses. It investigates accidents, unusual occurrences and allegations of improprieties involving licensed facilities or materials. It also directs, in conjunction with the Federal Emergency Management Agency, NRC activities related to emergency preparedness, including evaluation of State and local emergency preparedness plans.

iv) Financing

NRC receives about 85% of its financial resources from the United States Treasury after Congressional appropriation of funds. NRC obtains income through bilateral and multilateral co-operative research agreements to which it is a party. The Commission also realizes income pursuant to contracts with DOE and other federal agencies. Although NRC collects fees for license applications, construction permits, operating licenses, license amendments and renewals, and inspection fees, NRC remits the fees to the federal treasury. The monies, therefore, are not available for direct Commission disbursement.

191

b) Department of Energy

i) Legal status

91 Stat. 565,
Section 201
42 USC 7101
et seq.

In 1977, Congress established the Department of Energy (DOE) to assume the responsibilities of the Energy Research and Development Administration (ERDA) and other energy-related Government organizations. DOE is a cabinet-level department in the executive branch, not an independent regulatory agency. However, it does have legal personality. Created by the DOE Organization Act, DOE administers programs pursuant to a broad variety of legislation such as the Energy Security Act, Energy Tax Act of 1978, Federal Power Act, and a myriad of other statutes.

ii) Responsibilities

DOE handles programs connected with fossil fuels and alternative energy sources in addition to tasks related to nuclear energy. The nuclear energy responsibilities constitute only a small portion of DOE's activities; for example, DOE also oversees the nation's strategic petroleum reserves, conducts electric and hybrid vehicle research and administers projects relating to geothermal and solar energy.

88 Stat. 1233,
Section 103
42 USC 5813

DOE exercises central responsibility for policy planning, co-ordination, support and management of research and development for all energy sources. It helps to shape the role of nuclear energy within the United States' total energy mix. DOE encourages demonstration projects to develop commercial feasibility and practical applications of extraction, conversion, storage, and use of nuclear energy. It supports environmental, biomedical, physical, and safety research related to nuclear energy, accumulating and disseminating data and providing assistance to industry and state and local governments. DOE also undertakes research on nuclear weaponry, and application of nuclear power systems to the space environment. It fosters competition among sectors of private industry marketing different kinds of fuel and power generated by various fuels.

91 Stat. 565,
Section 203
42 USC 7101 *et seq.*

DOE is the lead agency for nuclear waste management activities such as research, development, demonstration and planning. The NRC has authority for regulating waste management activities by non-federal entities (see Chapter on *Radioactive waste management,* above).

DOE, in consultation with NRC and the Department of State, negotiates bilateral and multilateral agreements related to energy and monitors the world energy market. It encourages development of commercial nuclear power as an energy source, and ensures that countries purchasing United States nuclear fuel conform to IAEA safeguards. Under the Nuclear Non-Proliferation Act of 1978, and the Atomic

Energy Act of 1954, DOE administers United States nuclear export policy in conjunction with NRC, the Department of State, and the Department of Commerce. DOE approves contracts for the sale of special nuclear materials and enrichment services to foreign nations; moreover, DOE participates in reviews of export licenses for equipment, reactors, and nuclear material. Finally, DOE approves re-transfers of United States origin nuclear material by foreign governments.

iii) Structure

91 Stat. 565,
Section 203
42 USC 7101 *et seq.*

DOE is a cabinet level executive department headed by the Secretary of Energy, who is appointed by the President with the advice and consent of the Senate. The Secretary decides major policy issues and is the energy advisor among cabinet officers.

91 Stat. 565,
Section 202
42 USC 7101 *et seq.*

The President appoints a Deputy Secretary, and an Under Secretary. The Deputy Secretary acts in the absence or disability of the Secretary. Like the Secretary, the Deputy Secretary deals with the overall administration of the Department. The Under Secretary, however, bears primary responsibility for energy conservation.

The President, with the advice and consent of the Senate, appoints eight Assistant Secretaries. Each is responsible for a segment of DOE's program (see below).

In 1981, DOE was reorganized in order to focus DOE's objectives more narrowly than at its inception. Presently, DOE emphasizes programs that require Government intervention. DOE is more involved in national security and defense, high cost or high risk research and development, and energy emergency preparedness and response.

– *Federal Energy Regulatory Commission*

91 Stat. 565,
Sections 204 and 401
42 USC 7107 *et seq.*

This Commission, part of the Department of Energy, operates independent of control or supervision by the Secretary; hence, although the Commission reports to the President through the Secretary, it is insulated from overt political pressure. The five members, no more than three of whom can be from the same political party, are appointed by the President with the advice and consent of the Senate. The members cannot be removed except for neglect of duty, inefficiency, or malfeasance.

The Commission oversees domestic interstate operations of electric utilities, hydroelectric plants, and oil and gas pipelines. Its goal is to ensure adequate energy supplies at reasonable prices while allowing producers sufficient latitude to operate in the free market place. The Commission deals with nuclear energy only to the extent that decisions influence the determination of an overall energy mix.

– Staff offices

Nine offices or administrative officials now report directly to the Secretary and Deputy Secretary.

91 Stat. 565,
Section 503
42 USC 7107 *et seq.*

The Office of Hearings and Appeals is responsible for DOE adjudications including reviewing applications for exemptions from DOE rules, regulations, or orders. It considers legal or factual issues before issuance of remedial orders to persons who have allegedly violated the regulations issued pursuant to the Emergency Petroleum Allocation Act of 1973. It also acts as the appeals authority for initial agency determinations made pursuant to the Freedom of Information Act and the Privacy Act.

The Energy Board of Contract Appeals hears and decides issues relating to contracts with DOE, and financial assistance programs. With respect to nuclear energy, this Board hears appeals on invention licensing for designs or products useful in producing or exploiting nuclear energy.

91 Stat. 565,
Section 202 *(b)*
42 USC 7107 *et seq.*

The Office of the General Counsel is responsible for all DOE legal services.

The Assistant Secretary for Management and Administration co-ordinates department support services. These include project construction and facility management, procurement policy and operations, financial assistance management, budget and financial policy and operations, and minority participation in department actions.

The Inspector General, appointed by the President and confirmed by the Senate, conducts audits, inspections and investigations of DOE programs and operations to promote efficiency and prevent fraud or abuse. This broad function extends to monitoring contractor activities.

The Assistant Secretary for Congressional Intergovernmental and Public Affairs, supervises five offices consolidating the department's external programs. The Congressional Affairs Office is the principal contact between Congress and DOE, co-ordinating appearances by officials at Congressional hearings and monitoring new legislation and bills affecting DOE. It in turn informs Congress of DOE activities. The Office of Intergovernmental Affairs encourages State, local, tribal and territorial governments in formulation of energy policy. Through this office, DOE solicits views of governors, local leaders, and non-governmental organizations. The Office of Public Affairs inventories department public information resources and makes exhibits, publications, and speakers available. The Office of Consumer Affairs provides citizens with information and promotes participation in notice and comment procedures and public hearings, a function assuming new importance now as hearings on waste management policy are held. The office tries to work toward public consensus on energy policy. The Office of Competition seeks solutions which would be the least intrusive on a free market economy.

Finally, the Office of Minority Economic Impact undertakes studies on the impact of energy policy, including reactor siting, on the minority community.

The Office of Policy Planning and Analysis co-ordinates policy with program development to ensure institutional coherence. It drafts major policy documents such as the National Energy Policy Plan of July 1981.

The Assistant Secretary for International Affairs is responsible for the international component of overall energy policy; therefore, he represents the Department in international and integovernmental discussions.

– *Operational Offices*

Eight officials or offices and all regional field offices report to the Secretary through the Under Secretary, the chief operating officer of the Department who integrates overall policy with program development and execution.

91 Stat. 565,
Section 203
42 USC 7107 *et seq.*

The Assistant Secretary for Nuclear Energy serves as the principal advisor to the Secretary on nuclear fission energy, and is responsible for DOE non-weapons related nuclear research and development. He is assisted by Deputy Assistant Secretaries for Uranium Enrichment and Assessment, Breeder Reactor Programs, and Naval Reactors and the Directors for Converter Reactor Deployment, Terminal Waste Disposal and Remedial Action, Spent Fuel Management and Reprocessing Systems. He supervises construction and operation of nuclear research and demonstration reactors and undertakes associated research and development activities. In conjunction with the Department of the Navy, this Office is responsible for all aspects of naval reactors. In conjunction with Assistant Secretaries for International Affairs and Defense Programs and the Department of State, the Assistant Secretary for Nuclear Energy speaks for the Department on nuclear non-proliferation. He also assumes responsibility for research in the area of safe and environmentally acceptable disposal of radioactive waste. Finally, he supervises uranium enrichment activities.

91 Stat. 565
Section 203
42 USC 7107 *et seq.*

The Assistant Secretary for Defense Programs advises the Secretary on national security matters, including authorization for unclassified nuclear activities outside of the United States. He directs design, testing and production of special nuclear material for weapons. He oversees safeguards and security related to facilities, material and information, overlapping into the civilian sector. Moreover, he directs United States efforts to verify test treaty compliance and collaborates with other authorities to assure non-proliferation. He ensures that nuclear exports are not contrary to national security. He oversees research and development on inertial confinement fusion technology (controlled thermonuclear fusion).

The Assistant Secretary for Environmental Protection, Safety and Emergency Preparedness guides environmental impact and assessment programs and reviews safety technology issues involving all energy technology. He carries out studies regarding the effects of radioactivity on health and engages in environmental risk analysis. He co-ordinates plans to respond to civilian and military nuclear incidents, accidents, and national emergencies.

The Director of Energy Research advises the Secretary of Energy on the Department's physical research programs, its overall energy research and development programs, environmental and health effects research, university-based education and training activities, grants and other forms of financial assistance. It is the Director's responsibility to advise the Secretary with respect to the well-being and management of the multi-program laboratories under the jurisdiction of the Department, excluding nuclear weapons laboratories. He co-ordinates the Department's Institutional Planning Process and the development of policy for the utilization of the multi-program laboratories.

DOE conducts programs at fifty-four plants and research and development laboratories which account for about half of DOE's annual budget. Nine are multi-program laboratories while the remainder are dedicated to a single program.

In general, the multi-program laboratories support two or more programs and are large multidisciplinary facilities with broad capabilities in physical, chemical, nuclear and life sciences, as well as nuclear, electrical, mechanical, and other branches of engineering. Program-dedicated research and development facilities, on the other hand, provide services primarily to a single program. These facilities are all government-owned and most are contractor-operated.

The Institutional Planning Process is the management tool for DOE overview of the direction and development of the multi-program national laboratories. The process results in an annually updated five-year plan, which is reviewed by the Field and Laboratory Co-ordination Council. The Council, a senior DOE management body, reviews, discusses and resolves significant issues and policy questions pertaining to the utilization and management of DOE research and development laboratories and pertaining to the co-ordination of related departmental activities.

Eight departmental field offices (Operations Offices) administer the work carried out by the DOE laboratory and plant facilities.

iv) Financing

The DOE receives most of its revenue from the United States Treasury, after Congressional appropriations. DOE, however, is a direct energy supplier. It markets hydroelectricity generated by federal water projects, provides uranium enrichment services to meet domestic and foreign customers and produces petroleum from the Naval Petroleum Reserves. DOE furnishes uranium enrichment services and hydroelectric power at prices based on the cost of providing these services.

c) Department of Labor

This cabinet-level Department has overall responsibility for worker safety. The *Occupational Health and Safety Administration* (OHSA) develops and promotes occupational health and safety standards, conducts inspections, and issues penalties. The *Mine Safety and Health Administration* develops mine safety and health standards, proposes penalties for violations of the standards, investigates accidents and co-operates with States in developing mine safety and health programs.

d) Department of Transportation

This cabinet-level Department works with DOE and NRC to co-ordinate transport of hazardous materials. The *Materials Transportation Bureau* (MTB) promulgates regulations for all modes of transport of nuclear materials and waste.

e) Environmental Protection Agency

This Agency (EPA) assumes overall responsibility for United States environmental quality. Within the agency, the *Office of Radiation Programs,* managed by the Office of the Assistant Administrator for Air, Noise, and Radiation, establishes generally applicable environmental standards for releases of radiation into the environment. It promulgates rules limiting emission of hazardous pollutants into the atmosphere. It provides technical assistance to State radiation protection agencies, setting up a surveillance and inspection system for measuring radiation levels in the environment. EPA also establishes standards for disposal of radioactive wastes.

2. ADVISORY BODIES

Federal Advisory Committees

Each federal agency may have a number of advisory committees which assist it in developing policies, priorities, or research plans. As an example the following listing is arranged according to the federal agency to which the panel is responsible.

a) NRC Advisory Committees

The following panels advise and assist the NRC

68 Stat. 919,
Section 161 *(a)*
42 USC 2201

The Advisory Panel for Decontamination of Three Mile Island Unit 2 consists of local residents and public officials residing in, or responsible for, Harrisburg, Pennsylvania. It was formed in October 1980 to provide advice on major stages of the clean-up. The panel solicits views of members of the public and interacts with Congress and other federal agencies to help assure the safe and expeditious clean-up of the damaged reactor.

10 CFR 1.21*(a)*

The Advisory Committee on the Medical Use of Isotopes, composed of physicians and scientists, considers medical questions referred to it by the NRC staff, rendering opinions on medical uses of radioactive material and providing advice on policy matters concerning those uses.

b) DOE Advisory Committees

68 Stat. 919,
Section 163
42 USC 2203

DOE established several advisory committees pursuant to authority conferred by the Department of Energy Organization Act. A few of them consult on nuclear energy matters.

The DOE/National Science Foundation (NSF) Nuclear Science Advisory Committee provides advice to DOE and NSF concerning needed basic nuclear research including experimental and theoretical physics. Recommendations concentrate on fundamental properties of atomic nuclei. Members assess adequacy of current facilities, institutional balance of support for optimized scientific productivity and training of nuclear scientists, and links with allied sciences, and then define research objectives.

In the summer of 1983, a new *Advisory Panel on Alternative Means of Financing and Managing Radioactive Waste Facilities* was formed to study and report to the DOE on alternative means of financing and managing civilian radioactive waste facilities, pursuant to Section 303 of the Nuclear Waste Policy Act of 1982. The panel's report will include a thorough and objective analysis of the advantages and disadvantages of each alternative approach.

The Energy Research Advisory Board, which advises the Secretary, the Deputy Secretary, the Director of Energy Research and the Assistant Secretary for Policy and Evaluations, guides overall research and development. The Board consists of representatives from industry, universities, utilities, government and public interest groups.

The High Energy Physics Advisory Panel also has responsibility for some nuclear related areas.

c) Department of Health and Human Services

Two Groups, the Medical Radiation Advisory Committee (Radiation Study Section), and the Radiopharmaceutical Drugs Advisory Committee help develop regulations and set research priorities for the Food and Drug Administration of the Public Health Service.

3. PUBLIC AND SEMI-PUBLIC AGENCIES

The following federal agencies sometimes exert regulatory authority over some aspects of nuclear energy; however, the major thrust of their activities is research oriented or advisory in nature. For example, while the Department of Commerce regulates the export of technology, it also develops measurement standardization schemes. The Department of Defense, responsible for military weaponry, overlaps into the civilian sector. Agencies are listed alphabetically by cabinet-level department. Then, independent federal agencies follow, and, finally, a few semi-public groups are noted.

A. CABINET-LEVEL DEPARTMENTS

a) Department of Agriculture

This cabinet-level department advises DOE and NRC about potential impact of nuclear facility siting in rural areas and on lands controlled by the Forest Service. Within the Department, the Science and Education Administration funds research in the life sciences and studies and promotes the use of radioisotopes in agriculture.

b) Department of Commerce

This Department licenses exports of certain components for nuclear plants. Within the Department, the *National Bureau of Standards* operates the *Centre for Radiation Research* which develops improvements in radiation measurement and instrument callibration. The *National Oceanic and Atmospheric Administration* researches the occurrence of radionuclides in estuaries. It studies the effect of radioactive materials on marine organisms and seeks application of radioactive tracers to fisheries problems.

c) Department of Defense

Within the Department of Defense (DOD), several agencies study medical applications of nuclear technology, such as the *Armed Forces Radiobiology Research Institute* which develops biomedical applications of isotopes and examines long-term effects of radiation exposure, and the Uniformed Services University of the Health Sciences, which does research on nuclear safety and dosimetry.

d) Department of Health and Human Services

Under the auspices of the Department of Health and Human Services (DHHS), the Public Health Service sponsors health research.

The Office of Radiological Health operates programs to reduce exposure to hazards of ionizing as well as non-ionizing radiation. It prepares standards for safe exposure limits, and develops methods for controlling exposure, especially to radiation emitted by electronic products.

The National Cancer Institute of Health, Radiation Oncology Branch undertakes clinical and laboratory research for direct medical management of cancer patients, concentrating on simulating cellular kinetics in the laboratory in order to better sequence radiotherapy.

e) Department of the Interior

Three separate agencies within this cabinet-level department assist in developing nuclear resources. The *United Stated Geological Survey (USGS)* conducts field and laboratory investigations supporting DOE waste disposal efforts, and collaborates with DOE on earth science technology. It conducts research on processes related to nuclear waste disposal and characterization of potential disposal sites. It consults with NRC on earth science matters related to regulation of waste repositories and the licensing of nuclear facilities. It assisted DOE with the National Uranium Resource Evaluation Program, and continues to perform limited assessment of uranium resources. Finally, USGS is implementing a nuclear hydrology program to study the movement of radioactive material in groundwater.

The Denver Federal Center makes field and laboratory studies of radioactive minerals and radiogenic isotopes related to geochronology. It is also conducting research to trace the movement of water, and is comparing geohydrologic environments for radioactive waste disposal.

The Bureau of Land Management, as custodian of federal lands, reviews proposals involving federally controlled land (e.g. waste disposal).

f) Department of State

DOE and NRC negotiate international accords in concert with the Department of State (DOS). The DOS negotiates agreements for co-operation and evaluates political, military and legal ramifications of export agreements. With the advent of the Nuclear Non-Proliferation Act of 1978, DOS plays a more active role, screening agreements and contracts for compliance with United States nuclear law and policy.

Within the State Department, the *Bureau of Oceans and International Environmental and Scientific Affairs* is responsible for formulation and implementation of policies and proposals concerning nuclear non-proliferation, nuclear exports, and other aspects of nuclear policy in relation to other nations and international organizations. The office assists DOE in negotiating contracts for technology transfers.

B. OTHER FEDERAL AGENCIES AND OFFICES

a) Federal Emergency Management Agency

This Agency (FEMA) assumes lead responsibility for all off-site nuclear emergency planning and response. With DOE and NRC, it co-ordinates federal, State and local efforts to develop and evaluate radiological emergency response plans and warning systems, with particular emphasis on the adequacy of State and local emergency plans.

b) National Aeronautics and Space Administration

This Agency (NASA), concerned with civilian and military aspects of space exploration, operates the *Lewis*

Research Center. The Center conducts projects in life sciences, nuclear medicine, and radiobiology. It has also studied the impact of radiation damage emanating from nuclear activities in space.

c) Tennessee Valley Authority

This federal Agency (TVA) conducts a co-ordinated resource conservation, development, and land use program in the Tennessee River Valley Region. It also produces and markets various types of power, including nuclear. TVA investigates options for waste disposal and nuclear safeguards.

d) White House Offices

Three offices are attached directly to the White House, and help decide priorities.

The *Office of Management and Budget (OMB)* develops the Administration's budget proposals each year. With authority to review individual agency requests subject to Congressional approval, OMB can influence which aspects of nuclear energy receive emphasis.

The *Office of Policy Development* advises the President on various policy alternatives. In the past, OPD had reviewed various options concerning nuclear power and other energy sources, and has prepared briefs regarding waste management alternatives, for example.

The *Office of Science and Technology Policy* co-ordinates research developments undertaken by various agencies, especially interdisciplinary approaches to waste disposal.

C. SEMI-PUBLIC BODIES

a) American National Standards Institute

This organization (ANSI) acts as a clearing-house to co-ordinate standards development. It consists of several management boards, one of which is the Nuclear Standard Board. Both NRC and DOE participate in that Board as voting members. The Board reviews standards developed by other organizations, such as the American Society of Mechanical Engineers and the American Society for Testing and Materials. The Institute deals with, among others, utilization or measurement of ionizing radiation, nuclear energy, fissionable materials, and chemical processing of nuclear materials. ANSI represents the United States in the

International Standards Organisation (ISO) and the International Electrotechnical Commission.

b) National Academy of Sciences

This umbrella group (NAS) conducts research in all areas of science and engineering, including the physical and social sciences. It published a report on the Biological Effects of Ionizing Radiation, and has set up a standing board dealing with radioactive waste management.

c) National Council on Radiation Protection and Measurement

This group studies nuclear physics, nuclear medicine and waste disposal as they relate to radiation protection. The Council formulates recommendations on radiation protection and measurement by compiling available scientific information from many disciplines. The Scientific Committee of the Council drafts recommendations which are in turn adopted by the Council. The recommendations cover consumer protection, occupational health, environmental protection, and nuclear waste disposal.

d) National Nuclear Data Center

The Center, a part of Brookhaven National Laboratory, co-operates with OECD, IAEA and the Soviet Union in publishing CINDA, the Computer Index of Nuclear Data. The Center assists in computer data retrievals and evaluates a broad range of technical multidisciplinary data.

CONVENTIONS RELEVANT
TO
NUCLEAR ACTIVITIES

I. THIRD PARTY LIABILITY

CONVENTION ON THIRD PARTY LIABILITY
IN THE FIELD OF NUCLEAR ENERGY
(PARIS CONVENTION)

Depositary: Organisation for Economic Co-operation and Development, Paris

Date of adoption: 29th July 1960

Date of entry into force: 1st April 1968

The Paris Convention was amended the first time by the "Additional Protocol to the Convention on Third Party Liability in the Field of Nuclear Energy" which was adopted on 28th January 1964 and entered into force at the same time as the Convention itself. The Convention was next amended by the "Protocol to amend the Convention on Third Party Liability in the Field of Nuclear Energy of 29th July 1960, as amended by the Additional Protocol of 28th January 1964", adopted on 16th November 1982; this latter Protocol has not yet entered into force.

Contracting Parties	Date of Ratification	
	Convention	1964 Additional Protocol
Belgium	3rd August 1966	3rd August 1966
Denmark	4th September 1974	4th September 1974
Finland (accession)	16th June 1972	16th June 1972
France	9th March 1966	9th March 1966
Germany, Federal Republic of	30th September 1975	30th September 1975
Greece	12th May 1970	12th May 1970
Italy	17th September 1975	17th September 1975
Netherlands	28th December 1979	28th December 1979
Norway	2nd July 1973	2nd July 1973
Portugal[1]	29th September 1977	29th September 1977
Spain	31st October 1961	30th April 1965
Sweden[1]	1st April 1968	1st April 1968
Turkey	10th October 1961	5th April 1968
United Kingdom	23rd February 1966	23rd February 1966

1. Sweden and Portugal ratified the 1982 Protocol on 8th March 1983 and 28th May 1984, respectively.

CONVENTION OF 31st JANUARY 1963
SUPPLEMENTARY TO THE PARIS CONVENTION OF 29th JULY 1960 ON THIRD PARTY LIABILITY IN THE FIELD OF NUCLEAR ENERGY (BRUSSELS SUPPLEMENTARY CONVENTION)

Depositary:	Belgium
Date of adoption:	31st January 1963
Date of entry into force:	4th December 1974

The Brussels Supplementary Convention was amended the first time by the "Additional Protocol to the Convention of 31st January 1963 Supplementary to the Paris Convention of 29th July 1960 on Third Party Liability in the Field of Nuclear Energy", which was adopted on 28th January 1964 and entered into force at the same time as the Convention itself. The Convention was next amended by the "Protocol to amend the Convention of 31st January 1963 Supplementary to the Paris Convention of 29th July 1960 on Third Party Liability in the Field of Nuclear Energy, as amended by the Additional Protocol of 28th January 1964", adopted on 16th November 1982; this latter Protocol has not yet entered into force.

Contracting Parties	Date of Ratification Convention and 1964 Additional Protocol
Denmark	4th September 1974
Finland (accession)	14th January 1977
France	30th March 1966
Germany, Federal Republic of	1st October 1975
Italy	3rd February 1976
Netherlands	28th September 1979
Norway	7th July 1973
Spain	27th July 1966
Sweden[1]	3rd April 1968
United Kingdom	24th March 1966

1. Sweden ratified the 1982 Protocol on 22nd March 1983.

CONVENTION ON CIVIL LIABILITY
FOR NUCLEAR DAMAGE
(VIENNA CONVENTION)

Depositary: International Atomic Energy Agency, Vienna
Date of adoption: 21st May 1963
Date of entry into force: 12th November 1977

Contracting Parties	Date of Ratification/ Accession
Argentina	25th April 1967
Bolivia (acc.)	10th April 1968
Cameroon (acc.)	6th March 1964
Cuba	25th October 1965
Egypt	5th November 1965
Niger (acc.)	24th July 1979
Peru (acc.)	26th August 1980
Philippines	15th November 1965
Trinidad and Tobago (acc.)	31st January 1966
Yugoslavia	12th August 1977

acc. = accession.

CONVENTION RELATING TO CIVIL LIABILITY IN THE FIELD OF MARITIME CARRIAGE OF NUCLEAR MATERIAL

Depositary: International Maritime Organisation, London
Date of adoption: 17th December 1971
Date of entry into force: 15th July 1975

Contracting Parties	Date of Ratification/ Accession
Argentina (acc.)	18th May 1981
Denmark	4th September 1974
France	2nd February 1973
Gabon (acc.)	21st January 1982
Germany, Federal Republic of	1st October 1975
Italy	21st July 1980
Liberia (acc.)	17th February 1981
Norway	16th April 1975
Spain (acc.)	21st May 1974
Sweden	22nd November 1974
Yemen (acc.)	6th March 1979

acc. = accession.

CONVENTION ON THE LIABILITY OF OPERATORS OF NUCLEAR SHIPS

Depositary: Belgium
Date of adoption: 25th May 1962

This Convention has not entered into force as the conditions stipulated by Article XXIV(1) thereof have not yet been met.

Signatories	Date of signature	Date of Ratification
Belgium	25th May 1962	
Republic of China	25th May 1962	
Egypt	25th May 1962	
Germany, Federal Republic of	25th October 1974	
India	25th May 1962	
Indonesia	25th May 1962	
Ireland	25th May 1962	
Republic of Korea	25th May 1962	
Lebanon	3rd June 1975	3rd June 1975
Liberia	25th May 1962	
Malaysia	25th May 1962	
Monaco	25th May 1962	
Netherlands	30th December 1968	20th March 1974
Panama	25th May 1962	
Philippines	25th May 1962	
Portugal	25th May 1962	31st July 1968
Yugoslavia	25th May 1962	

Accessions	Date of accession	
Malagasy Republic	13th July 1965	
Syria	1st August 1974	
Zaire	17th July 1967	

II. RADIATION PROTECTION

RADIATION PROTECTION CONVENTION, 1960 (No. 115)

Depositary: International Labour Organisation/
International Labour Office, Geneva
Date of adoption: 22nd June 1960
Date of entry into force: 17th June 1962

Contracting Parties	Date of Ratification
Argentina	15th June 1978
Barbados	8th May 1967
Belgium	2nd July 1965
Brazil	5th September 1966
Byelorussian SSR	26th February 1968
Czechoslovakia	21st January 1964
Denmark	7th February 1974
Djibouti	3rd August 1978
Ecuador	9th March 1970
Egypt	18th March 1964
Finland	16th October 1978
France	18th November 1971
German Democratic Republic	7th May 1975
Germany, Federal Republic of	26th September 1973
Ghana	7th November 1961
Greece	4th June 1982
Guinea	12th December 1966
Guyana	8th June 1966
Hungary	8th June 1968
India	17th November 1975
Iraq	26th October 1962
Italy	5th May 1971
Japan	31st July 1973
Lebanon	6th December 1977
Netherlands	29th November 1966
Nicaragua	1st October 1981
Norway	17th June 1961
Paraguay	10th July 1967
Poland	23rd December 1964
Spain	17th July 1962
Sweden	12th April 1961
Switzerland	29th May 1963
Syrian Arab Republic	15th January 1964
Turkey	15th November 1968
Ukranian SSR	19th June 1968
United Kingdom	9th March 1962
USSR	22nd September 1967

III. SAFEGUARDS AND PHYSICAL PROTECTION

TREATY ON THE NON-PROLIFERATION OF NUCLEAR WEAPONS

Depositaries:	United Kingdom, United States, USSR
Date of adoption:	1st July 1968
Date of entry into force:	5th March 1970

Contracting Parties	Date of Ratification/ Accession/Succession
Afghanistan	4th February 1970
Antigua and Barbuda (succ.)	1st November 1981
Australia	23rd January 1973
Austria	27th June 1969
Bahamas (acc.)	10th July 1973
Bangladesh (acc.)	27th September 1979
Barbados	21st February 1980
Belgium	2nd May 1975
Benin	31st October 1972
Bolivia	26th May 1970
Botswana	28th April 1969
Bulgaria	5th September 1969
Burundi (acc.)	19th March 1971
Cameroon, United Republic of	8th January 1969
Canada	8th January 1969
Cape verde (acc.)	24th October 1979
Central African Republic (acc.)	25th October 1970
Chad	10th March 1971
China, Republic of	27th January 1970
Congo (acc.)	23rd October 1978
Costa Rica	3rd March 1970
Cyprus	10th February 1970
Czechoslovakia	22nd July 1969
Democratic Kampuchea (acc.)	2nd June 1972
Democratic Yemen	1st June 1979
Denmark	3rd January 1969
Dominican Republic	24th July 1971
Ecuador	7th March 1969
Egypt	26th February 1981
El Salvador	11th July 1971
Ethiopia	5th February 1970
Fiji (acc.)	14th July 1972
Finland	5th February 1969
Gabon (acc.)	19th February 1974
Gambia	12th May 1975

acc. = accession   succ. = succession

Contracting Parties	Date of Ratification/ Accession/Succession
German Democratic Republic	31st October 1969
Germany, Federal Republic of	2nd May 1975
Ghana	5th May 1970
Greece	11th March 1970
Grenada (acc.)	19th August 1974
Quatemala	22nd September 1970
Guinea Bissau (acc.)	20th August 1976
Haiti	2nd June 1970
Holy See (acc.)	25th February 1971
Honduras	16th May 1973
Hungary	27th May 1969
Iceland	18th July 1969
Indonesia	12th July 1979
Iran	2nd February 1970
Iraq	29th October 1969
Ireland	1st July 1968
Italy	2nd May 1975
Ivory Coast	6th March 1973
Jamaica	5th March 1970
Japan	8th June 1976
Jordan	11th February 1970
Kenya	11th June 1970
Korea, Republic of	23rd April 1975
Lao People's Democratic Republic	20th February 1970
Lebanon	15th July 1970
Lesotho	20th May 1970
Liberia	5th March 1970
Libyan Arab Jamahiriya	26th May 1975
Liechtenstein (acc.)	20th April 1978
Luxembourg	2nd May 1975
Madagascar	8th October 1970
Malaysia	5th March 1970
Maldives	7th April 1970
Mali, Republic of	10th February 1970
Malta	6th February 1970
Mauritius	25th April 1969
Mexico	21st January 1969
Mongolia	14th May 1969
Morocco	27th November 1970
Nepal	5th January 1970
Netherlands	2nd May 1975
New Zealand	10th September 1969
Nicaragua	6th March 1973
Nigeria	27th Septembre 1968
Norway	5th February 1969
Panama	13th January 1977

acc. = accession   succ. = succession

Contracting Parties	Date of Ratification/ Accession/Succession
Papua New Guinea (acc.)	25th January 1982
Paraguay	4th February 1970
Peru	3rd March 1970
Philippines	5th October 1972
Poland	12th June 1969
Portugal (acc.)	15th December 1977
Romania	4th February 1970
Rwanda	20th May 1975
St. Lucia (acc.)	28th December 1979
San Marino	10th August 1970
Senegal	17th December 1970
Sierra Leone (acc.)	26th February 1975
Singapore	10th March 1976
Solomon Islands (succ.)	17th June 1981
Somalia	5th March 1970
Sri Lanka	5th March 1979
Sudan	31st October 1973
Suriname (succ.)	30th June 1976
Swaziland	11th December 1969
Sweden	9th January 1970
Switzerland	9th March 1977
Syrian Arab Republic	24th September 1969
Thailand (acc.)	7th December 1972
Togo	26th February 1970
Tonga (acc.)	7th July 1971
Tunisia	26th February 1970
Turkey	17th April 1980
Tuvalu (succ.)	19th January 1979
United Kingdom	27th November 1968
United States	5th March 1970
Upper Volta	3rd March 1970
Uruguay	31st August 1970
USSR	5th March 1970
Venezuela	26th September 1975
Viet Nam, Socialist Republic of (acc.)	14th June 1982
Western Samoa (acc.)	17th March 1975
Yugoslavia	3rd March 1970
Zaire	4th August 1970

acc. = accession   succ. = succession

CONVENTION ON THE ESTABLISHMENT OF A SECURITY CONTROL IN THE FIELD OF NUCLEAR ENERGY

Depositary: Organisation for Economic Co-operation and Development, Paris

Date of adoption: 20th December 1957

Date of entry into force: 22nd July 1959

Contracting Parties	Date of Ratification
Austria	30th October 1959
Belgium	22nd July 1959
Denmark	23rd May 1959
France	23rd February 1959
Germany, Federal Republic of	22nd July 1959
Ireland	2nd December 1958
Italy	3rd April 1963
Luxembourg	19th May 1961
Netherlands	9th July 1959
Norway	12th February 1959
Portugal	26th September 1959
Spain (acc.)	22nd July 1959
Sweden	5th January 1960
Switzerland	21st January 1959
Turkey	20th July 1959
United Kingdom	10th May 1958

The application of the Security Control Regulations under the Convention was suspended on 14th October 1976.

TREATY ESTABLISHING THE EUROPEAN ATOMIC ENERGY COMMUNITY (EURATOM)

Depositary: Italy
Date of adoption: 25th March 1957
Date of entry into force: 1st January 1958

The Euratom Treaty makes provision in Chapter VII for the establishment of a security control which applies to the territories of Member States of the European Community.

Contracting Parties
Belgium
Denmark
France
Germany, Federal Republic of
Greece
Ireland
Italy
Luxembourg
Netherlands
United Kingdom

CONVENTION ON THE PHYSICAL PROTECTION OF NUCLEAR MATERIAL

Depositaries: International Atomic Energy Agency, Vienna; United Nations, New York

Date of adoption: 3rd March 1980

This Convention is not yet in force.

Signatories	Date of Signature	Date of Ratification
Australia	22nd February 1984	
Austria	3rd March 1980	
Belgium*	13th June 1980	
Brazil	15th May 1981	
Bulgaria	23rd June 1981	10th April 1984
Canada	23rd September 1980	
Czechoslovakia	14th September 1981	23rd April 1982
Denmark*	13th June 1980	
Dominican Republic	3rd March 1980	
Finland	25th June 1981	
France*	13th June 1980	
German Democratic Republic	21st May 1980	5th February 1981
Germany, Federal Republic of*	13th June 1980	
Greece	3rd March 1980	
Guatemala	12th March 1980	
Haiti	9th April 1980	
Hungary	17th June 1980	4th May 1984
Ireland*	13th June 1980	
Israel	17th June 1983	
Korea, Republic of	29th December 1981	7th April 1982
Luxembourg*	13th June 1980	
Morocco	25th July 1980	
Netherlands*	13th June 1980	
Norway	26th January 1983	
Panama	18th March 1980	
Paraguay	21st May 1980	
Philippines	19th May 1980	22nd September 1981
Poland	6th August 1980	5th October 1983
Romania	15th January 1981	
South Africa	18th May 1981	
Sweden	2nd July 1980	1st August 1980
Turkey	23rd August 1983	
United Kingdom*	13th June 1980	
United States	3rd March 1980	13th December 1982
USSR	22nd May 1980	25th May 1983
Yugoslavia	15th July 1980	
European Atomic Energy Community (Euratom)	13th June 1980	

* Signed as a Member State of Euratom.

IV. DENUCLEARISATION

ANTARCTIC TREATY

Depositary: United States
Date of adoption: 1st December 1959
Date of entry into force: 23rd June 1961

Contracting Parties	Date of Ratification/ Accession
Argentina	23rd June 1961
Australia	23rd June 1961
Belgium	26th July 1960
Bulgaria (acc.)	11th September 1978
Brazil (acc.)	16th May 1975
Republic of China (acc.)	8th June 1983
Chile	23rd June 1961
Czechoslovakia (acc.)	14th June 1962
Denmark (acc.)	20th May 1965
France	16th September 1960
German Democratic Republic (acc.)	19th November 1974
India (acc.)	23rd August 1983
Japan	4th August 1960
Netherlands (acc.)	30th March 1967
New Zealand	1st November 1960
Norway	24th August 1960
Papua New Guinea (acc.)	16th September 1975
Peru (acc.)	10th April 1981
Poland (acc.)	8th June 1961
Romania (acc.)	15th September 1971
Spain (acc.)	31st March 1982
South Africa	21st June 1960
United Kingdom	31st May 1960
Uruguay (acc.)	11th January 1980
USSR	2nd November 1960
United States	18th August 1960

acc. = accession.

TREATY FOR THE PROHIBITION OF NUCLEAR WEAPONS IN LATIN AMERICA AND ADDITIONAL PROTOCOLS (TLATELOLCO TREATY)

Depositary: Mexico
Date of adoption: 14th February 1967
Date of entry into force: 22nd April 1968

Contracting Parties	Date of Ratification/ Accession/Approval
Bahamas	26th April 1977
Barbados	25th April 1969
Bolivia	18th February 1969
Brazil	29th January 1968
Columbia	4th August 1972
Costa Rica	25th August 1969
Chile	9th October 1974
Dominican Republic	14th June 1968
Ecuador	11th February 1969
El Salvador	22nd April 1968
Grenada	20th June 1975
Guatemala	6th February 1970
Haiti	23rd May 1969
Honduras	23rd September 1968
Jamaica	26th June 1969
Mexico	20th September 1967
Nicaragua	24th October 1968
Panama	11th June 1971
Paraguay	19th March 1969
Peru	4th March 1969
Suriname	10th June 1977
Trinidad & Tobago	3rd December 1970
Uruguay	20th August 1968
Venezuela	23rd March 1970

PROTOCOL I

Netherlands	26th July 1971
United Kingdom	11th December 1969
United States	23rd November 1981

PROTOCOL II

China, Republic of	12th June 1974
France	22nd March 1974
United Kingdom	11th December 1969
United States	12th May 1971
USSR	8th January 1979

TREATY ON THE PROHIBITION OF THE EMPLACEMENT OF NUCLEAR WEAPONS AND OTHER WEAPONS OF MASS DESTRUCTION ON THE SEABED AND THE OCEAN FLOOR AND IN THE SUBSOIL THEREOF

Depositaries: United Kingdom, United States, USSR
Date of adoption: 11th February 1971
Date of entry into force: 18th May 1972

Contracting Parties	Date of Ratification/ Accession
Afghanistan	21st May 1971
Australia	23rd January 1973
Austria	10th August 1972
Belgium	20th November 1972
Botswana	10th November 1972
Bulgaria	7th May 1971
Byelorussian SSR	14th September 1971
Canada	17th May 1972
Central African Republic	9th July 1981
China, Republic of	22nd February 1972
Congo (acc.)	23rd October 1978
Cyprus	30th December 1971
Czechoslovakia	11th January 1972
Denmark	15th June 1971
Dominican Republic	11th February 1972
Ethiopia	14th July 1977
Finland	8th June 1971
German Democratic Republic	27th July 1971
Germany, Federal Republic of	18th November 1975
Ghana	9th August 1972
Hungary	13th August 1971
Iceland	30th May 1972
India (acc.)	20th July 1973
Iran	26th August 1971
Iraq (acc.)	13th September 1972
Ireland	19th August 1971
Italy	3rd September 1974
Ivory Coast (acc.)	14th January 1972
Japan	21st June 1971
Jordan	17th August 1971
Laos	3rd November 1971
Lesotho	3rd April 1973
Luxembourg	11th November 1982
Malaysia	21st June 1972
Malta	4th May 1971
Mauritius	23rd April 1971

acc. = accession

Contracting Parties	Date of Ratification/ Accession
Mongolia	15th November 1971
Morocco	5th August 1971
Nepal	9th August 1971
Netherlands	14th January 1976
New Zealand	24th February 1972
Nicaragua	7th February 1973
Niger	9th August 1971
Norway	29th June 1971
Panama	20th March 1974
Poland	15th November 1971
Portugal (acc.)	24th June 1975
Romania	10th July 1972
Rwanda	20th May 1975
Saudi Arabia	23rd June 1972
Seychelles (acc.)	29th June 1976
Singapore	10th September 1976
South Africa	14th November 1973
Swaziland	9th August 1971
Sweden	28th April 1972
Switzerland	4th May 1976
Togo	28th June 1971
Tunisia	29th October 1971
Turkey	19th October 1972
Ukranian SSR	3rd September 1971
United Kingdom	18th May 1972
United States	18th May 1972
USSR	18th May 1972
Yugoslavia	25th October 1973
Zambia (acc.)	1st November 1972

acc. = accession.

V. MARINE POLLUTION

CONVENTION ON THE PREVENTION OF MARINE POLLUTION BY DUMPING OF WASTES AND OTHER MATTER (LONDON CONVENTION)

Depositaries: Mexico, United Kingdom, United States, USSR
Date of adoption: 29th December 1972
Date of entry into force: 30th August 1975

Contracting Parties	Date of Ratification/ Accession
Afghanistan	2nd April 1975
Argentina	11th September 1979
Brazil	26th July 1982
Byelorussian SSR	29th January 1976
Canada	13th November 1975
Cape Verde	26th May 1977
Chile	4th August 1977
Cuba	1st December 1975
Denmark	23rd October 1974
Dominican Republic	7th December 1973
Finland	3rd May 1979
France	3rd February 1977
Gabon	5th February 1982
German Democratic Republic	20th August 1976
Germany, Federal Republic of	8th November 1977
Greece	10th August 1981
Guatemala	14th July 1975
Haiti	28th August 1975
Honduras	2nd May 1980
Hungary	5th February 1976
Iceland	24th May 1973
Ireland	17th February 1982
Japan	15th October 1980
Jordan	11th November 1973
Kenya	17th December 1975
Kiribati	12th May 1982
Libyan Arab Jamahiriya	22nd November 1976
Mexico	7th April 1975
Monaco	16th May 1977
Morocco	18th February 1977
Nauru	26th July 1982
Netherlands	2nd December 1977
New Zealand	30th April 1975
Nigeria	19th March 1976
Norway	4th April 1974

Contracting Parties	Date of Ratification/ Accession
Panama	31st July 1975
Papua New Guinea	10th March 1980
Philippines	10th August 1973
Poland	23rd January 1979
Portugal	14th April 1978
South Africa	7th August 1978
Spain	31st July 1974
Suriname	21st October 1980
Sweden	21st February 1974
Switzerland	31st July 1979
Tunisia	13th April 1976
Ukrainian SSR	5th February 1976
United Arab Emirates	9th August 1974
USSR	15th December 1975
United Kingdom	17th November 1975
United States	29th April 1974
Yugoslavia	25th June 1976
Zaire	16th September 1975

CONVENTION FOR THE PREVENTION OF MARINE POLLUTION BY DUMPING FROM SHIPS AND AIRCRAFT (OSLO CONVENTION)

Depositary: Norway

Date of adoption: 15th February 1972

Date of entry into force: 7th April 1974

Contracting Parties	Date of Ratification
Belgium	28th February 1978
Denmark	28th July 1972
Finland	2nd May 1979
France	8th March 1974
Germany, Federal Republic of	23rd November 1977
Iceland	27th June 1973
Ireland	25th January 1982
Netherlands	29th September 1975
Norway	2nd June 1972
Portugal	30th January 1973
Spain	14th June 1973
Sweden	13th September 1972
United Kingdom	30th June 1975

CONVENTION ON THE PROTECTION OF THE MARINE ENVIRONMENT OF THE BALTIC SEA AREA

Depositary: Finland
Date of adoption: 22nd March 1974
Date of entry into force: 3rd May 1980

Contracting Parties	Date of Ratification
Denmark	20th July 1977
Finland	27th June 1975
German Democratic Republic	6th January 1977
Germany, Federal Republic of	3rd May 1980
Poland	11th November 1979
Sweden	30th July 1976
USSR	2nd November 1978

CONVENTION FOR THE PREVENTION OF MARINE POLLUTION FROM LAND-BASED SOURCES (PARIS CONVENTION)

Depositary: France
Date of adoption: 4th June 1974
Date of entry into force: 6th May 1978

Contracting Parties	Date of Ratification
Denmark	1st March 1976
France (approval)	19th January 1977
Germany, Federal Republic of	2nd March 1982
Iceland	19th June 1981
Netherlands	10th November 1977
Norway	6th April 1977
Portugal	10th May 1978
Spain	17th April 1980
Sweden	30th July 1976
United Kingdom	6th April 1978
European Economic Community	23rd June 1975

CONVENTION FOR THE PROTECTION OF
THE MEDITERRANEAN SEA AGAINST POLLUTION
(BARCELONA CONVENTION)

Depositary: **Spain**
Date of adoption: **16th February 1976**
Date of entry into force: **12th February 1978**

Contracting Parties	Date of Ratification/ Accession/Approval
Algeria (acc.)	16th February 1981
Cyprus	19th November 1979
Egypt (app.)	24th August 1978
France (app.)	11th March 1978
Greece	3rd January 1979
Israel	3rd March 1978
Italy	3rd February 1979
Lebanon (acc.)	8th November 1977
Libyan Arab Jamahiriya	31st January 1979
Malta	30th December 1977
Monaco	20th September 1977
Morocco	15th January 1980
Spain	17th December 1976
Syrian Arab Republic	26th December 1978
Tunisia	30th July 1977
Turkey	6th April 1981
Yugoslavia	13th January 1978
European Economic Community (app.)	16th March 1978

acc. = accession   app. = approval.

OECD SALES AGENTS
DÉPOSITAIRES DES PUBLICATIONS DE L'OCDE

ARGENTINA – ARGENTINE
Carlos Hirsch S.R.L., Florida 165, 4° Piso (Galería Guemes)
1333 BUENOS AIRES, Tel. 33.1787.2391 y 30.7122

AUSTRALIA – AUSTRALIE
Australia and New Zealand Book Company Pty, Ltd.,
10 Aquatic Drive, Frenchs Forest, N.S.W. 2086
P.O. Box 459, BROOKVALE, N.S.W. 2100. Tel. (02) 452.44.11

AUSTRIA – AUTRICHE
OECD Publications and Information Center
4 Simrockstrasse 5300 Bonn (Germany). Tel. (0228) 21.60.45
Local Agent/Agent local :
Gerold and Co., Graben 31, WIEN 1. Tel. 52.22.35

BELGIUM – BELGIQUE
Jean De Lannoy, Service Publications OCDE
avenue du Roi 202, B-1060 BRUXELLES. Tel. 02/538.51.69

BRAZIL – BRÉSIL
Mestre Jou S.A., Rua Guaipa 518,
Caixa Postal 24090, 05089 SAO PAULO 10. Tel. 261.1920
Rua Senador Dantas 19 s/205-6, RIO DE JANEIRO GB.
Tel. 232.07.32

CANADA
Renouf Publishing Company Limited,
2182 ouest, rue Ste-Catherine,
MONTRÉAL, Qué. H3H 1M7. Tel. (514)937.3519
OTTAWA, Ont. K1P 5A6, 61 Sparks Street

DENMARK – DANEMARK
Munksgaard Export and Subscription Service
35, Nørre Søgade
DK 1370 KØBENHAVN K. Tel. +45.1.12.85.70

FINLAND – FINLANDE
Akateeminen Kirjakauppa
Keskuskatu 1, 00100 HELSINKI 10. Tel. 65.11.22

FRANCE
Bureau des Publications de l'OCDE,
2 rue André-Pascal, 75775 PARIS CEDEX 16. Tel. (1) 524.81.67
Principal correspondant :
13602 AIX-EN-PROVENCE : Librairie de l'Université.
Tel. 26.18.08

GERMANY – ALLEMAGNE
OECD Publications and Information Center
4 Simrockstrasse 5300 BONN HM. (0228) 21.60.45

GREECE – GRÈCE
Librairie Kauffmann, 28 rue du Stade,
ATHÈNES 132. Tel. 322.21.60

HONG-KONG
Government Information Services,
Publications/Sales Section, Baskerville House,
2nd Floor, 22 Ice House Street

ICELAND – ISLANDE
Snaebjörn Jónsson and Co., h.f.,
Hafnarstraeti 4 and 9, P.O.B. 1131, REYKJAVIK.
Tel. 13133/14281/11936

INDIA – INDE
Oxford Book and Stationery Co. :
NEW DELHI-1, Scindia House. Tel. 45896
CALCUTTA 700016, 17 Park Street. Tel. 240832

INDONESIA – INDONÉSIE
PDIN-LIPI, P.O. Box 3065/JKT., JAKARTA, Tel. 583467

IRELAND – IRLANDE
TDC Publishers – Library Suppliers
12 North Frederick Street, DUBLIN 1 Tel. 744835-749677

ITALY – ITALIE
Libreria Commissionaria Sansoni :
Via Lamarmora 45, 50121 FIRENZE. Tel. 579751/584468
Via Bartolini 29, 20155 MILANO. Tel. 365083
Sub-depositari :
Ugo Tassi
Via A. Farnese 28, 00192 ROMA. Tel. 310590
Editrice e Libreria Herder,
Piazza Montecitorio 120, 00186 ROMA. Tel. 6794628
Costantino Ercolano, Via Generale Orsini 46, 80132 NAPOLI. Tel. 405210
Libreria Hoepli, Via Hoepli 5, 20121 MILANO. Tel. 865446
Libreria Scientifica, Dott. Lucio de Biasio "Aeiou"
Via Meravgli 16, 20123 MILANO Tel. 807679
Libreria Zanichelli
Piazza Galvani 1/A, 40124 Bologna Tel. 237389
Libreria Lattes, Via Garibaldi 3, 10122 TORINO. Tel. 519274
La diffusione delle edizioni OCSE è inoltre assicurata dalle migliori librerie nelle
città più importanti.

JAPAN – JAPON
OECD Publications and Information Center,
Landic Akasaka Bldg., 2-3-4 Akasaka,
Minato-ku, TOKYO 107 Tel. 586.2016

KOREA – CORÉE
Pan Korea Book Corporation,
P.O. Box n° 101 Kwangwhamun, SÉOUL. Tel. 72.7369

LEBANON – LIBAN
Documenta Scientifica/Redico,
Edison Building, Bliss Street, P.O. Box 5641, BEIRUT.
Tel. 354429 – 344425

MALAYSIA – MALAISIE
University of Malaya Co-operative Bookshop Ltd.
P.O. Box 1127, Jalan Pantai Baru
KUALA LUMPUR. Tel. 51425, 54058, 54361

THE NETHERLANDS – PAYS-BAS
Staatsuitgeverij, Verzendboekhandel,
Chr. Plantijnstraat 1 Postbus 20014
2500 EA S-GRAVENHAGE. Tel. nr. 070.789911
Voor bestellingen: Tel. 070.789208

NEW ZEALAND – NOUVELLE-ZÉLANDE
Publications Section,
Government Printing Office Bookshops:
AUCKLAND: Retail Bookshop: 25 Rutland Street,
Mail Orders: 85 Beach Road, Private Bag C.P.O.
HAMILTON: Retail: Ward Street,
Mail Orders, P.O. Box 857
WELLINGTON: Retail: Mulgrave Street (Head Office),
Cubacade World Trade Centre
Mail Orders: Private Bag
CHRISTCHURCH: Retail: 159 Hereford Street,
Mail Orders: Private Bag
DUNEDIN: Retail: Princes Street
Mail Order: P.O. Box 1104

NORWAY – NORVÈGE
J.G. TANUM A/S
P.O. Box 1177 Sentrum OSLO 1. Tel. (02) 80.12.60

PAKISTAN
Mirza Book Agency, 65 Shahrah Quaid-E-Azam, LAHORE 3.
Tel. 66839

PHILIPPINES
National Book Store, Inc.
Library Services Division, P.O. Box 1934, MANILA.
Tel. Nos. 49.43.06 to 09, 40.53.45, 49.45.12

PORTUGAL
Livraria Portugal, Rua do Carmo 70-74,
1117 LISBOA CODEX Tel. 360582/3

SINGAPORE – SINGAPOUR
Information Publications Pte Ltd,
Pei-Fu Industrial Building,
24 New Industrial Road N° 02-06
SINGAPORE 1953, Tel. 2831786, 2831798

SPAIN – ESPAGNE
Mundi-Prensa Libros, S.A.
Castelló 37, Apartado 1223, MADRID-1. Tel. 275.46.55
Libreria Bosch, Ronda Universidad 11, BARCELONA 7.
Tel. 317.53.08, 317.53.58

SWEDEN – SUÈDE
AB CE Fritzes Kungl Hovbokhandel,
Box 16 356, S 103 27 STH, Regeringsgatan 12,
DS STOCKHOLM. Tel. 08/23.89.00
Subscription Agency/Abonnements:
Wennergren-Williams AB,
Box 13004, S104 25 STOCKHOLM.
Tel. 08/54.12.00

SWITZERLAND – SUISSE
OECD Publications and Information Center
4 Simrockstrasse 5300 BONN (Germany). Tel. (0228) 21.60.45
Local Agents/Agents locaux
Librairie Payot, 6 rue Grenus, 1211 GENÈVE 11. Tel. 022.31.89.50

TAIWAN – FORMOSE
Good Faith Worldwide Int'l Co., Ltd.
9th floor, No. 118, Sec. 2,
Chung Hsiao E. Road
TAIPEI. Tel. 391.7396/391.7397

THAILAND – THAILANDE
Suksit Siam Co., Ltd., 1715 Rama IV Rd,
Samyan, BANGKOK 5. Tel. 2511630

TURKEY – TURQUIE
Kültur Yayinlari Is-Türk Ltd. Sti.
Atatürk Bulvari No : 191/Kat. 21
Kavaklidere/ANKARA. Tel. 17 02 66
Dolmabahce Cad. No : 29
BESIKTAS/ISTANBUL. Tel. 60 71 88

UNITED KINGDOM – ROYAUME-UNI
H.M. Stationery Office,
P.O.B. 276, LONDON SW8 5DT.
(postal orders only)
Telephone orders: (01) 622.3316, or
49 High Holborn, LONDON WC1V 6 HB (personal callers)
Branches at: EDINBURGH, BIRMINGHAM, BRISTOL,
MANCHESTER, BELFAST.

UNITED STATES OF AMERICA – ÉTATS-UNIS
OECD Publications and Information Center, Suite 1207,
1750 Pennsylvania Ave., N.W. WASHINGTON, D.C.20006 – 4582
Tel. (202) 724.1857

VENEZUELA
Libreria del Este, Avda. F. Miranda 52, Edificio Galipan,
CARACAS 106. Tel. 32.23.01/33.26.04/31.58.38

YUGOSLAVIA – YOUGOSLAVIE
Jugoslovenska Knjiga, Knez Mihajlova 2, P.O.B. 36, BEOGRAD.
Tel. 621.992

Les commandes provenant de pays où l'OCDE n'a pas encore désigné de dépositaire peuvent être adressées à :
OCDE, Bureau des Publications, 2, rue André-Pascal, 75775 PARIS CEDEX 16.

Orders and inquiries from countries where sales agents have not yet been appointed may be sent to:
OECD, Publications Office, 2, rue André-Pascal, 75775 PARIS CEDEX 16.

67738-06-1984

OECD PUBLICATIONS, 2, rue André-Pascal, 75775 PARIS CEDEX 16 - No. 42853 1984
PRINTED IN FRANCE
(66 84 05 1) ISBN 92-64-12602-3